Fundame[illegible]

Drawing & Painting

Fundamentals of Drawing & Painting

Tips and Techniques

General Editor: Richard Taylor

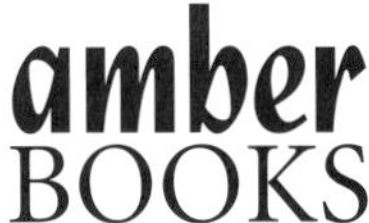

First published in 2006 by
Amber Books Ltd
Bradley's Close
74–77 White Lion Street
London N1 9PF
www.amberbooks.co.uk

ISBN-13: 978-1-904687-73-3
ISBN-10: 1-904687-73-3

Distributed in the UK by
Bookmart Ltd
Blaby Road
Wigston
Leicester LE18 4SE

Contributing Artists:
Dave Jordan: 40–43, 48–51, 84–86; Xiaopeng Huang: 76–83; Melvyn Petterson: 22–25; Ian Sidaway: 8–9, 87–94; Albany Wiseman: 26–33, 43–47

Picture Credits:
All DeAgostini/George Taylor except the following: DeAgostini/Shona Wood: 6–10

Printed in Singapore

Contents

GETTING STARTED
Organizing your workspace 6
Tricks of the trade 8
Choosing the best easel 11

DRAWING TECHNIQUES
Keeping a sketchbook 13
Pens for drawing 17
Introducing marker pens 20
Drawing with ballpoints 22
Drawing with fibre-tipped pens 26
Using graphite sticks 30
Oil pastels 34
Soft pastels 37
Experimenting with textured papers 40
Capturing reflections 43
Drawing with a grid 48

PAINTING TECHNIQUES
Choosing the best palette 52
Brushes 54
Using oil mediums 57
Using acrylic mediums 59
Using mixed media 61
Wash-off techniques 66
Mixing orange 70
Mixing green 72
Mixing purple 74
Details and textures in watercolour 76
Applying paint without a brush 84
Seasonal palette – spring 87
Seasonal palette – summer 89
Seasonal palette – autumn 91
Seasonal palette – winter 93

Glossary 95
Index 96

Organizing your work space

You'll save yourself both time and money if you keep your art materials readily to hand and in good condition. So get organized!

A place for everything and everything in its place is the golden rule for the artist, especially when space is limited. Spend some time finding a home for your equipment and you'll be able to work more comfortably and effectively. You will also save money. Remember, art materials are costly, so it is worth making them last. On the following pages, various storage methods are described to help you keep your materials and artworks in perfect condition.

Looking after your brushes

Store your brushes bristle-end up in a jar or tin, but make sure they are dry first. Always dry brushes flat – if they are dried upright, water runs down under the ferrule, loosening the hairs.

If you have a large collection of brushes, group those of a similar size together so that you can find what you want when you want it. You should always separate brushes used for oil painting from those used for water-based media, as traces of oil on a brush can ruin a water-based mix or wash. For long-term storage, put brushes away in a box or tin, but make sure they are thoroughly dry first. Lay them flat and add a few mothballs to ward off insect attacks.

A temporary home

You also need somewhere to put your brushes while you are working on a painting. Acrylic brushes should be rinsed out as soon as you stop using them because the paint is almost impossible to remove once it has dried. If you have to leave the painting for a short time, plunge the bristles into the water jar – resting a brush on its bristle end won't do it any harm for a few moments.

Other media are more forgiving, so you can leave brushes loaded with paint during a short break. Simply put the brushes on a ridged brush rest or in a piece of florist's oasis, as shown right.

SORTING OUT YOUR ART TOOLS

Keep frequently used pencils, brushes and pens upright in a jar or pot, where they are easily accessible. Alternatively, store coloured and pastel pencils in shallow tins, organizing them by colour – warm to cool, for example. A piece of foam cut to size and laid on top will keep them in place. If you work with a range of media, store them in separate boxes or a set of labelled, small plastic drawers. A plastic toolbox or fishing-tackle box with cantilevered trays is ideal for items such as pencils, erasers, brushes, palettes and nibs. These are sold in art supply shops as 'art bins', but often at a higher price. When you are actually painting, use a ridged rest or piece of oasis to hold your brushes.

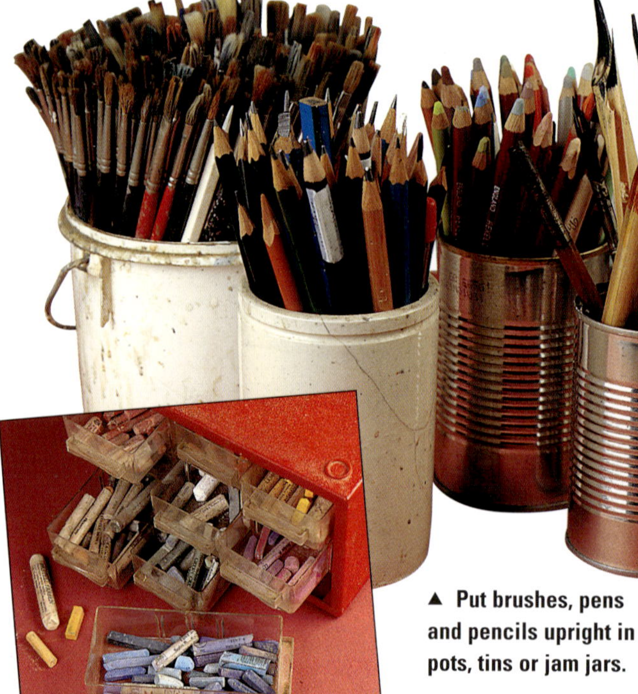

▲ Put brushes, pens and pencils upright in pots, tins or jam jars.

▲ Store pastels by colour in a transparent plastic drawer unit – you can then put your hand on the right stick straight away.

▶ A slab of florist's oasis is a useful temporary resting place for oil paint brushes. Simply stab the brushes, bristle-end up, into the oasis.

▶ A brush rest is a cheap and useful piece of equipment when painting. The ridges prevent the brushes from rolling off.

STORING PAPER AND ARTWORKS

The best form of storage for plain paper, or drawings and paintings on paper, is a plan chest. These substantial items of furniture have shallow drawers designed for storing artwork. They are available in a range of sizes and materials. Wooden plan chests are cumbersome and heavy, but lighter and cheaper styles in tubular metal and plastic are available from specialist suppliers, often by mail order. The size you choose will be dictated by the scale at which you work.

Interleave your drawings and paintings with sheets of acid-free tissue paper or tracing paper. Pastel and charcoal drawings need to be handled with special care. Fix them using an aerosol fixative, or fixative and a diffuser.

Always spray your work in a well-ventilated place away from other surfaces, ideally out of doors. Prop the drawing so that it is vertical and spray lightly, keeping the spray moving over the surface to get an even coverage.

If you don't have the funds or the space for a plan chest, a portfolio is a good alternative. Consider investing in two, one for finished works and one for pristine paper. They should be stored somewhere dry – in a cupboard, in the loft or under a bed, for example.

Paper should be handled as little as possible, as the edges become grubby and tattered with constant handling and fingers leave greasy marks that can disrupt a watercolour wash. For easy identification of each weight and type of paper, place sheets of coloured paper or sticky notes between different batches, then write a description on each one.

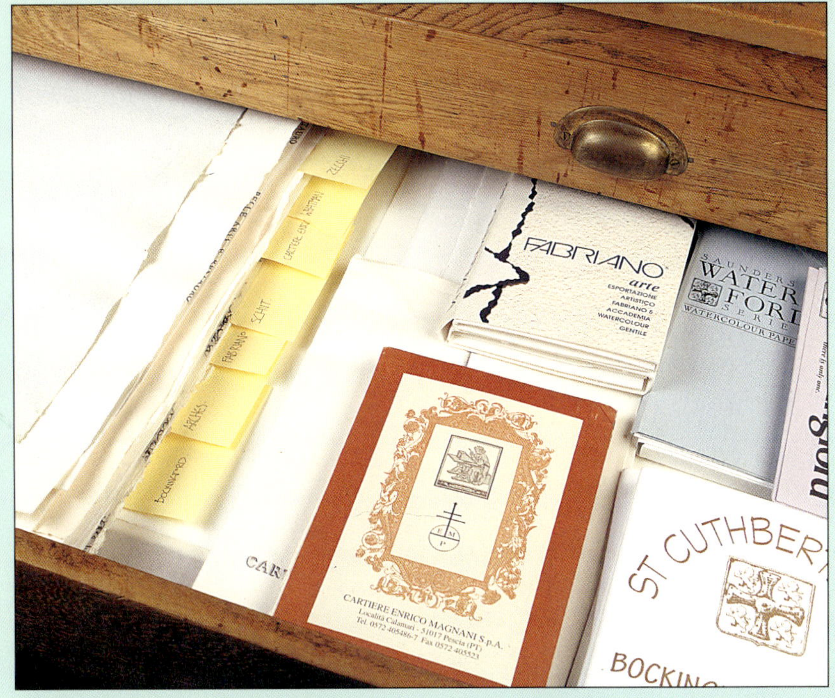

▲ Use sticky notes to label different types and weights of paper. This avoids having to rifle through the plan chest or portfolio, and possibly damaging or marking the papers. And keep sample packs of papers, as they are useful for practising on.

▼ Charcoal and pastel drawings are easily smudged, so fix them (see right) before storing them. Interleave drawings with tissue or tracing paper to protect them.

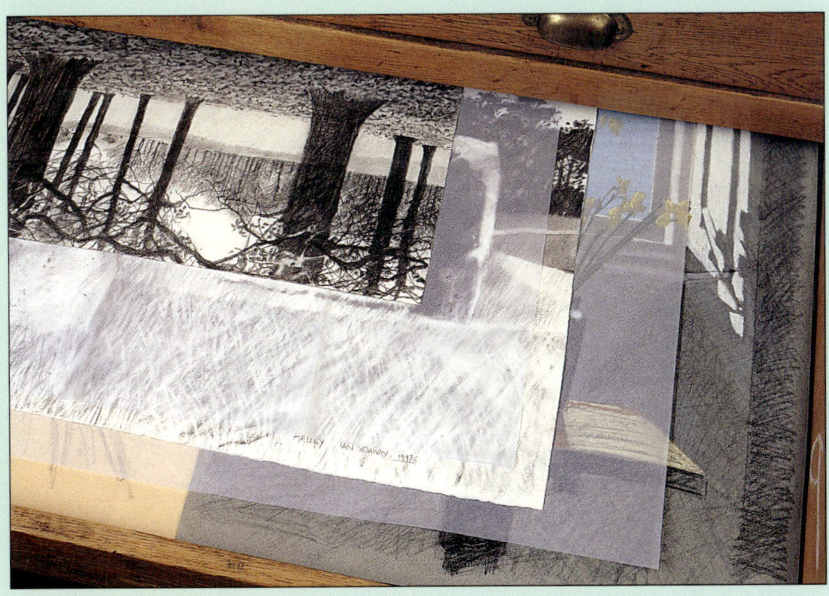

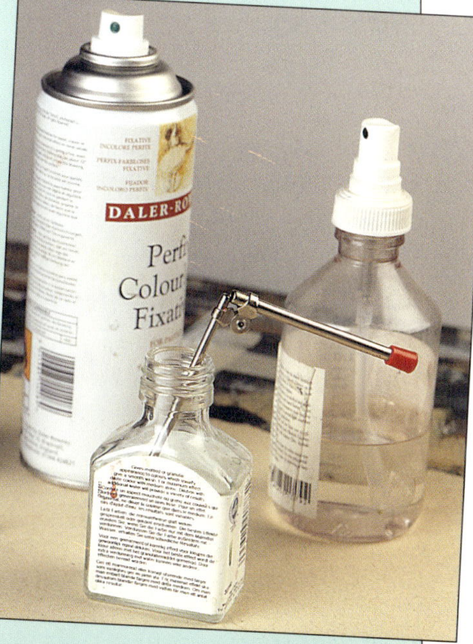

▲ The most convenient way of fixing a powdery medium is with an aerosol fixative, but a diffuser is the traditional method. Bend the diffuser to create a right angle, immerse one end in the fixative, then blow briskly through the mouthpiece to create a fine spray. Practise on scrap paper first until you can achieve an even coverage.

Tricks of the trade

Art materials are expensive – but with a little care you can extend the life of your equipment and even rescue materials that have seen better days.

To keep your costs as low as possible but maintain the quality of your painting, it really pays to look after and restore equipment – and, indeed, improvise tools if necessary. The handy tips that follow will help you to extend the life of your materials.

New life for old brushes

Brushes last longer if you clean and dry them properly; however, you can often rescue neglected brushes with a little special treatment. A brush that has lost its condition can be washed in warm, soapy water, then treated with hair or fabric conditioner. Rinse off the product, reshape the brush with your fingers and leave it to dry.

If stray hairs are sticking out, or the fibres are misshapen, you can sometimes restore the shape by suspending the brush in a jar of water for a few days. Push the brush handle through thin card and rest this on the rim of the jar so that the brush hangs in the water without resting on its bristles.

If this process fails to restore the brush to its intended shape, take a little gum arabic between your fingertips and smooth the bristles into shape. Leave to dry. Hair gel can also be used to reshape an unruly brush. Whatever you use, rinse the brush carefully before you next use it.

Another good way to reshape a brush is to wrap toilet paper around the wet bristles. The paper contracts as it dries, pulling the bristles into shape.

IMPROVISED EASEL

If you enjoy working on big canvases but don't have the space or cash for a large easel, metal shelving with adjustable brackets provides a neat and flexible alternative.

Fix the metal uprights to the wall a suitable width apart, then insert the brackets at the required height. Alternatively, a pair of angled brackets screwed to the wall is fine if you tend to work on the same size of canvas and don't need to adjust the height.

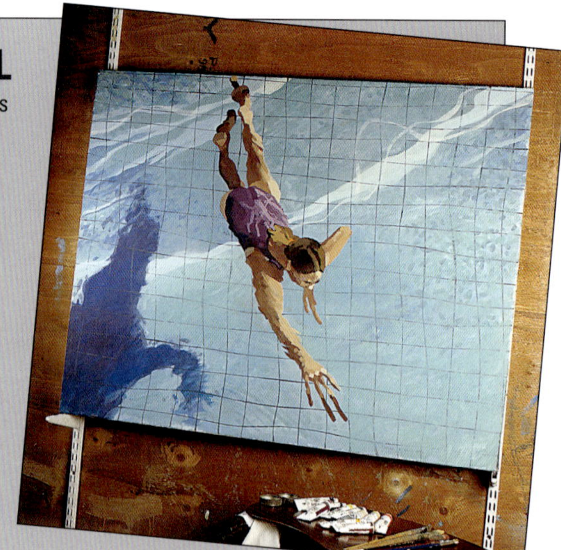

Flattening dented canvases

Remove bulges from a canvas by dampening the back. As it dries, the cotton or linen fibres shrink to give a smooth surface. If this does not work, you might need to apply heat. Dampen the canvas, then steam off the water by holding a hot iron just above the surface (test first on a scrap snipped from the edge). Try not to put the iron directly on the canvas, as this will stretch it.

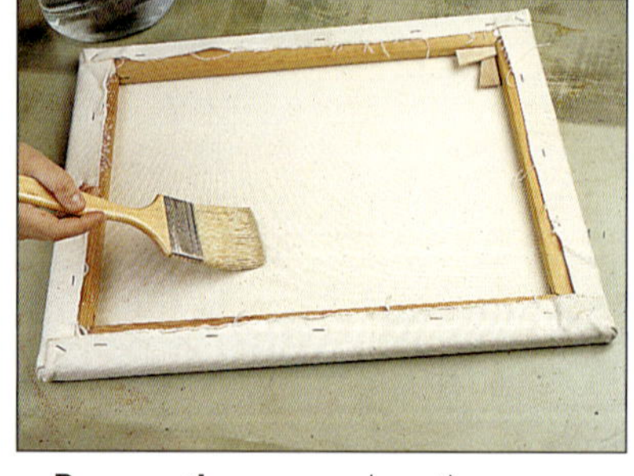

▲ **Dampen the canvas** Lay the canvas face down on a surface protected by a blanket. Dampen with a brush, cloth or sponge, and leave to dry.

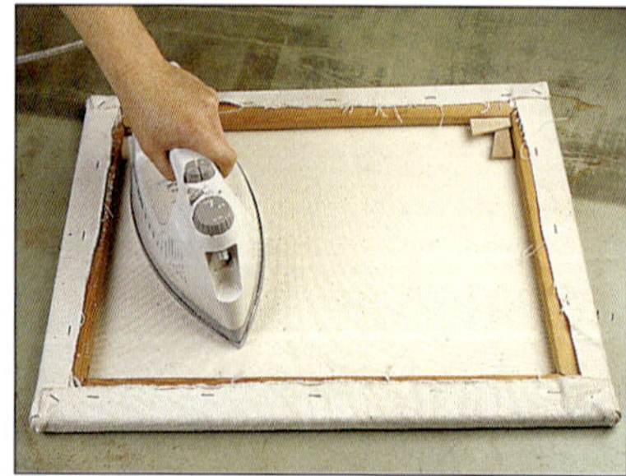

▲ **Heat the canvas** To eradicate serious dents, dampen the back then hold a hot iron over the area. The rapid drying will flatten the canvas.

Dried-on acrylics

Acrylic paint dries quickly and is then almost impossible to remove from a brush. It is a good idea to use two jars of water for acrylic painting – one for cleaning brushes, the other for diluting the paint. Add a drop of washing-up liquid to the cleaning water to prevent paint accumulating on the brush.

If you leave your brushes too long and the acrylic paint has dried on the bristles, soak them in methylated spirit for up to 12 hours, then wash them under running water.

Dealing with masking fluid

Masking fluid is particularly tough on brushes. Apply it with old brushes (kept in a separate jar) or use a dip pen or a stick. If you rub a brush on household soap before you dip it into masking fluid, it will be easier to clean.

Making your paints last

To prevent your paints from drying out, always replace the cap on the tube when you have finished with a colour. Wipe the threads at the top of the tube clean before replacing the cap – a little lubricating jelly or glycerine applied to the threads will prevent the cap from sticking. If a cap does stick, a brisk tap with a heavy object is sometimes all that is needed to loosen it. A strip of sandpaper wrapped around the cap will improve your grip.

To loosen caps on watercolour or gouache paint tubes, run hot water over the neck. If that fails to loosen them, soak the tube upside down in hot water overnight. For oil paint tubes, substitute turpentine or white spirit for hot water.

You can also use a pair of pliers or a jar opener to shift unyielding caps. Alternatively, wedge the cap between the edge of the door and the jamb – pull the door towards you so that it acts as a vice, then twist the paint tube.

Reviving dried-out paint

Always squeeze tubes of paint from the bottom upwards, as this keeps the paint together and prevents it drying out too quickly. Get the last drop of paint out of a tube by laying it on a flat surface and scraping a palette knife along its length from bottom to top. If a tube of paint has dried out, however, you can sometimes access usable paint at the base of the tube by piercing it with a pin. Stick masking tape over the hole to seal it.

For dried-out watercolour or gouache, cut the end off the tube and add a few drops of water through the newly made opening. Leave the water to work its way into the paint, then mix it into a paste. Alternatively, cut the tube open and use the paint as pan colour.

CLEANING AND CARING FOR BRUSHES

Get into the habit of cleaning your brushes after every session. Wipe excess paint on tissue, a rag or an old telephone directory – tear off the top page after you have wiped your brush on it, leaving a clean sheet ready for next time. Rinse the brush in the correct solvent – turpentine or white spirit for oils, water for watercolour, gouache and acrylic. Next, hold it under cold running water, rub it over a bar of plain household soap or solid brush cleaner, then work up a lather. Rinse under the tap until the water runs clear.

Flick your wrist to remove excess water. If necessary, shape the brush with your fingers, then leave to dry flat.

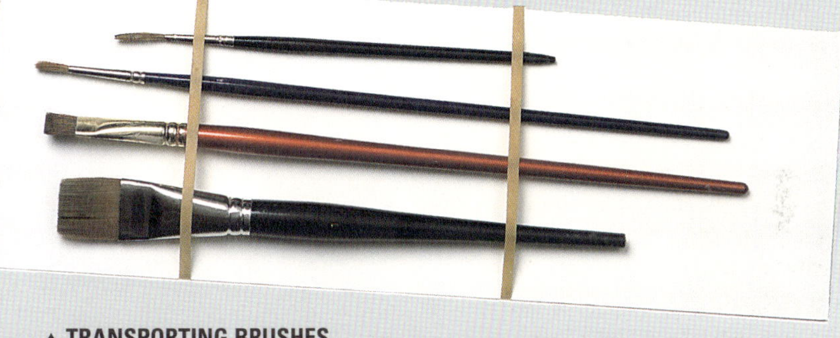

▲ **TRANSPORTING BRUSHES**
Make sure you protect your brushes when you're on the move. Cut a piece of stiff card wide enough to accommodate your collection of brushes side by side and longer than your biggest brush. Stretch two elastic bands around the card, one at the top and one at the bottom. Insert your brushes under the elastic bands.

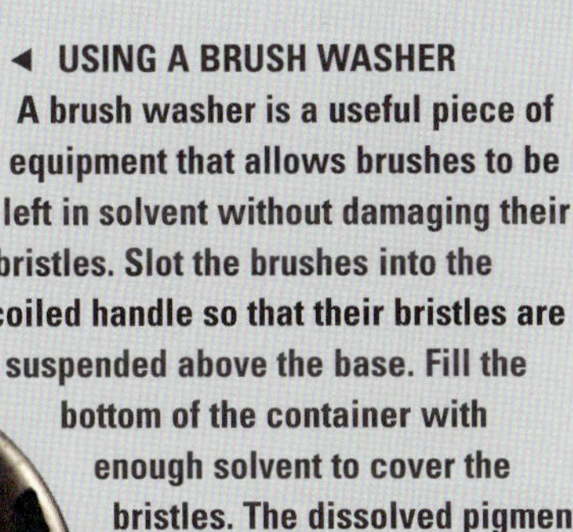

◄ **USING A BRUSH WASHER**
A brush washer is a useful piece of equipment that allows brushes to be left in solvent without damaging their bristles. Slot the brushes into the coiled handle so that their bristles are suspended above the base. Fill the bottom of the container with enough solvent to cover the bristles. The dissolved pigment from the bristles settles at the bottom of the pot – some designs have a filter so that the pigment can be removed and the solvent re-used.

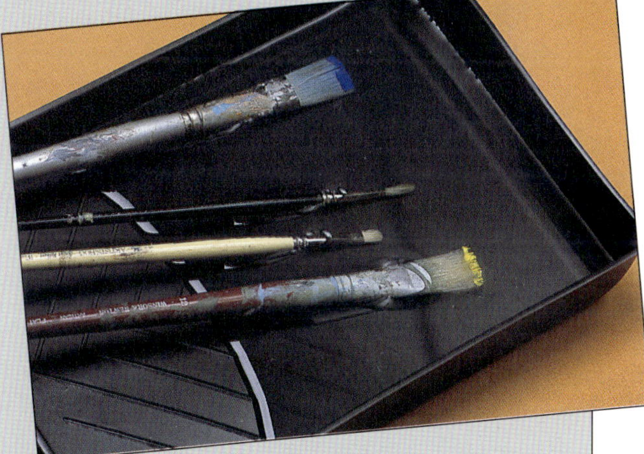

▲ **KEEPING ACRYLIC BRUSHES WORKABLE**
Acrylic paint dries quickly and, once dry, is almost impossible to remove. During a painting session, keep brushes workable by laying them in a shallow dish of water, such as a decorator's roller tray – rest the handles on the rim to avoid pressure on the bristles.

HOME-MADE PALETTES

Palettes can be improvised very easily. Use old white plates and saucers for watercolour and gouache. Mix larger washes in yoghurt pots.

You can make palettes for acrylics and oil paints from offcuts of wood, ply or laminates. Seal timber or ply with several layers of varnish or paint first. Glass makes an excellent mixing surface, too, as it is smooth and easy to clean.

Acrylic paint dries quickly on the palette and, once dry, cannot be re-wetted. You can make a moisture-retaining palette (see below) that works in the same way as those available from art suppliers.

If you are planning a long break from your painting, cover watercolours, acrylics or oils with cling film and put the palette in the freezer. Allow it to thaw for about an hour before you plan to use it.

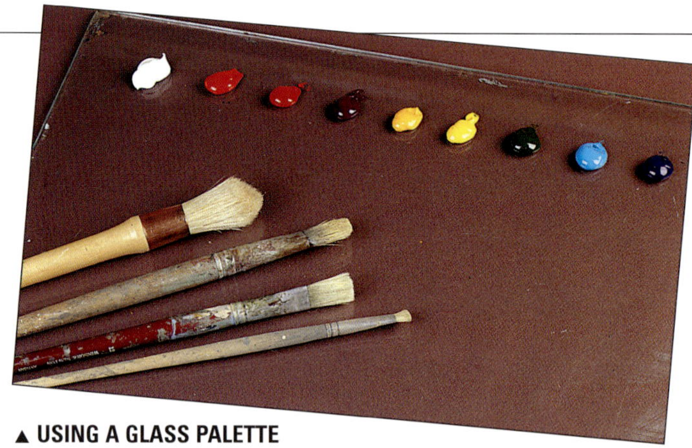

▲ USING A GLASS PALETTE
A sheet of glass makes a good palette. Make sure the glass has a bevelled edge so that you don't cut yourself. Put a sheet of paper underneath, in a shade that matches your ground so you can judge how the mixes will appear when applied. Lay out the colours in an orderly way – here they are organized warm to cool, with white at the end.

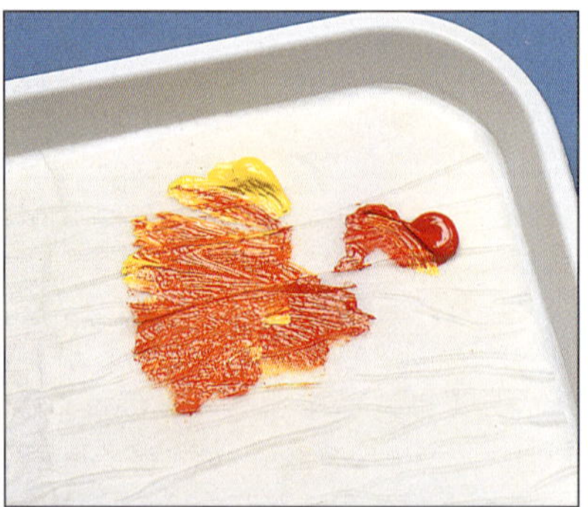

▲ MOIST PALETTE FOR ACRYLICS
To keep acrylic paint workable for longer, make a moisture-retaining palette. Line the base of a shallow plastic tray with wet blotting paper. Lay a sheet of greaseproof paper on top to form the mixing surface.

▼ COVERING WITH CLING FILM
If you have unused acrylics left at the end of a session, cover the tray with cling film to keep the paints moist.

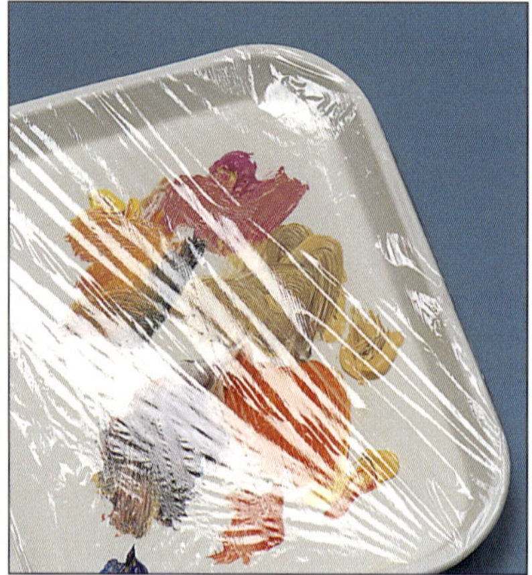

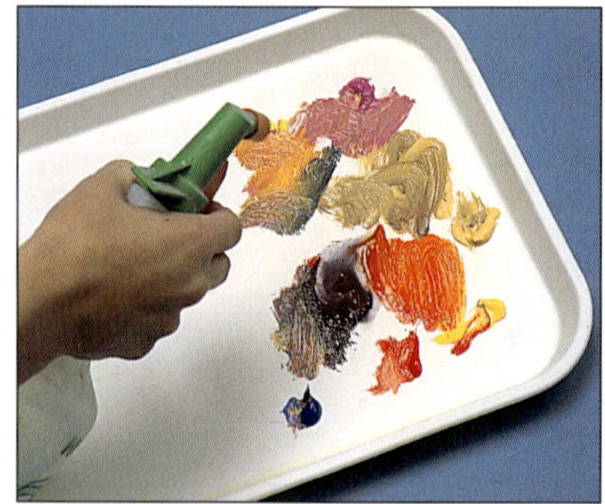

▲ SPRAYING YOUR PALETTE
Use a plant sprayer to mist the palette if watercolour or acrylic paints are drying out. You can also spray the support to keep the paint surface wet and workable, but don't overdo it or the paint will run.

PASTELS

When working in pastel, lay out your sticks on a sheet of corrugated card, arranged in colour groups. The hollows will prevent them rolling off the work surface.

If different coloured pastels are stored together, the colours rub off on each other and the sticks begin to look grubby. To remove surface dirt, put the pastels in a jar of rice and shake.

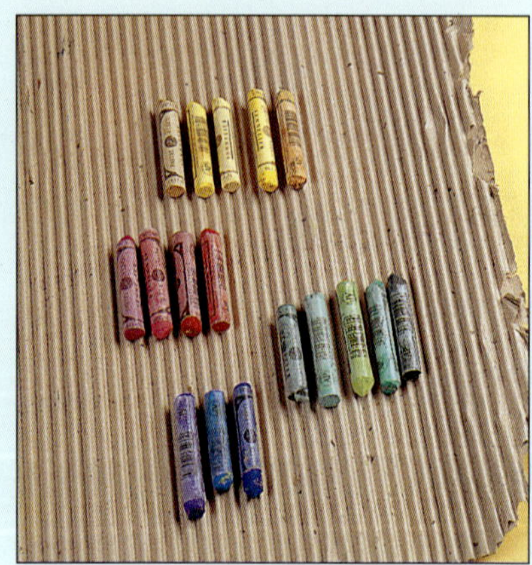

▲ ORGANIZING PASTELS ON CARD
Corrugated card prevents the pastels you are using from getting mixed up – and they won't roll off the work surface.

▼ CLEANING PASTEL STICKS
Rice in a small jar will brighten dirty pastel sticks. Put the pastels in the jar and shake for about a minute or so.

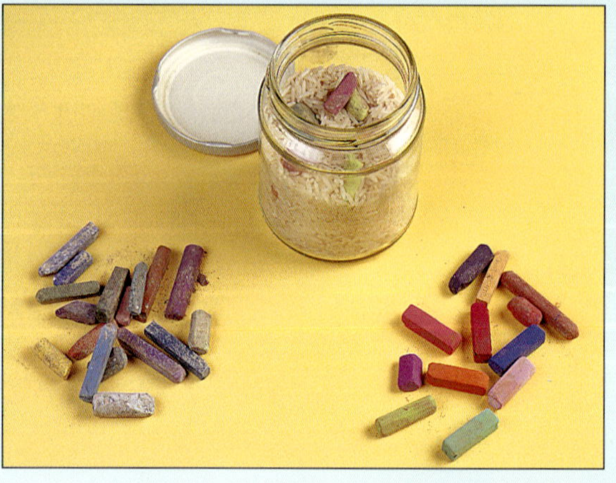

Choosing the best easel

A stable easel, which holds your work rigidly in one position, will avoid the frustration of trying to work with your picture precariously propped up on a table or on your lap. You'll soon find it's a necessity rather than a luxury.

A good easel is an artist's best friend. It will last a lifetime and is one of the most important and permanent pieces of studio equipment, so take time to look around and buy a model that meets all your requirements. Your choice of easel depends on various factors – the available space in your working area, whether you like to work standing up or sitting down, and whether you tend to work mostly indoors or outdoors. It also depends on the medium you generally use and on the scale of your work. For example, watercolours are much easier to use with an easel that can be tilted to the horizontal, so your washes won't run down the paper.

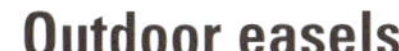

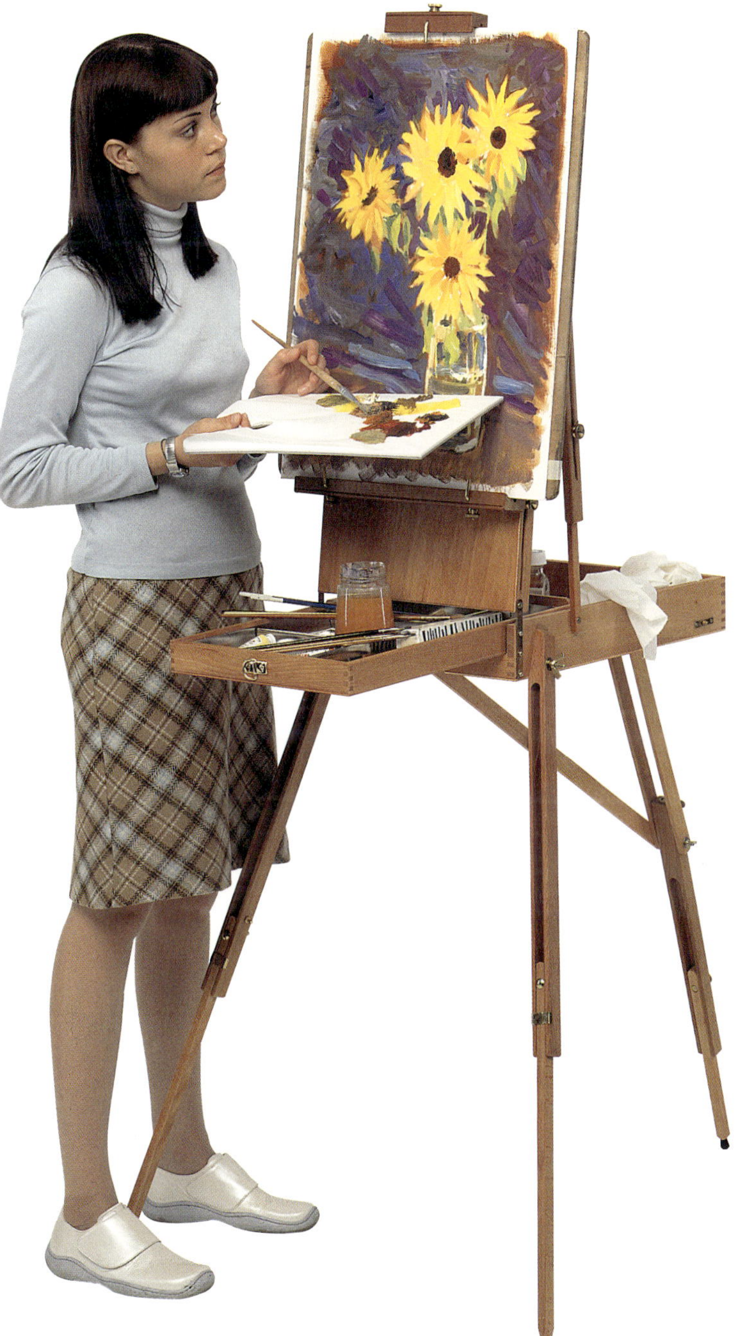

Outdoor easels

Lugging a heavy easel on painting expeditions is no fun at all, so choose a compact, portable model for outdoor work. A sketching easel (see easels E–H overleaf) could be the answer, being both lightweight and foldable. These are made in wood or aluminium, are fully adjustable and can usually be positioned for both watercolour and vertical painting.

Sketching easels can accommodate surprisingly large boards and canvases, but this depends on the make and type. Check the distance between the top and bottom easel grips to make sure that the easel will take the size of support you prefer.

A box easel (see left, below and easel N overleaf) is more stable, though slightly heavier than an ordinary sketching easel. However, it is easy to fold up and carry, and also incorporates a box or drawer for holding paints, brushes and other materials.

Easels for indoor work

For large or heavy canvases, a traditional upright studio easel (easels I-L overleaf) is probably your best bet. These can be bulky – some even have castors, so that they can be moved around more easily – but they are reassuringly solid.

If your work space is limited, a radial easel (J) is a versatile alternative. This consists of an upright spine with tripod-type legs. The whole easel can be adjusted, so you can angle your work to suit the light, though not to the horizontal position necessary for watercolour painting. When it is not in use, the radial easel can be folded for easy storage.

A tilting radial easel is also known as a 'combination' easel (K) because it brings together features of both the radial and the sketching easel. It has a central joint, so

◄ The versatile box easel is ideal for the artist who likes to work both in the studio and out-of-doors. For storage and carrying, the easel folds down to a box shape with a handle for easy carrying (right).

that it can be adjusted to any position from upright to completely horizontal, and it is therefore an ideal choice for the artist who works in a variety of media.

If your studio space or work area is limited, a sketching easel or a box easel will be just as versatile indoors as out. Alternatively, if you work on a fairly small scale, a table-top easel in wood or aluminium (see easels A–D below) might be all you need.

Looking after your easel

Apart from the lightweight sketching easels made from aluminium, most artists' easels are robustly constructed from hardwood, traditionally beechwood. They require little regular maintenance, although the wood benefits from an occasional coat of wax polish, especially when an easel is used outside or in damp conditions. Also, the metal adjusting nuts can become stiff and should be kept lubricated with oil.

THE RIGHT EASEL FOR THE JOB

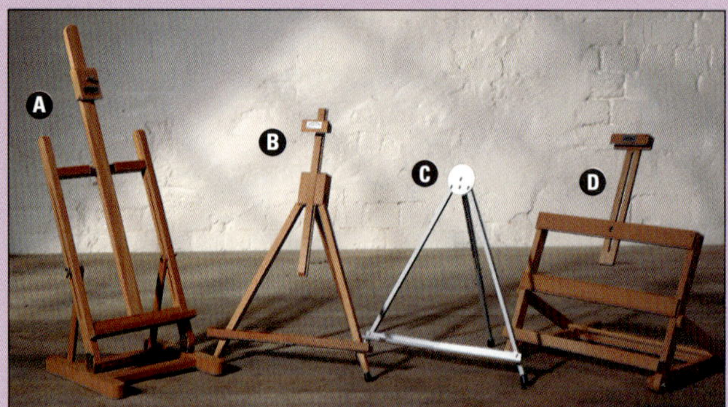

TABLE EASELS

A Sturdy wooden easel with an 'H' frame, which can be tilted to provide the ideal working angle.

B Light, portable tripod-type wooden easel with rubber-tipped non-slip feet.

C Extremely light aluminium easel with adjustable telescopic back leg and rubber-tipped feet.

D Wooden easel, which can be set at four different angles and folds flat when not in use.

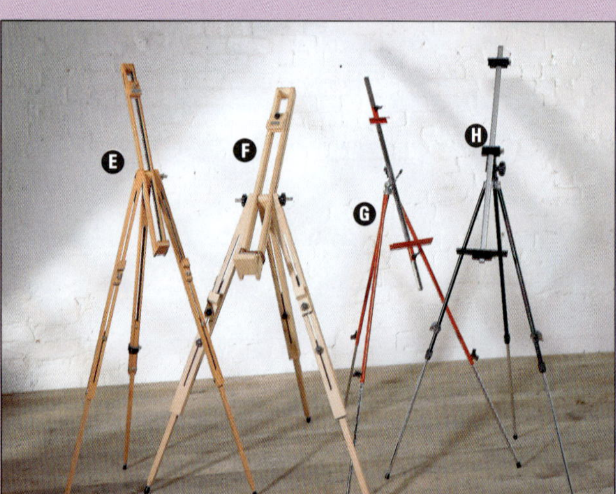

SKETCHING EASELS

E Lightweight easel with an adjustable tilting facility, making it suitable for all media, including watercolour.

F Substantial tilting, sketching easel appropriate for all media.

G Folding, tilting metal easel with telescopic legs and adjustable canvas grip.

H Fully adjustable metal easel with a camera mount fixing, so that it can be used as a photographic tripod.

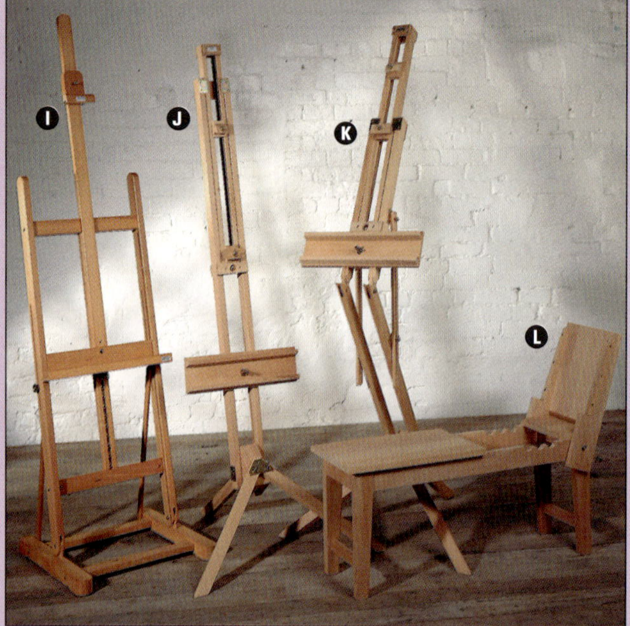

STUDIO EASELS

I Sturdy studio easel with an adjustable lower shelf for the canvas or board, allowing simple adjustment of the working height.

J Rigid, adjustable radial easel, which can be tilted backwards and forwards, but not horizontally, for watercolour work.

K Combination easel, which can be secured in any position and is suitable for use with all media.

L Artist's 'donkey' or platform easel – a comfortable sitting easel which takes up very little space when folded.

M Simple, popular 'A' frame easel with a metal ratchet on the lower support for adjusting the working height.

N Box easel with a container for paints, brushes and other art materials. Ideal for studio or outdoor work.

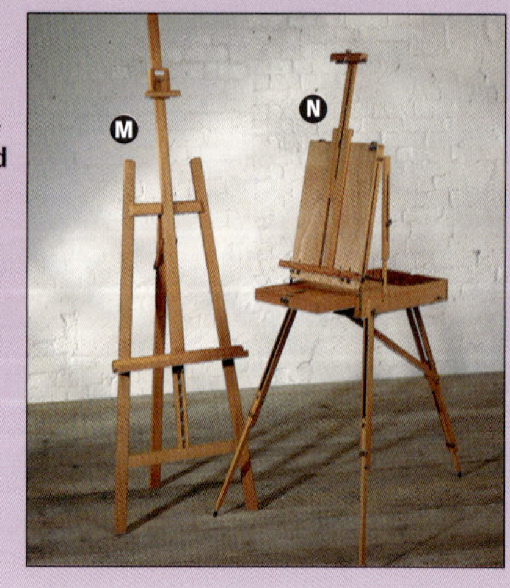

Keeping a sketch book

Whether you use it to make preparatory drawings, try out different mediums or create a visual diary, the sketch book is an invaluable tool for the artist.

Artists have been known to make sketches on old envelopes, on shopping lists – and even on the back of the hand! It is much simpler, however, if you carry a sketch book at all times. In this way you can make on-the-spot drawings and jot down visual ideas whenever and wherever you like – and you always know where to find them when you need them.

The sketchbook habit

For most artists, carrying a sketch book is more effective than carrying a camera. True, you can take a photograph in a fraction of a second and it will give you a detailed rendition of a particular scene. Unless you are a skilled photographer, however, you cannot use the camera as creatively, as it tends to render everything in the same way.

A sketch book, on the other hand, provides a personal record. In it, you can record not only what you see, but also what you feel. You can emphasize certain elements, and leave out others entirely. If you are struck by a particular facial expression, for example, you can make a quick sketch, capturing the essence of that expression without worrying about detail, colour, texture and so on.

It is a good idea to buy a small sketch book – one which fits into your pocket or a bag that you always carry – and to use it whenever the opportunity arises. Record people and places, and sketch details of what is happening around you. Above all, jot down any ideas you might have for future paintings. Your sketch book – unlike your memory – won't let you down. Once you have made a drawing, it is there for ever to provide you with inspiration.

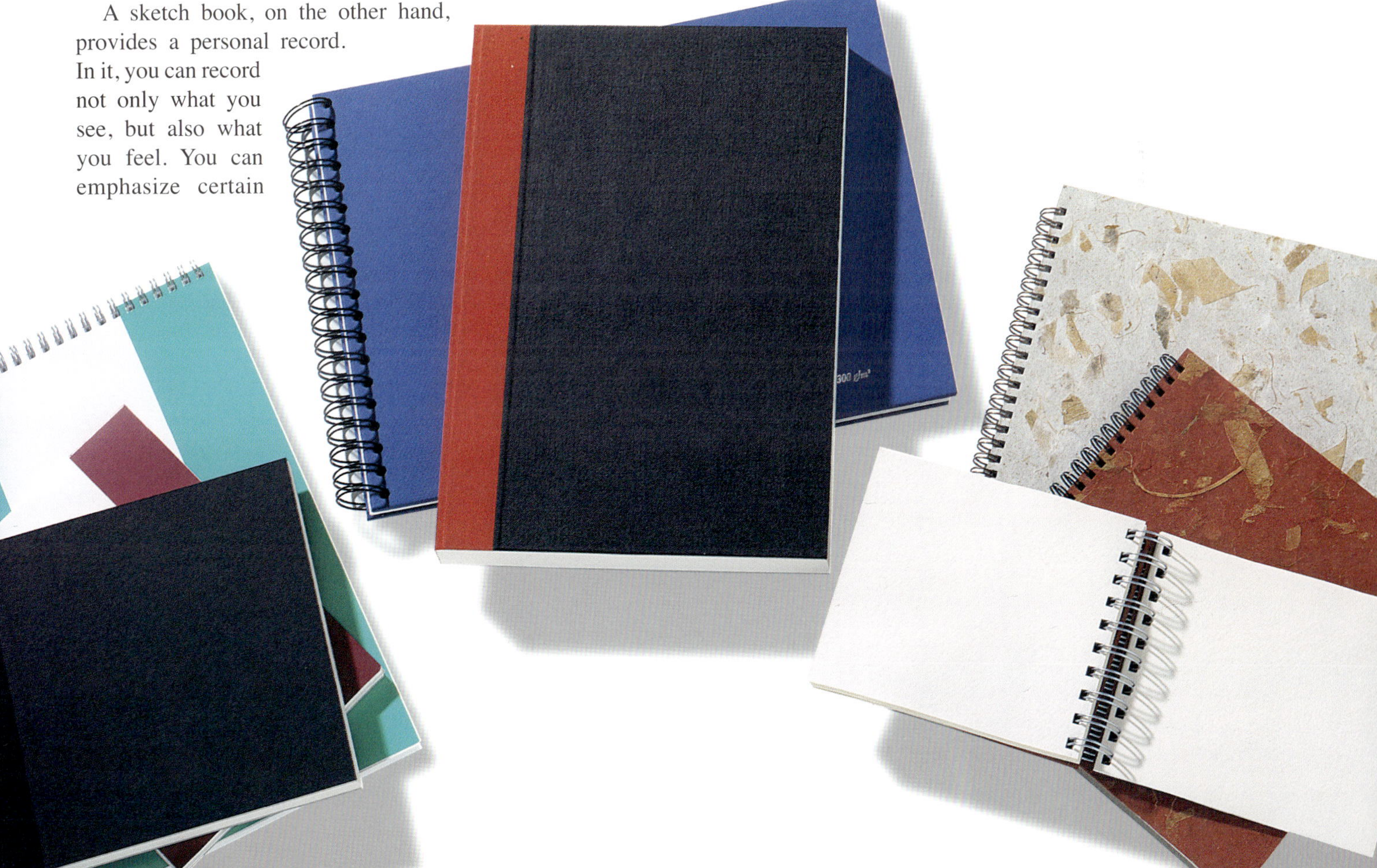

▼ **Large or small, spiral-bound or case-bound, landscape or portrait, there is a sketch book to meet the needs of every artist.**

The quality of the paper in sketch books varies enormously. You can, for example, buy books of handmade paper, often bound with elaborately marbled or fabric covers. These sketch books are beautiful objects in their own right.

The right paper

However, a very expensive sketch book can be quite daunting for the amateur artist, who might be afraid to ruin it with poor sketches. Remember also that a sketch book with a delicate, ornate cover will get damaged easily if you intend to carry it around with you.

It is probably better to begin by using an inexpensive book – but avoid very cheap pads that contain thin, shiny paper. These are generally bought from stationers rather than art shops. Usually, the paper they are filled with is too hard to use with anything except a ballpoint or fountain pen.

Most art shops stock sketch books in a range of cartridge and drawing papers, from 95gsm (45lb) sketching paper to the heavier 290gsm (140lb). Also available are pads of assorted coloured and tinted papers, ideal for pastel and coloured pencil work. However, these are not usually made in pocket sizes, A5 generally being the smallest.

Choosing a sketch book

To a large extent your choice of sketch book will depend on what drawing materials you use. Cartridge paper is a good all-rounder, suitable for most drawing tools. However, bear in mind that pen and ink and technical pens are best used on very smooth papers, while chunky mediums such as soft pencil, pastel and charcoal are served well by coarse surfaces.

Sketch books come in various shapes and sizes. Some are rectangular and upright ('portrait' format); others are rectangular and horizontal ('landscape' format). The portrait format is perhaps the most versatile choice because you can always work across two pages, taking your drawing over the spine for a landscape subject.

Spiral- or case-bound?

The spine of a sketch book can be either case-bound (that is, stitched or gummed) or spiral-bound. The spiral-bound ones don't allow you to sketch across two pages, but they do let you remove pages without ruining the book. This means you can discard substandard sketches and mount and frame exceptional ones.

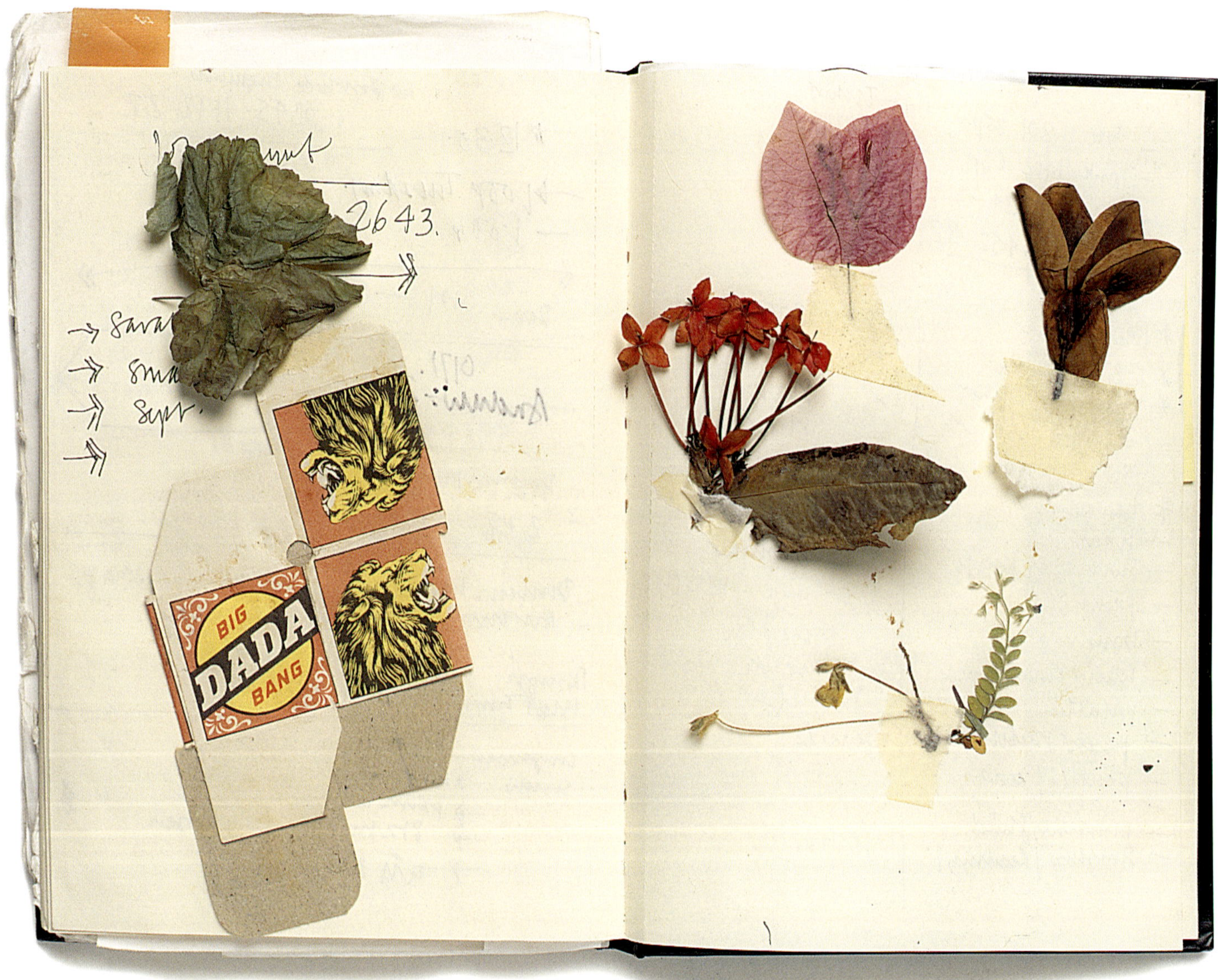

What's more, the spiral-bound books can easily accommodate mounted materials. To make your book really attractive, feel free to include visually interesting items such as pressed flowers and leaves, postcards, tickets, invitations and even scraps of fabric – anything, in fact, that may prove useful as a reference, inspiration or memory jogger. Your sketch book is, in effect, a visual diary.

You can also use your sketch book for painting outdoors. Most heavier sketchbook papers of around 290gsm (140lb) are fine for light watercolour washes. However, for very wet colour, you should always use a watercolour pad (see above right).

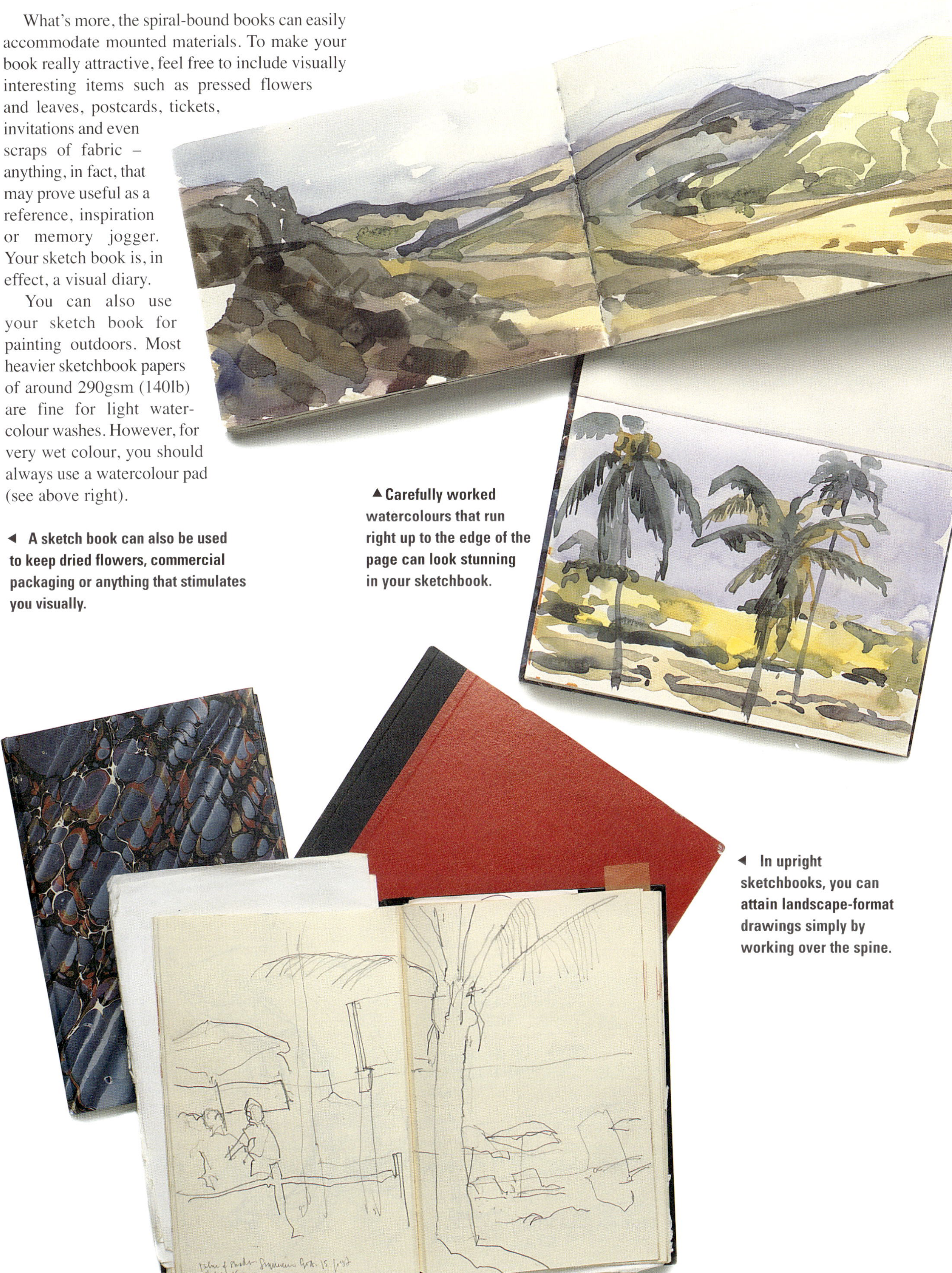

◄ **A sketch book can also be used to keep dried flowers, commercial packaging or anything that stimulates you visually.**

▲ **Carefully worked watercolours that run right up to the edge of the page can look stunning in your sketchbook.**

◄ **In upright sketchbooks, you can attain landscape-format drawings simply by working over the spine.**

Watercolour pads

Like sketch books, watercolour pads come in a range of sizes starting from around 180 x 130mm (7 x 5in). They are made with proper watercolour paper and have a strong backing board for rigidity and stability. The papers range from very rough to smooth hot-pressed. They are available either spiral-bound or as a block which is gummed on all four edges to reduce the need for stretching.

For sketching with acrylic paints, you can buy pads of canvas-textured paper. Oil paints are not really a suitable sketching medium because they take so long to dry.

Colour notes

Painting out-of-doors can be a delight, but you often find yourself running out of time or stopped in your tracks by a change in the weather. It is difficult to finish the painting at home because you cannot remember the colours.

The answer is to make colour notes in your sketch book before you start work on the painting. Make a very rough line drawing of the subject in your sketch book. Then you can write the names of the colours on the sketch or, even better, paint an actual blob of colour in the relevant area. These approximate colour guides will provide the reference you need to complete the painting at home.

One sketch book, many styles

Use your sketch book to experiment with different drawing styles and mediums. The sketches below – which are all by the same artist – give some indication of the styles you might like to include in your book. The top picture is a line drawing in pencil, but has blocks of tone dotted across the composition to add variety. The middle picture is also in pencil – but colour has been added with washes of coffee.

The bottom sketch was done in watercolours. Paints might not seem the ideal sketching medium – but you can easily carry around a small watercolour set that contains all you need.

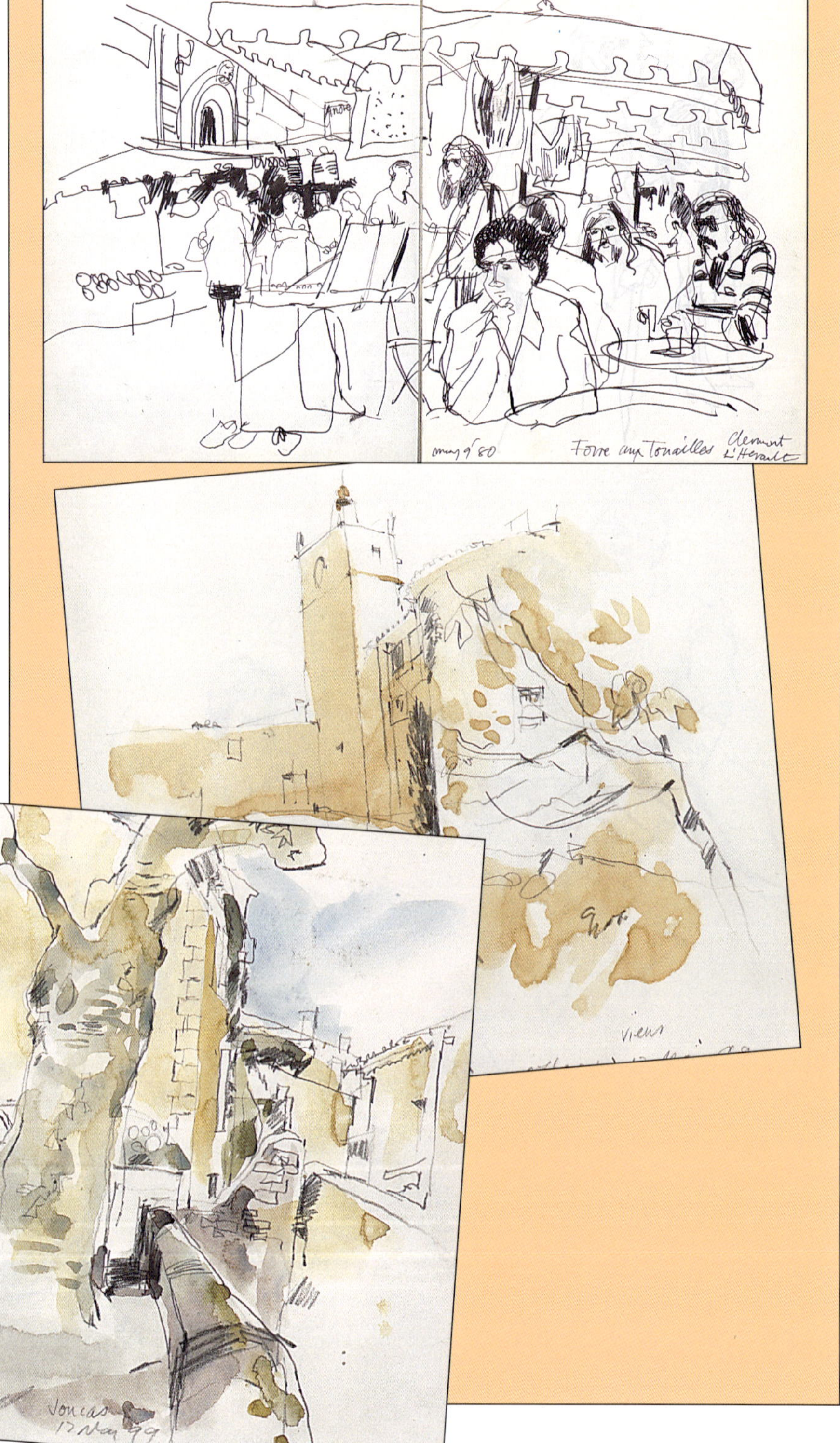

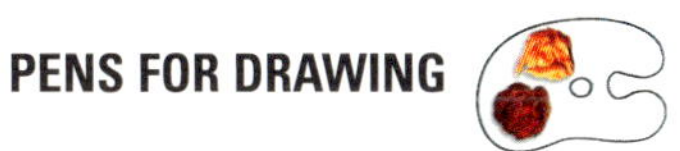

Pens for drawing

The range of pens available to the artist is vast and inspiring, ranging from traditional dip pens made from quill, bamboo or reed to fibre-tipped pens in many shapes, sizes and colours. Here we review the choices available.

Your choice of pen is very personal and most artists have a favourite. Still, it is worth knowing what is on the market because you might have special requirements from time to time.

Dip pens are the most basic type. As their name suggests, they are loaded by being dipped into ink and have to be recharged at intervals. At the other end of the scale is an ever-expanding range of innovative markers and brush pens which come in a vast array of colours.

Traditional dip pens

These are made from quills, bamboo and reed. Quill pens are cut from the flight feathers of birds such as swans, ravens, ducks or geese, and they usually produce a slightly scratchy line. This type of pen is particularly popular with calligraphers. Bamboo pens are very tough and vary in size depending on the piece of bamboo used. Reed pens are more flexible than bamboo pens, but tend to chip easily. Both reed and bamboo pens are still used in Japanese and Chinese art today.

Metal dip pens

The metal pen has been traced back as far as Roman times, but it wasn't widely used until the nineteenth century, when technical innovations made it possible to mass-produce steel nibs. From this time, steel nibs became more popular than quill, bamboo and reed. Most metal dip pens consist of a shaft or handle into which a separate metal nib is slotted. It is worth experimenting with some of the many different nibs available to discover the marks they are capable of producing and to find out which most ideally suits your needs and your style of drawing.

Script pens Old-fashioned script nibs consist of a shaped piece of metal with a slit cut in it down which the ink can flow. Some have fine or rounded points, while others are chiselled for italic lettering. They are ideal for sketching.

Mapping pens These pens have slender, straight nibs with very fine drawing points. They are specially designed for detailed work such as technical drawing and map-making.

Lettering pens The nibs used for lettering pens are available in various shapes,

VARYING THE LINE WIDTH

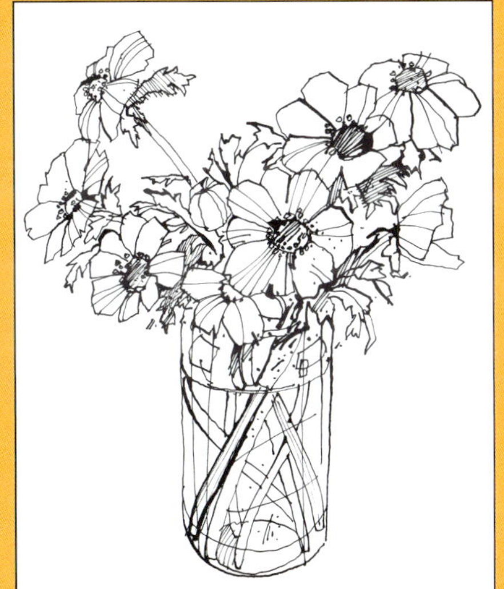

Technical pen
The fine lines produced by a technical pen are ideal for delicate drawings with a lot of detail. Use hatching for darker areas.

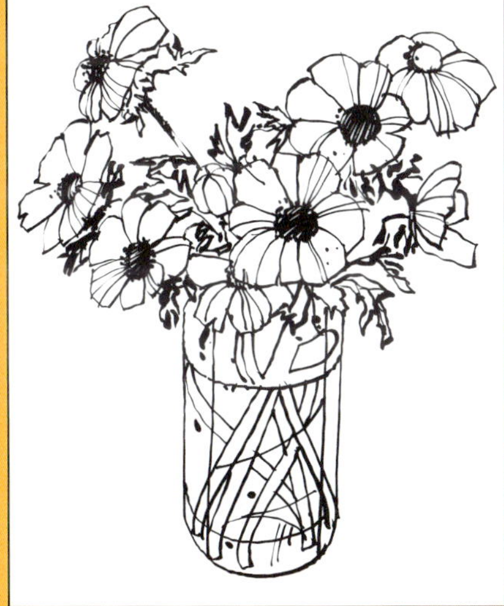

Brush pen
With the flexible tip of a brush pen, you can adopt a more fluid approach, using both thick and thin lines in a sketch.

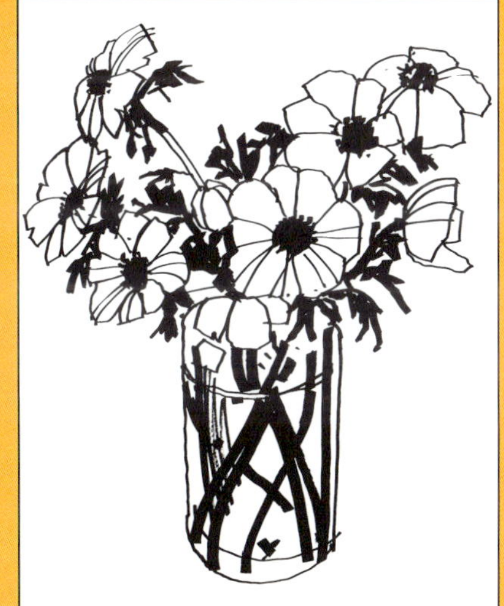

Marker
A marker with a chisel tip makes thick, bold lines that can fill shapes such as the flowers' stalks with a single stroke.

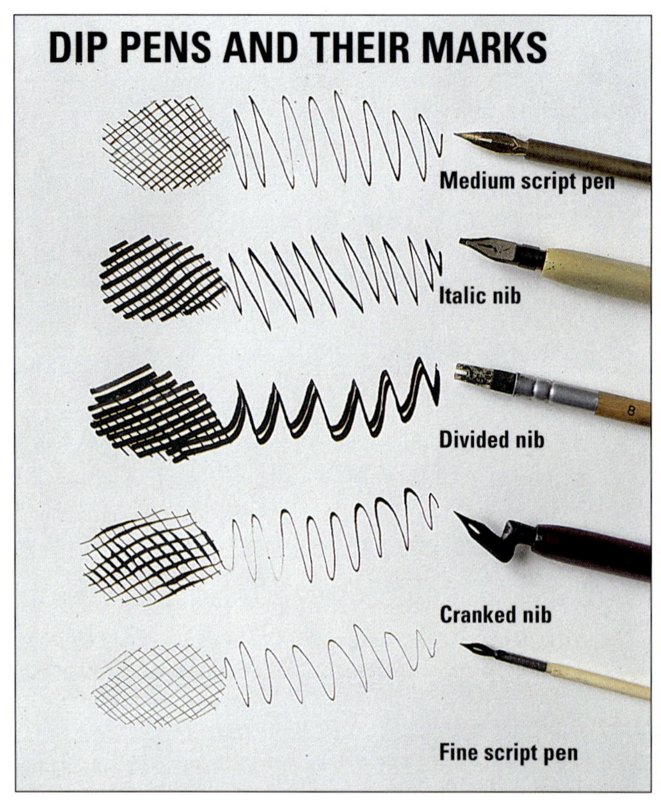

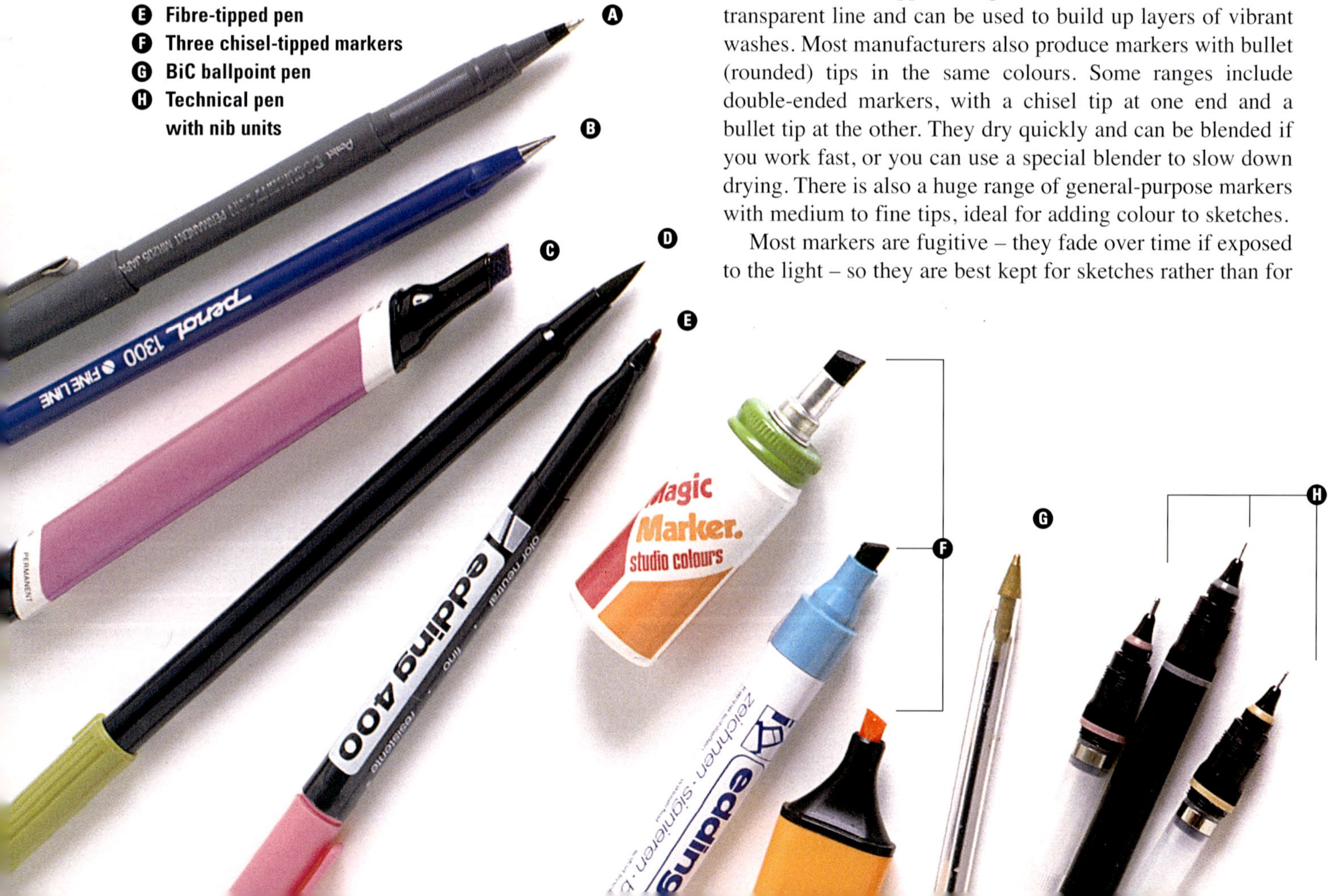

which are designed to produce the special serifs, flourishes and ribbon shapes used in calligraphy. Nibs consisting of two pieces of metal are designed to hold more ink. Some lettering pens have broad nibs with two or three splits in them, making it possible to produce a wide line. Others are divided, giving parallel lines for calligraphy. Pens for musical notation are cranked (bent at an angle so that the tip of the nib is not in line with the pen shaft), which makes them more springy.

Reservoir pens

These pens contain their own store of ink and are ideal for use on location, as you don't have to carry a bottle of ink with you.

Fountain pens The ink for these pens is carried in either a replaceable cartridge or a refillable, pump-action reservoir. Most are designed for writing, but others are for sketching.

Technical pens Originally designed for illustrators and draughtsmen, these pens produce consistent lines in specific widths. The nib units fit into a holder and can be changed when you require a different line width. Use technical pens with the correct ink, never leave the nib exposed and wash out the units from time to time.

Ruling pens These are also specialist drawing tools. The reservoir is filled using a brush or dropper, and the size of the tip can be adjusted by turning a screw. They give a consistent line and don't have to be recharged as often as dip pens.

Markers and fibre-tipped pens

This category includes a wide and colourful range of pens, some of which are designed for professional applications, while others are intended for everyday use.

Markers Chisel-tipped felt pens, or markers, leave a broad, transparent line and can be used to build up layers of vibrant washes. Most manufacturers also produce markers with bullet (rounded) tips in the same colours. Some ranges include double-ended markers, with a chisel tip at one end and a bullet tip at the other. They dry quickly and can be blended if you work fast, or you can use a special blender to slow down drying. There is also a huge range of general-purpose markers with medium to fine tips, ideal for adding colour to sketches.

Most markers are fugitive – they fade over time if exposed to the light – so they are best kept for sketches rather than for

TYPES OF DRAWING PEN

- **A** Ballpoint
- **B** Fineline ballpoint
- **C** Chisel-tipped marker
- **D** Brush pen
- **E** Fibre-tipped pen
- **F** Three chisel-tipped markers
- **G** BiC ballpoint pen
- **H** Technical pen with nib units

images that will be displayed. Solvent-based markers should always be used in a well-ventilated space.

Fineliners These allow you to work with more precision, although the tip will eventually become blunt. Some fineliners are available in specific line widths.

Brush pens The tip on a brush pen is longer and more pliable than on other markers, and some ranges have a huge choice of colours. By varying the pressure, you can produce fine, medium or bold strokes. Some double-ended pens have a brush pen on one end and a fine fibre tip on the other.

Ballpoint pens

The first ballpoint pen was invented in 1938 by a Hungarian journalist called Laszlo Biro, who was inspired by the quick-drying, smudge-proof ink used for commercial printing presses. The thicker ink would not flow from an ordinary nib, so he devised a pen with a tiny ball-bearing in its tip. Biro is often used as a generic term to describe ballpoint pens. One of the most popular ballpoint pens today is the BiC, launched by the French Baron Bich in 1950. Ballpoints are cheap and convenient, and can be a useful addition to your sketching kit.

Rollerballs These pens work on the same principle as ballpoints, but the ink in them is more like that used in cartridge pens or fibre-tipped pens. It dries quickly by evaporation and does not create blotches as ballpoints sometimes do.

Inks

The main distinction between inks is whether they are waterproof or water-soluble. Waterproof ink allows you to lay a wash over a line without dissolving it, whereas a water-soluble ink will spread and run. Indian ink is the best-known drawing ink – it is black, permanent and waterproof. Coloured waterproof drawing inks are dye-based and not lightfast, so are best used in sketchbooks where they won't be exposed to light for long periods. Waterproof inks should not be used in fountain pens, as they will clog the mechanism.

Liquid watercolours and acrylics Like coloured inks, these can be used with dip pens and are available in a wide array of shades. Liquid watercolours are soluble once dry, while liquid acrylics are not.

Liquid acrylic

Indian ink

Liquid watercolour

Waterproof drawing ink

Bamboo pens

- **I** Selection of nibs for a dip pen
- **J** Divided nib for parallel lines
- **K** Mapping pen
- **L** Cranked nib for music notation
- **M** Script pen
- **N** Ruling pen
- **O** Sketching fountain pen
- **P** Selection of coloured fibre-tipped pens
- **Q** Bullet-tipped pen
- **R** 3mm (1/8in) chisel-tipped pen
- **S** Fineliner

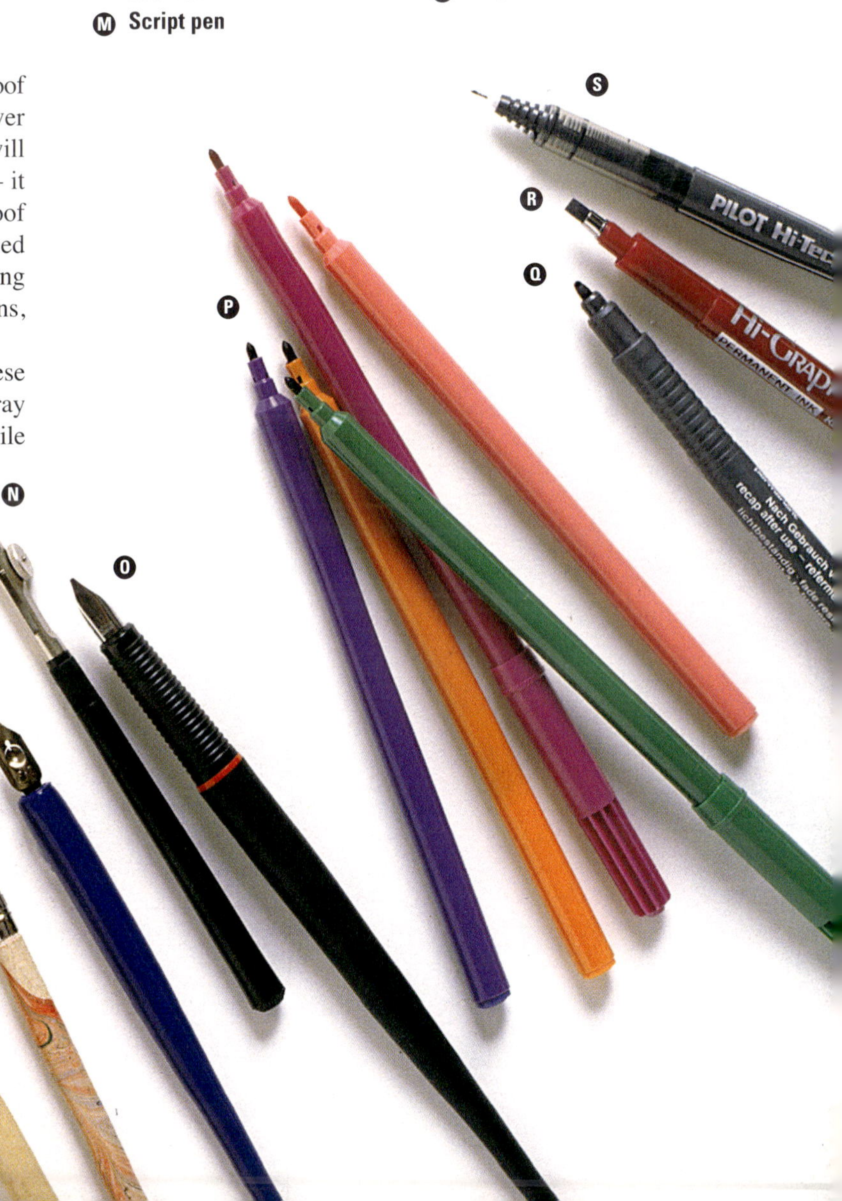

Introducing marker pens

Whether you're sketching outdoors or working on a finished drawing indoors, marker pens provide a colourful and convenient medium.

If you thought marker pens belonged in the office or the children's playroom – think again! Vigorous, brilliantly coloured drawings can be made with this modern medium, which is especially convenient for outdoor sketching. A set of marker pens is light, compact and clean, allowing you to make full-colour sketches without the need for cumbersome paints, palettes and jars of water.

The only drawback with markers is that they contain dyes rather than pigments, so the colours tend to fade in time when exposed to strong sunlight. You can, however, minimize the risk of fading by keeping your drawings in a portfolio or hanging them well away from direct sunlight.

Types of marker

There is an enormous range of markers to choose from, in literally hundreds of colours and with various sizes and shapes of tip. Art and graphic suppliers sell the best-quality pens, but the ones sold in stationers and supermarkets are cheaper and perfectly adequate for sketching and practice work.

- **Fibre tips** have tips made from nylon or fibreglass. They are hard-wearing and smooth-flowing.
- **Felt tips** have thicker, slightly more flexible tips made from wool or a synthetic substitute. They flow smoothly and make soft, dense marks.
- **Fineliners** have tips made from plastic or a similar synthetic material. They are hard and durable and produce thin, spidery lines.

Tip shapes

As well as being made from a variety of materials, felt and fibre tips have a range of tip shapes, varying from fine points to broad, chisel-shaped wedges.

- **Wedge-shaped tips** are the most versatile. By turning the marker as you draw, you can use the edge and the different sides of the tip to make broad, medium and thin lines. You can also fill in areas of flat colour by working quickly in broad, horizontal lines, taking each line over the previous one before it has time to dry.
- **Bullet-shaped tips** produce medium and bold marks, and the rounded tip can be used for stippling effects.

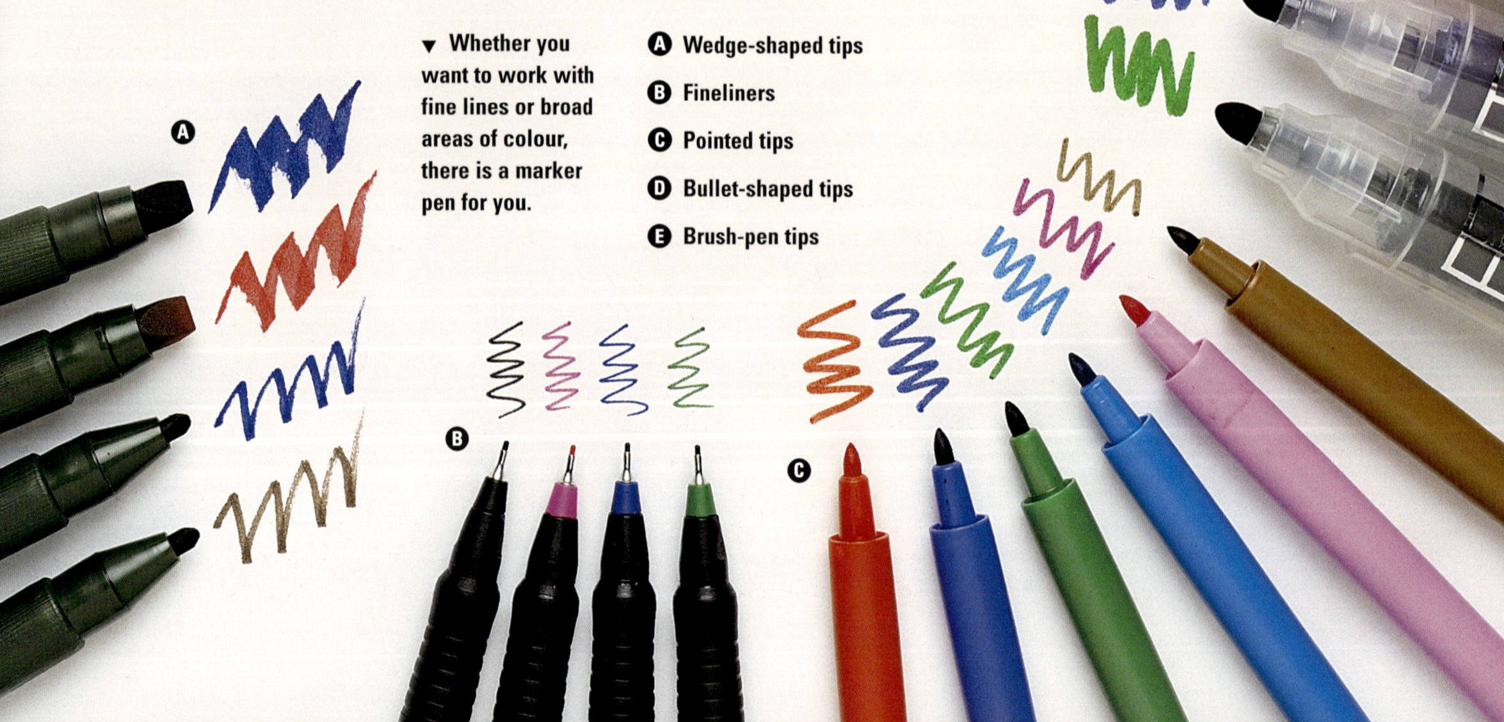

▼ **Whether you want to work with fine lines or broad areas of colour, there is a marker pen for you.**

A Wedge-shaped tips
B Fineliners
C Pointed tips
D Bullet-shaped tips
E Brush-pen tips

- **Pointed tips** produce thin lines of uniform thickness. They are good for defining outlines and for rendering fine details.
- **Brush-pen tips** are made of elongated, flexible fibres that come to a point, and these create a variety of marks that look similar to those that are made with a watercolour brush.

Two types of ink

Another important consideration when it comes to marker pens is whether they contain water-based or spirit-based inks. The water-based inks tend to lie on the paper surface for longer, making it easier to blend colours. Interesting soft, feather-like effects can be achieved by drawing on dampened paper.

The spirit-based colours, by contrast, are readily absorbed into the paper, permanent and waterproof. They tend to 'bleed' beyond the shape drawn by the nib, although for fine-art purposes this doesn't usually matter. They also tend to bleed right through the paper, so, when working on a sketch pad, place a sheet of scrap paper beneath the drawing surface.

Spirit-based pens that are drying out can be rejuvenated by tipping a few drops of lighter fuel into the cap before putting it back on the pen. After a few hours, the nib should have absorbed the fuel and, although the colour will be lighter, the pen will last longer.

Papers

It is fun to experiment with different drawing surfaces, as each influences the character of the drawn lines, depending on how readily they absorb the marker dyes. You can buy special marker paper which resists colour bleeding. This paper has a hard, non-absorbent surface and is ideal when you want to produce crisp, clear marks and fine details. Alternatively, try drawing on smooth white card or even white scraperboard.

Delicate effects

If you want a more delicate effect, try drawing on ordinary cartridge paper or watercolour paper. The marks produced will be softer and fatter as the colour sinks into the surface and spreads slightly. On the highly absorbent Japanese rice papers, the marker dye spreads rapidly, like ink on blotting paper, producing effects similar to watercolour painting.

Practice is the key to successful marker work. Bear in mind that markers are not a subtle medium, and they do have certain limitations. The colours are bright and brash – they cannot be lightened with water or white paint, and mistakes cannot be rectified. Also, the marks cannot be blended on the paper as easily as, say, watercolour or pastel.

On the plus side, a single marker can produce a whole range of lines, tones and textural effects according to how you hold it and the pressure you apply. So buy a selection of pens with different nib shapes and experiment by making marks on sheets of scrap paper.

Different strokes

Marker pens lend themselves to a surprisingly wide range of drawing techniques. Fineliners are ideal for stippling or cross-hatching (see top row of apples below). By cross-hatching in colour, you can create great optical mixing effects by overlaying different hues. On the bottom-left apple, look at the way red has been hatched over green to create a brown suitable for the shadowed side. With chisel- and bullet-shaped pens, try making use of the transparency of the inks by laying flat areas of colour over each other (see bottom-right apple). To avoid getting muddy tones, limit the colours you overlay to three or four.

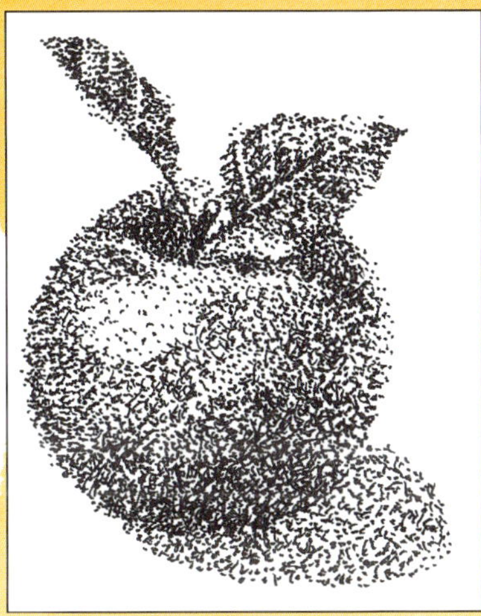

Stippling in monochrome

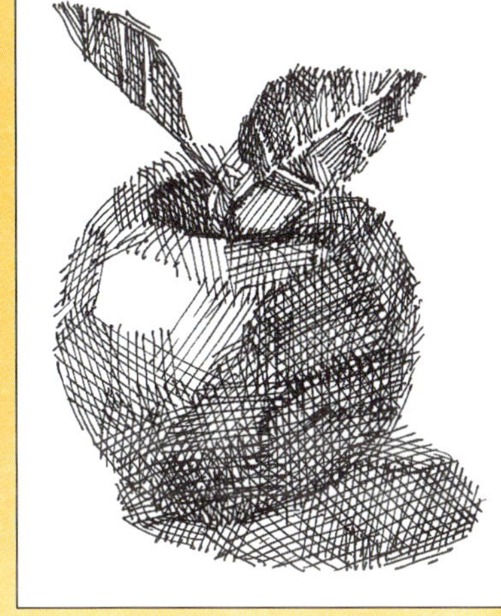

Cross-hatching in monochrome

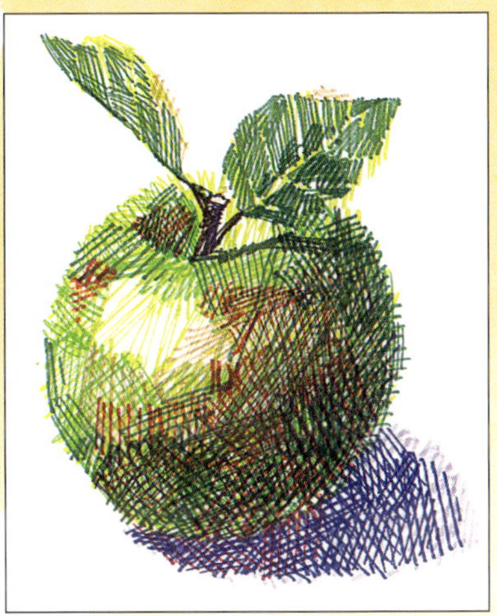

Cross-hatching in colour

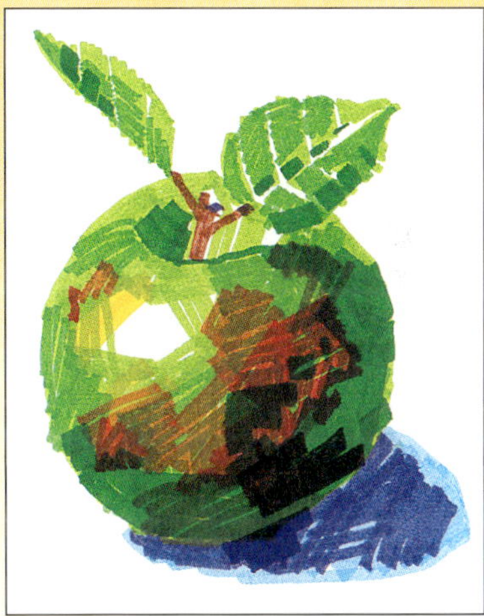

Building up layers of colour

Drawing with ballpoints

The everyday ballpoint pen, or Biro, is not usually considered an artist's medium, but this humble writing tool has much to recommend it.

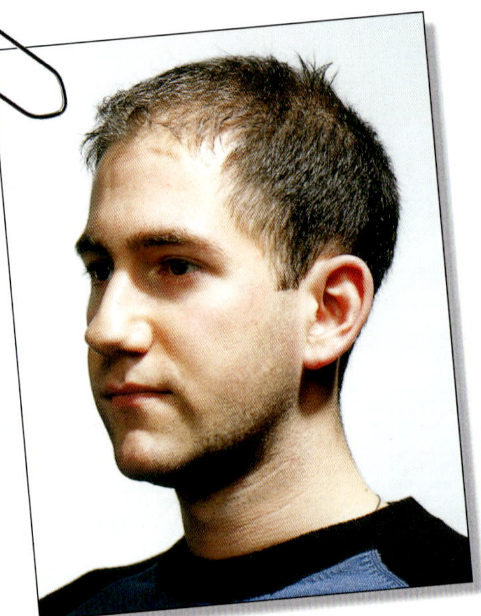

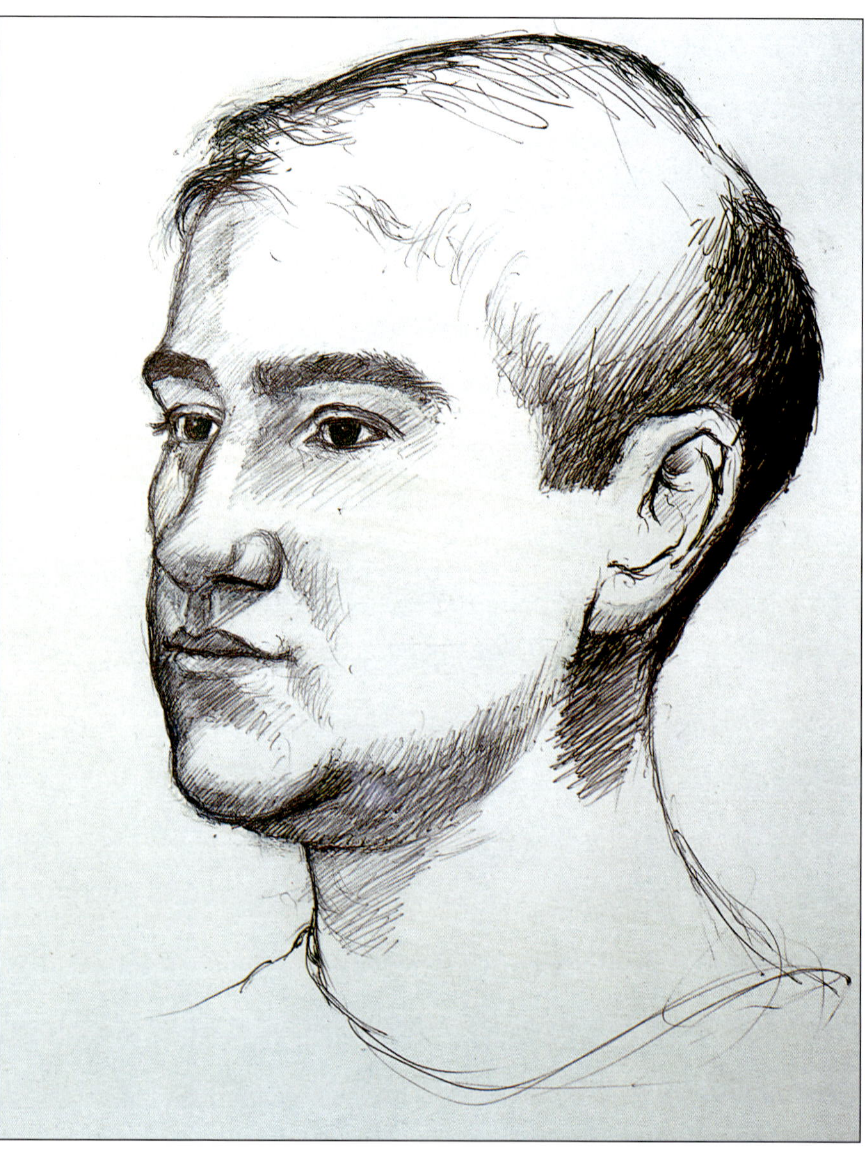

▲ **A combination of ballpoint, rollerball and fibre-tip pens was used for this portrait.**

Ballpoint pens, invented in the 1930s by Hungarian journalist Lazlo Biro (1899–1985), make interesting if slightly unconventional drawing tools. They have many advantages, as they are cheap, easily portable and can be used on most types of paper.

Black and blue

For the artist, black is probably the most useful ballpoint shade. It gives a strong, positive image, as you can see from this portrait. And it is also the least likely to fade.

Blue, although not quite as lightfast, makes a useful alternative colour for the artist, creating a brighter and perhaps more unusual effect. Experiment by trying a little sketching and drawing with both colours to see which you prefer.

Fine lines

Ballpoints produce fine lines of consistent width – you can't vary the character much by applying more or less pressure to the pen. The line has a wiry, mechanical quality and is ideal for hatching, cross-hatching, scribbled hatching and stippling. Even the broken line of a pen that is about to run out can be exploited.

In the portrait, the darker areas of shadow were applied with black rollerball and fibre-tip pens. These types of pen produce marks that are significantly bolder than the ballpoint lines, and so create a strong contrast of tone.

YOU WILL NEED

Piece of cartridge paper 35.5 x 25.5cm (14 x 10in)

3 black pens: ballpoint; fibre-tip; rollerball

Bleedproof white gouache paint

No. 4 round brush

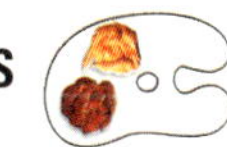

FIRST STEPS

1 ▶ **Establish the left eye** Using the fine black ballpoint pen, locate the sitter's nearer (left) eye – this is the pivot for the entire portrait. Draw the edges of the lids and the line of the eye socket. Outline the iris and hatch shadows under the eye and beside the bridge of the nose. Sketch in the curve of the eyebrow.

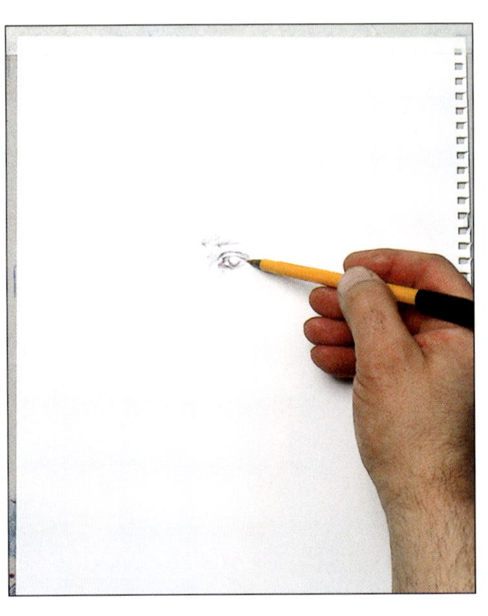

TROUBLESHOOTER

WHITE IT OUT

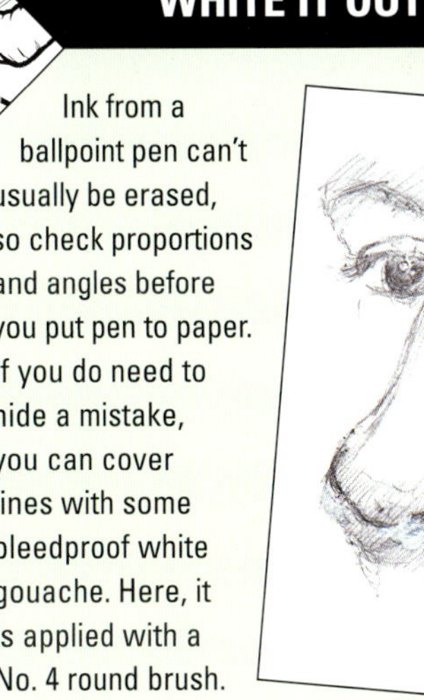

Ink from a ballpoint pen can't usually be erased, so check proportions and angles before you put pen to paper. If you do need to hide a mistake, you can cover lines with some bleedproof white gouache. Here, it is applied with a No. 4 round brush.

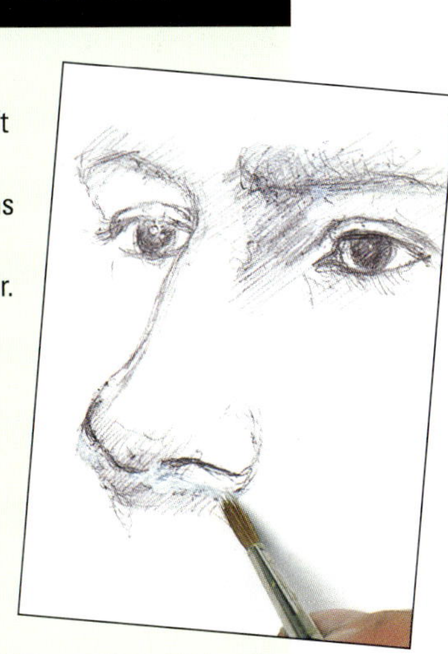

2 ▼ **Develop the eye** Darken the iris, leaving a highlight to give sparkle to the eye. Develop the eyebrow and indicate the lower lashes. Start to build up the tone, using loose hatching.

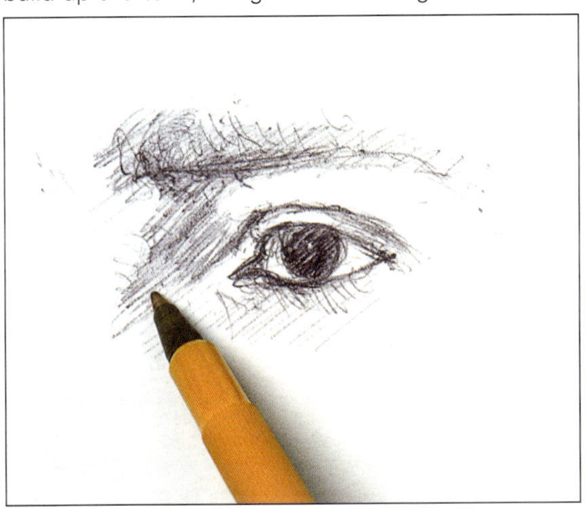

3 ▼ **Position the second eye** Measure with your pen to locate the position of the right eye, which is partially hidden behind the bridge of the nose. Establish the upper and lower lids, the pupil, the iris and the curve of the eyebrow.

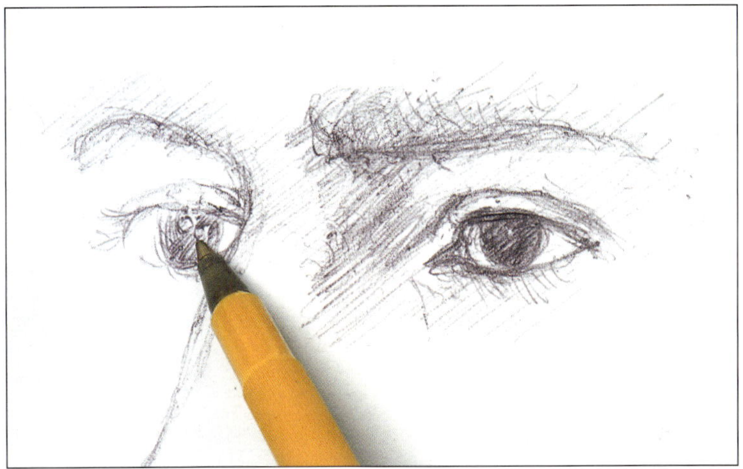

4 ▼ **Draw the nose** Use your pen to measure the length and width of the nose. In this view, the base of the nose looks broader than the eye. Add dark tone under the nose to make the tip advance and the underside recede.

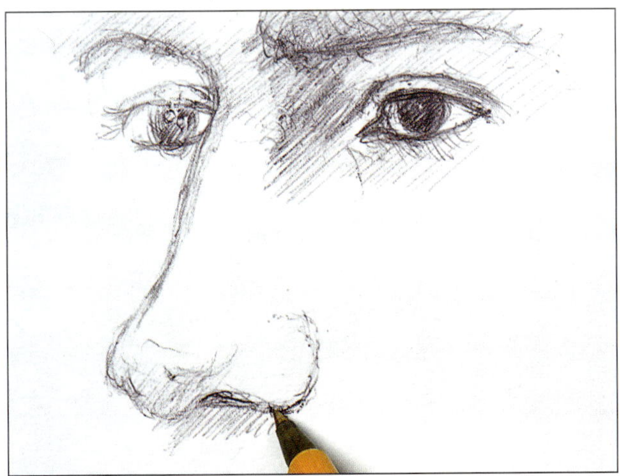

DEVELOPING THE FEATURES

Continue working up the features to complete the face, then start to work outwards to establish the shape of the whole head.

5 ▶ **Add the mouth** Lightly sketch the edge of the right cheek, using short pen strokes – these are easier to correct and look more natural than a single hard line. Draw the outline of the lips and the indentation between the nose and top lip.

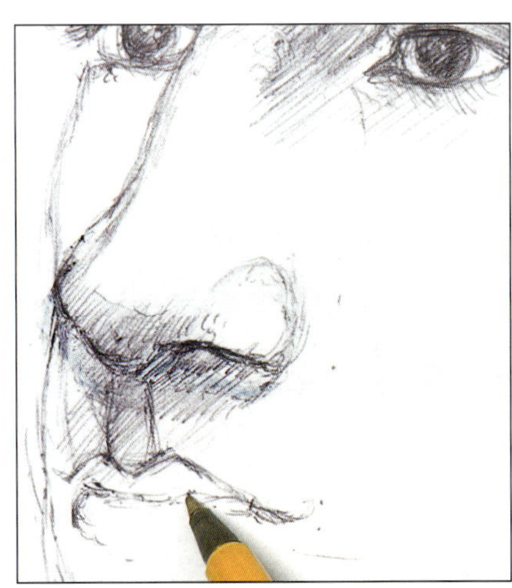

6 ▶ Work on the face Finish drawing the mouth and plot the line of the chin. Add shadows on and around the lips and on the tip of the chin. Work across the drawing, developing the graduations of tone. The sitter has dark, well-defined eyebrows, so use small strokes of the ballpoint pen to add more texture and tone to these.

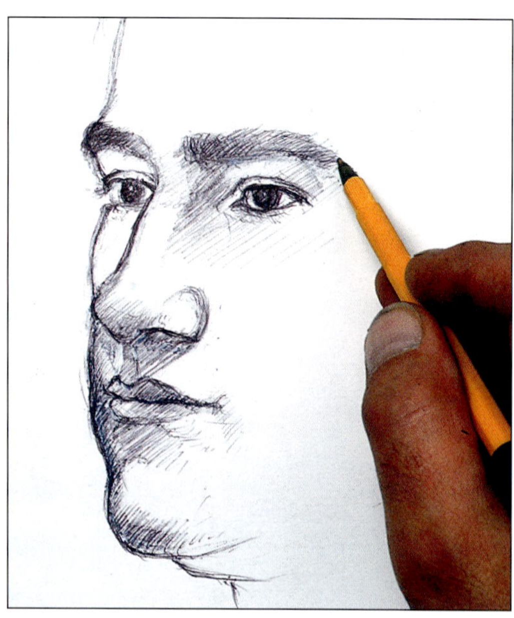

7 ▼ Plot the skull Add shadow under the right eye. Now outline the skull and ear. Notice how the skull is an egg shape, broader at the top. Note, too, how the top of the ear lines up with the eyebrow, while the bottom aligns with the area under the nose.

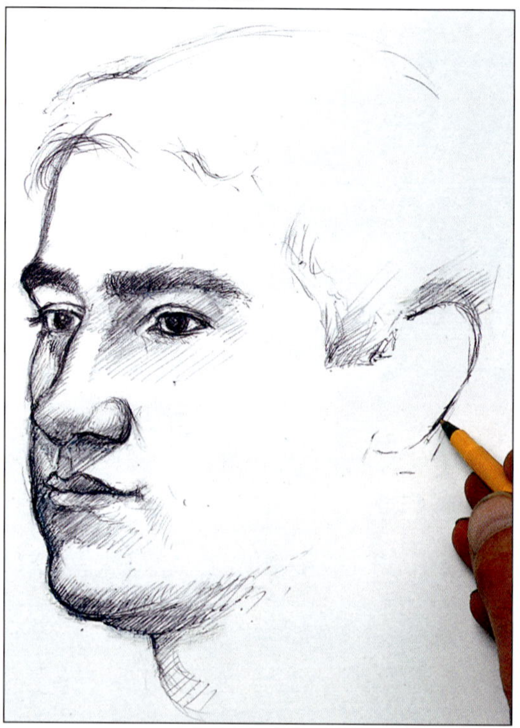

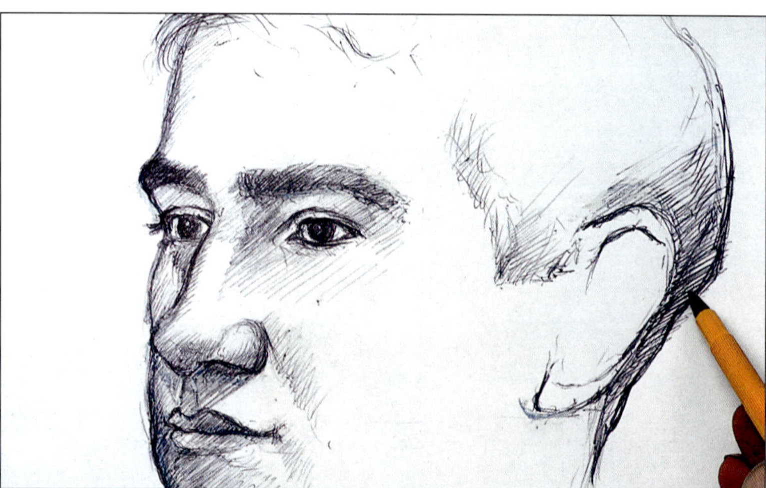

8 ▲ Develop the skull Continue working on the head, adding the dark shadow at the back of the skull that helps to convey the volume and roundness of the form. Use regular hatched strokes for this.

9 ▶ Define the left eyebrow Use bleedproof white gouache applied with a No. 4 round brush to tidy up the outline of the left eyebrow. Apply the white paint above and below the brow. Leave to dry.

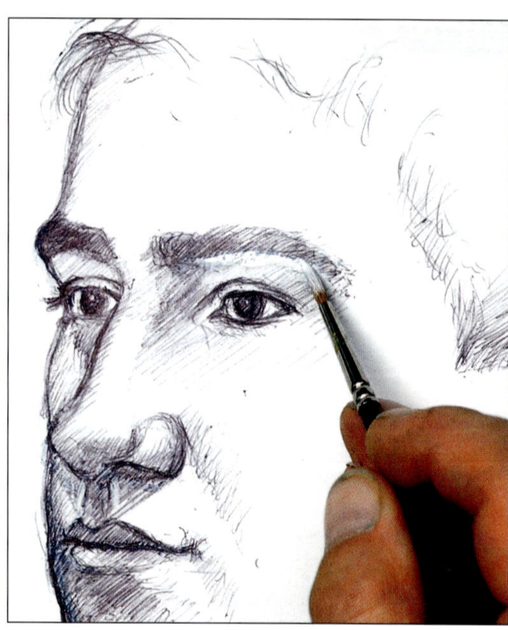

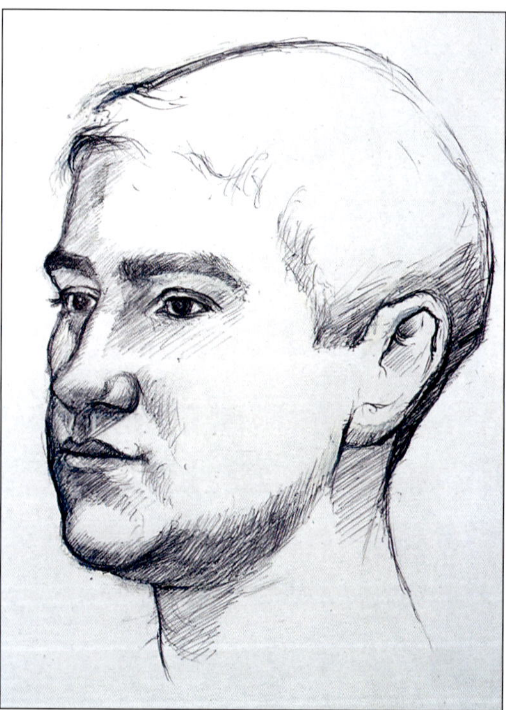

10 ▲ Add more tone Using regular hatched strokes, apply the shadow cast by the ear on to the neck, and the shadow within the whorl of the ear. Use a curving stroke for the shadow under the jaw to suggest the softness of the flesh. Add light shading across the forehead.

A FEW STEPS FURTHER

Stand back and review your progress. The likeness is excellent, and the head has a sense of solidity and volume. Study the way the light falls across the sitter's head and consider developing the tonal contrasts in the finishing stages.

11 ▶ Add more tone and texture A black fibre-tip pen gives a darker, more emphatic mark. Use it to add definition to the shadow at the back of the head.

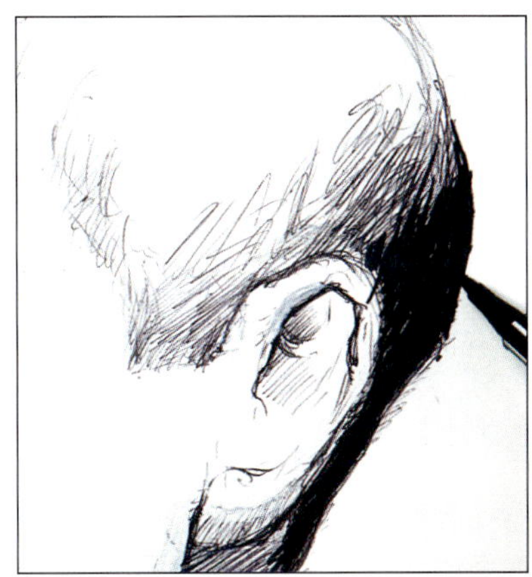

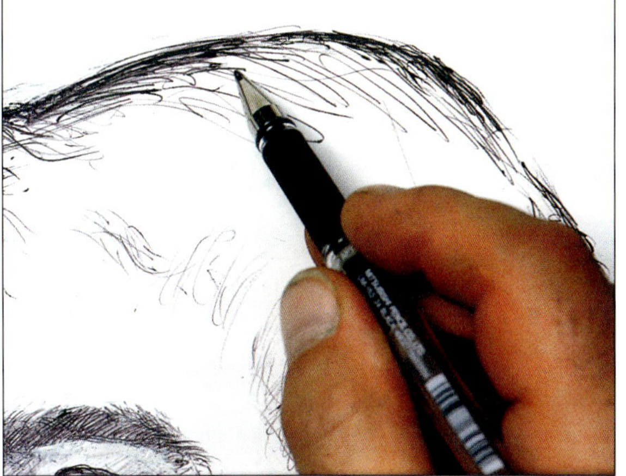

12 ▲ Suggest the hair Using a black rollerball pen, make loose, scribbled marks to indicate the hair on the top of the head. It isn't necessary to work up the hair over the entire head – simply indicate its texture at key points, such as the crown and around the ears, and the viewer's eye will fill in the areas between.

THE FINISHED PICTURE

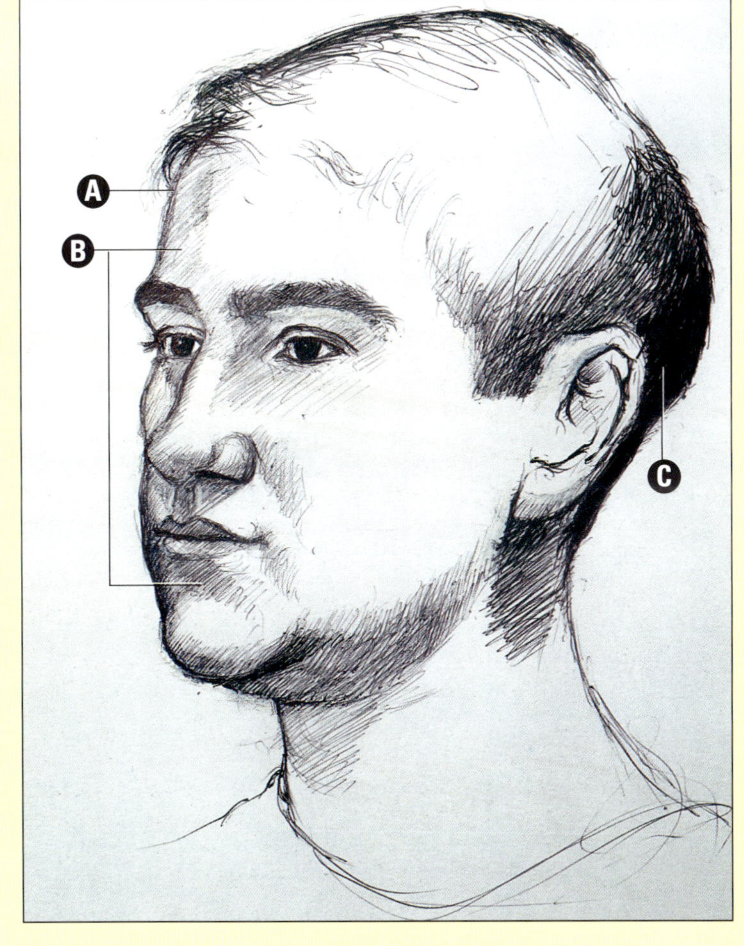

A Broken line
The outline was built up from an overlapping series of short lines applied with the fine tip of a ballpoint pen.

B Hatched tones
Mid and dark tones were created with closely laid hatched strokes – straight and regular on flat planes such as the forehead, and curving around more rounded surfaces such as the jaw.

C Fibre tip for emphasis
The darkest darks – at the back of the head – were applied with a fibre-tipped pen. This has a blacker line that is more fluid and less wiry than the marks of the ballpoint.

Drawing with fibre-tipped pens

Interpret the fascinating geometric pattern and sharp, spiky leaves of a pineapple with the crisp, decisive lines produced by a fibre-tipped pen.

Drawing with a pen requires a different technique from drawing with a pencil, charcoal, pastel or other softer medium. A pen gives a well-defined line that cannot easily be erased or altered, so you need to be decisive in your approach from the beginning.

There are many different types of pen available to the artist, ranging from drawing pens with fine tips for graphic designers to dip pens handmade from goose quills and bamboo. Each has its own character and its own advantages and disadvantages to the artist, with some pens being more suitable for precision work and others for freer interpretations of a subject.

The pineapple in this project was drawn with a fibre-tipped pen rather than a dip pen and ink. You'll find a wide range of fibre-tipped pens to choose from at any art shop. Ideal for line illustrations, cartoons and quick sketches, as well as finished drawings, these pens come in a variety of tip sizes, graded in numbers from the very fine 005 and 01 to the thicker 08 and 10. Versatile brush pens are also available if you want more flexibility. When working with a fibre-tipped pen, remember to replace the cap each time you finish using it, or it will dry out.

Use cartridge paper when drawing with a pen – you'll find the nib moves easily over its smooth surface.

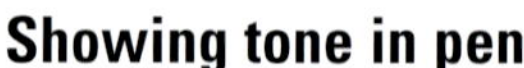

Showing tone in pen

While you can show tone with a soft pencil or a stick of charcoal simply by shading with the edge or pressing hard, you'll need a different approach with a fibre-tipped pen, as it creates lines which are all of a uniform thickness. One way to convey gradations of tone is to draw hatched lines either close together (for dark areas) or further apart (for paler areas). To create an even darker tone, add lines of cross-hatching as well. Alternatively, change to a pen with a thicker tip for areas of deep shadow.

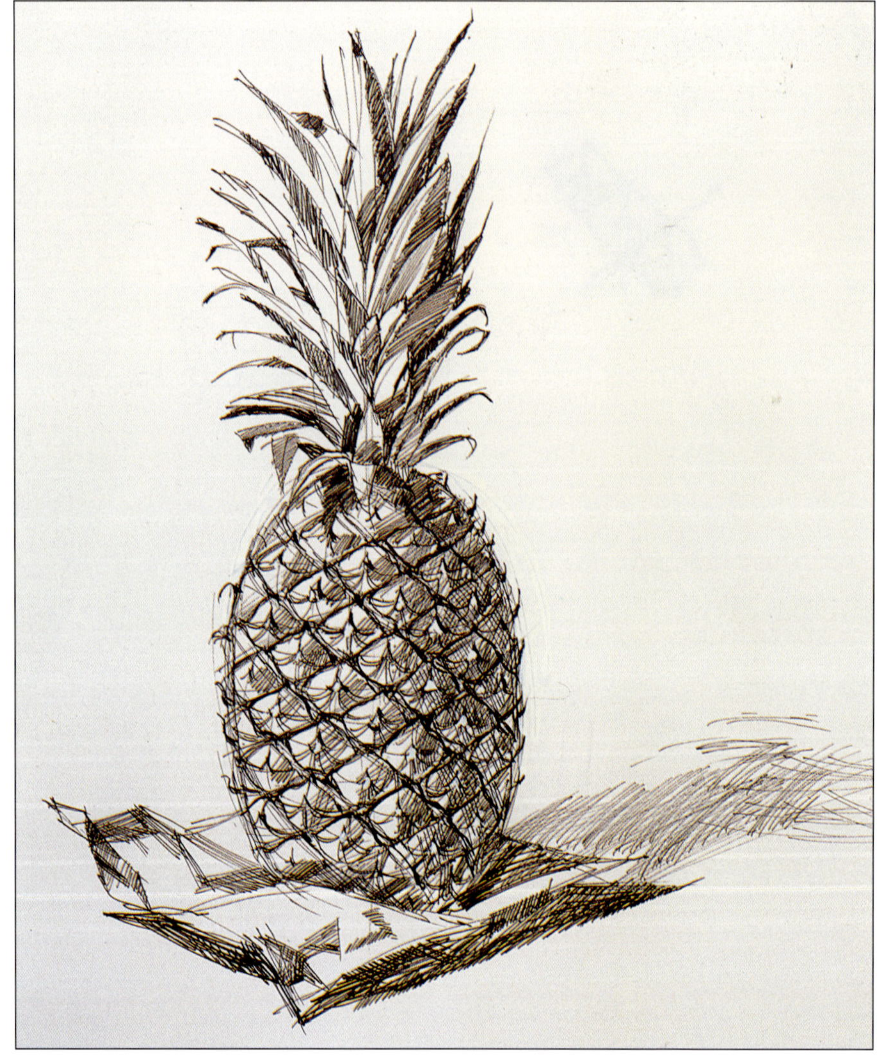

◄ This pen drawing of a pineapple combines well-defined outlines with subtly drawn areas of tone to give a highly realistic finished image.

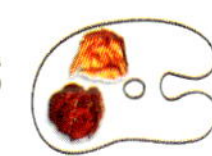

YOU WILL NEED

Large sheet of cartridge paper

3 fibre-tipped pens: 01, 07, 05

Bleedproof Designer's White

No. 5 round brush

FIRST STEPS

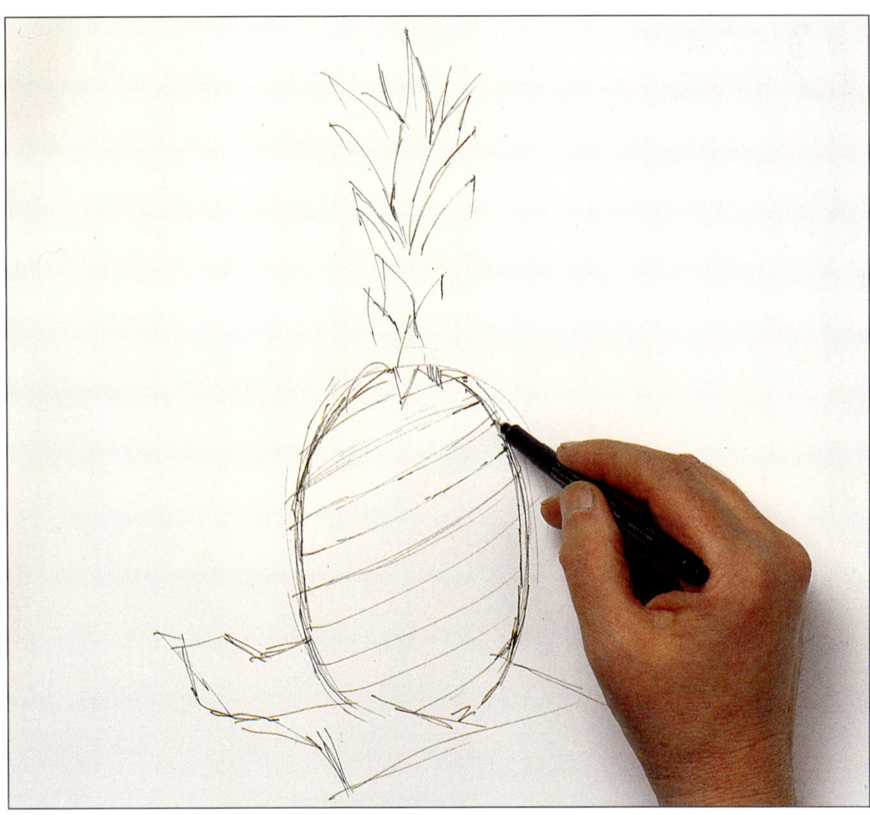

1 ▸ **Make a sketch** Holding one of the pens vertically, compare the height of the pineapple to the height of its leaves – the proportion is about half and half. Using an 01 pen, begin to sketch the pineapple, some of its leaves and the paper bag underneath it. Draw the body of the pineapple as a smooth oval, marking diagonal lines across it to help you interpret the regular growth pattern on the skin.

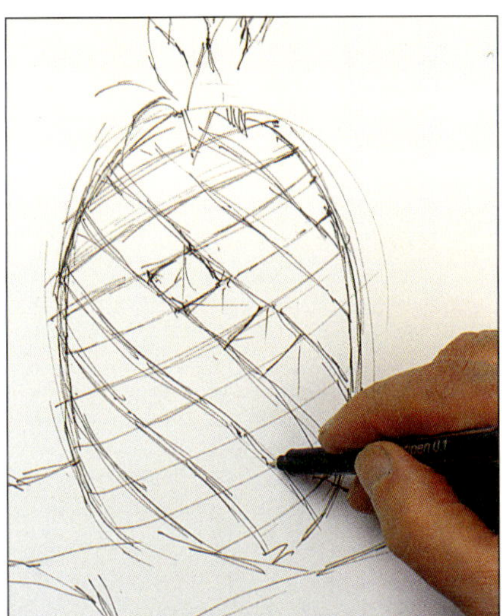

2 ◂ **Map out the pattern** Notice how the pattern on the pineapple forms a diagonal grid. Sketch in the crossing diagonals, curving the lines slightly to show the pineapple's rounded shape.

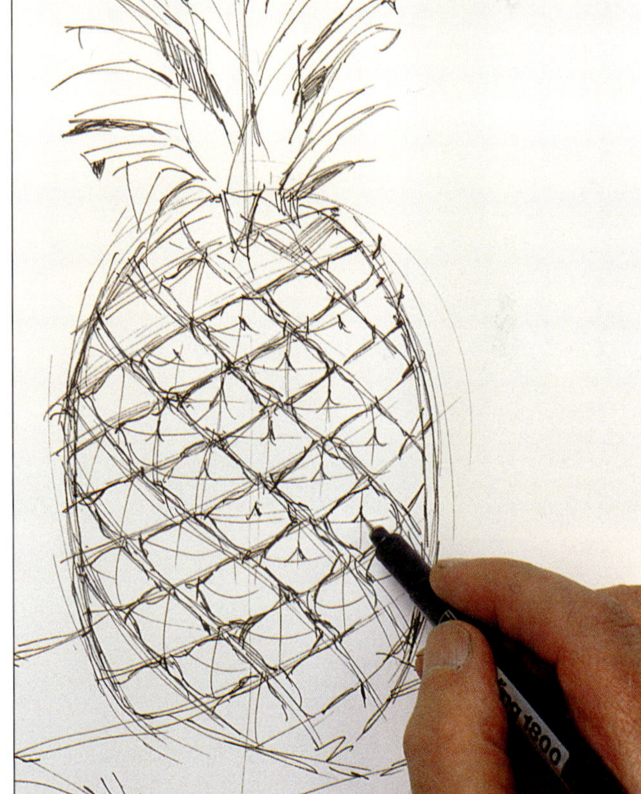

3 ▴ **Develop the leaves and pattern** Draw more leaves, checking that they emerge symmetrically from the top of the pineapple by lightly marking a centre line through the fruit. Hatch in a little dark tone where the leaves are in shadow. Begin to draw some of the distinctive segments inside each diamond shape on the pineapple.

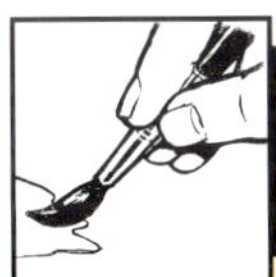

EXPERT ADVICE
Trying out the pattern

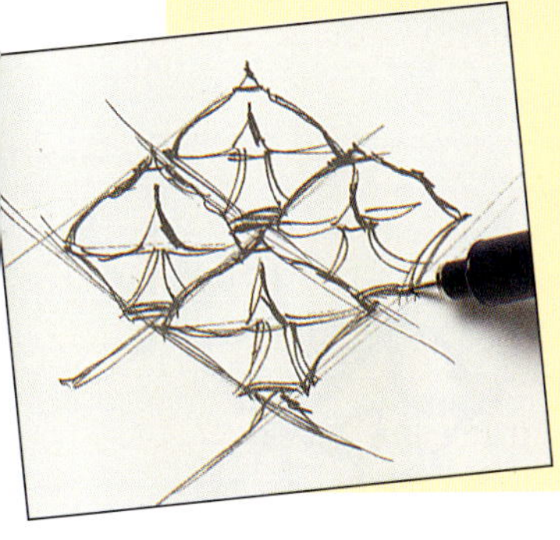

Practise sketching a small section of the pineapple's pattern before you begin the drawing. Each segment is based on a simple diamond shape. Build it up with a short, flat base, a point at the top and curves at the sides. Draw a horizontal line across the shape – the small spike sticks up from this with two lines below it.

HOW TO DEVELOP TONE

As the pineapple is in shadow on the right, you will need to develop darker tones on this side of the fruit. With fibre-tipped pens, the most effective way to achieve gradations of tone is with hatching and cross-hatching.

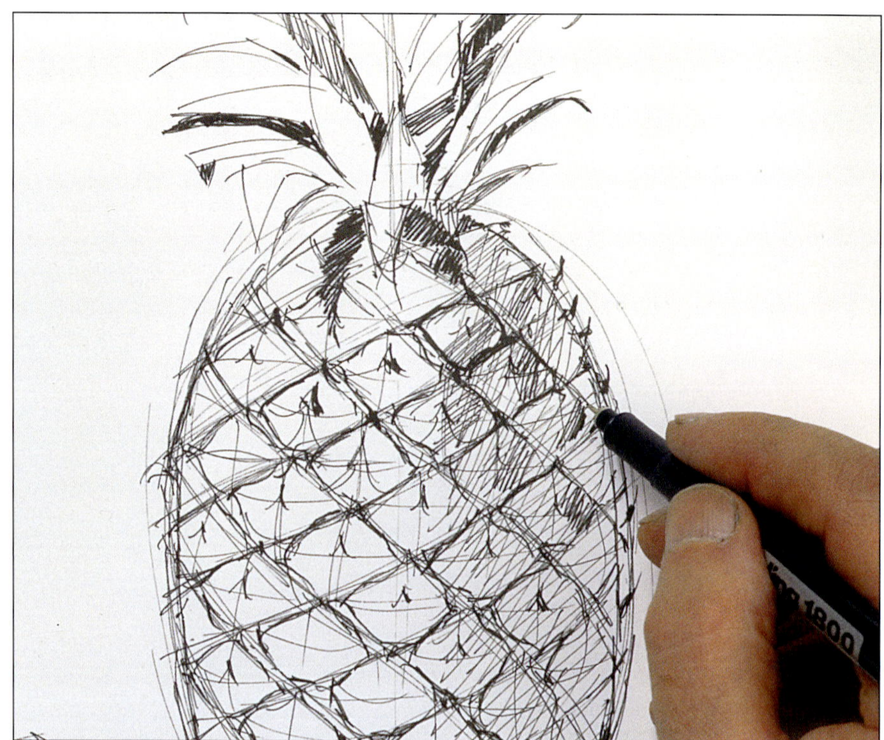

4 ▸ Shade with a thicker pen Change to an 07 pen and fill in the darkest areas of shade on the leaves and where they cast shadows on the pineapple. Return to the 01 pen to hatch in light tone across the shaded right-hand side of the fruit. Create texture with cross-hatching and add the spikes visible along the right-hand edge.

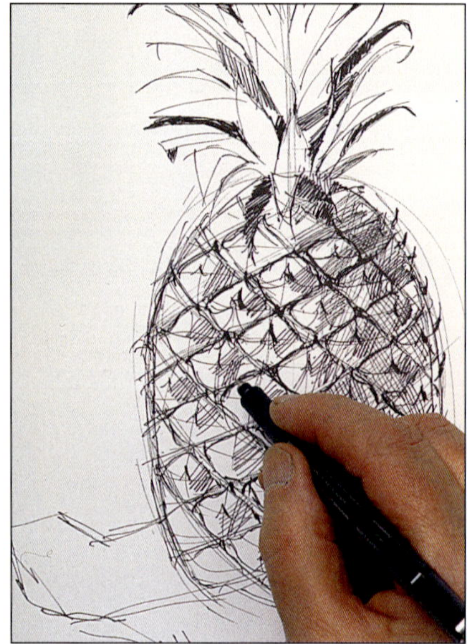

5 ◂ Define the segments further Use an 05 pen to work on each segment individually, emphasizing its features. Then change back to the 01 pen to hatch in a little light shading on the left side of the pineapple.

6 ▸ Work on the shadows Show the creases on the paper bag with directional lines and, changing to the 07 pen, fill in the dark tone with firm hatching lines. To depict the dark shadow under the bag, make long, feathered strokes with the 05 pen. Use the finest pen to build up the shadow of the pineapple with light, well-spaced hatching.

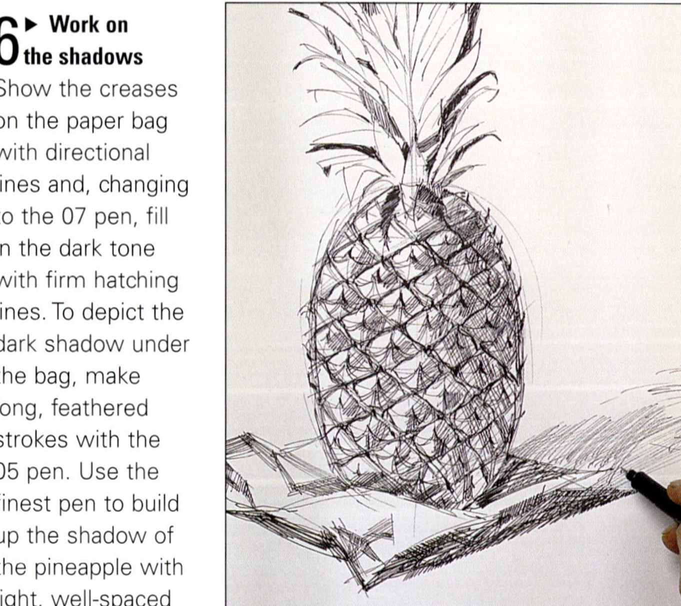

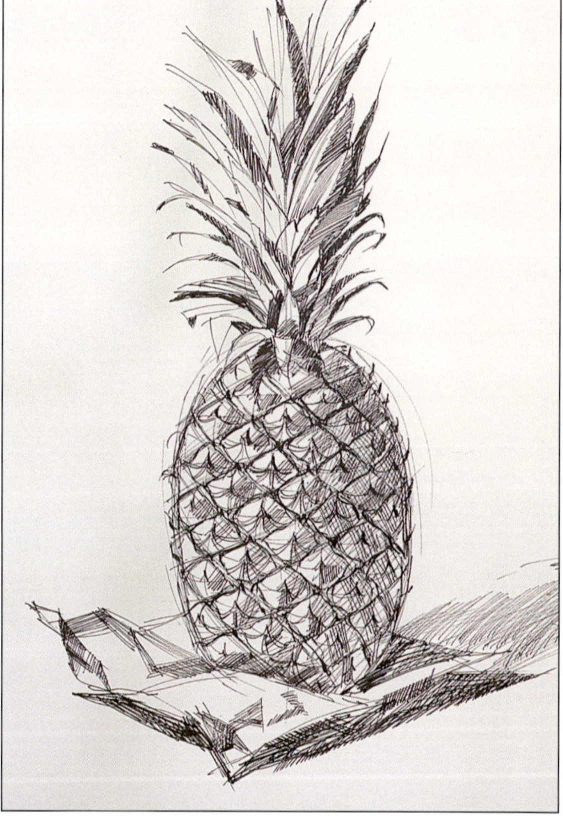

7 ▴ Return to the leaves Render areas of tone on the leaves with parallel marks made with the 05 pen, keeping the look crisp and well defined. Work the lines close together for dark tones and further apart for medium tones. Add the softest tones to the leaves with the 01 pen. These hatched lines also suggest the fibrous nature of the leaves.

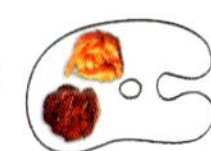

A FEW STEPS FURTHER

Apart from a few minor tonal adjustments, the illustration of the pineapple is finished. In spite of being built up entirely with line work and cross-hatching without any really solid shading, it is a very realistic image.

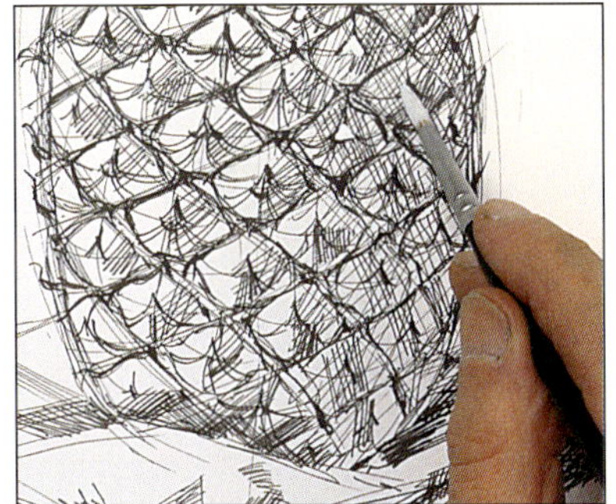

8 ▲ **Add highlights** If you want to add a few highlights to the drawing, you can blank out some of the pen lines with an opaque white liquid called Bleedproof Designer's White. Pick up a small amount on a No. 5 round brush and dab it on to the tips of the spikes to make them catch the eye. You can also remove the early construction lines around the pineapple by painting over them with this liquid.

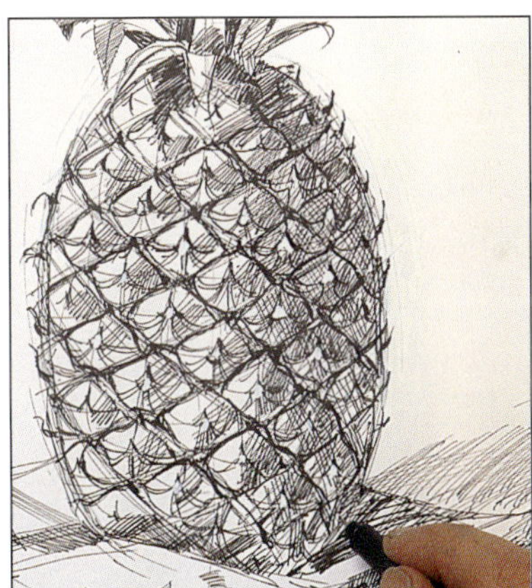

9 ▲ **Darken the overall tone** Outline the segments on the pineapple's skin with the 07 pen. Changing back to the 01 pen, darken the pineapple's right side, especially at the upper and lower edges, with more cross-hatching.

THE FINISHED PICTURE

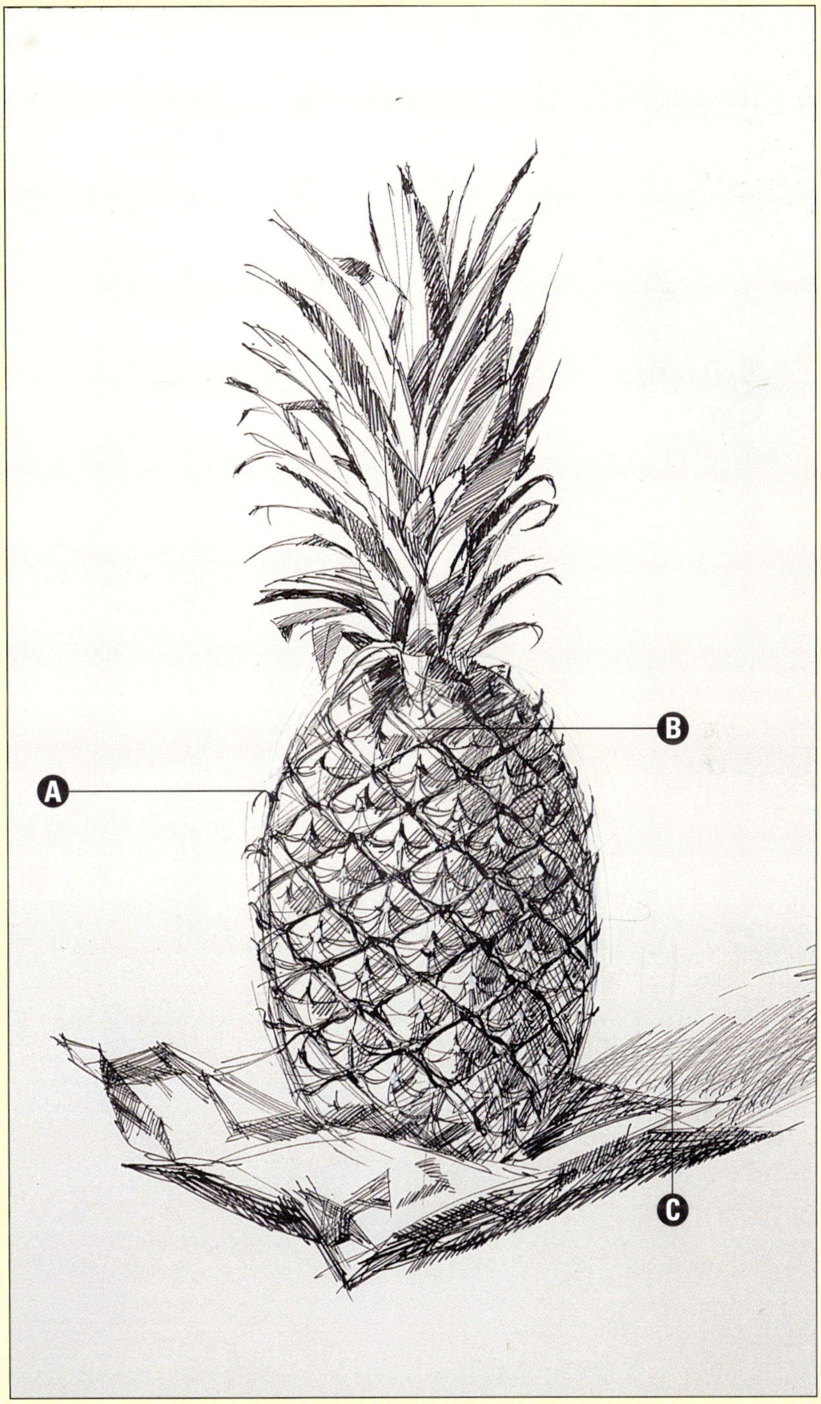

A Regular pattern
The distinctive pattern on the skin of the pineapple was built up gradually, using a diamond-shaped grid as a guide.

B Graded tone
Variations in tone on the surface of the pineapple were achieved with hatched and cross-hatched lines drawn either very close together or further apart.

C Light shadow
Long, fine lines made with a sweep of the wrist created a patch of light tone to represent the shadow cast by the pineapple on to the horizontal surface.

Using graphite sticks

The bold, expressive marks of chunky graphite sticks are perfect for capturing the hustle and bustle of this quayside fish market.

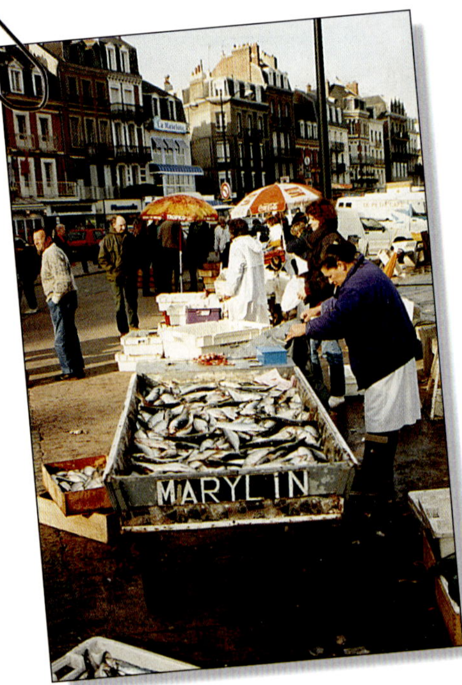

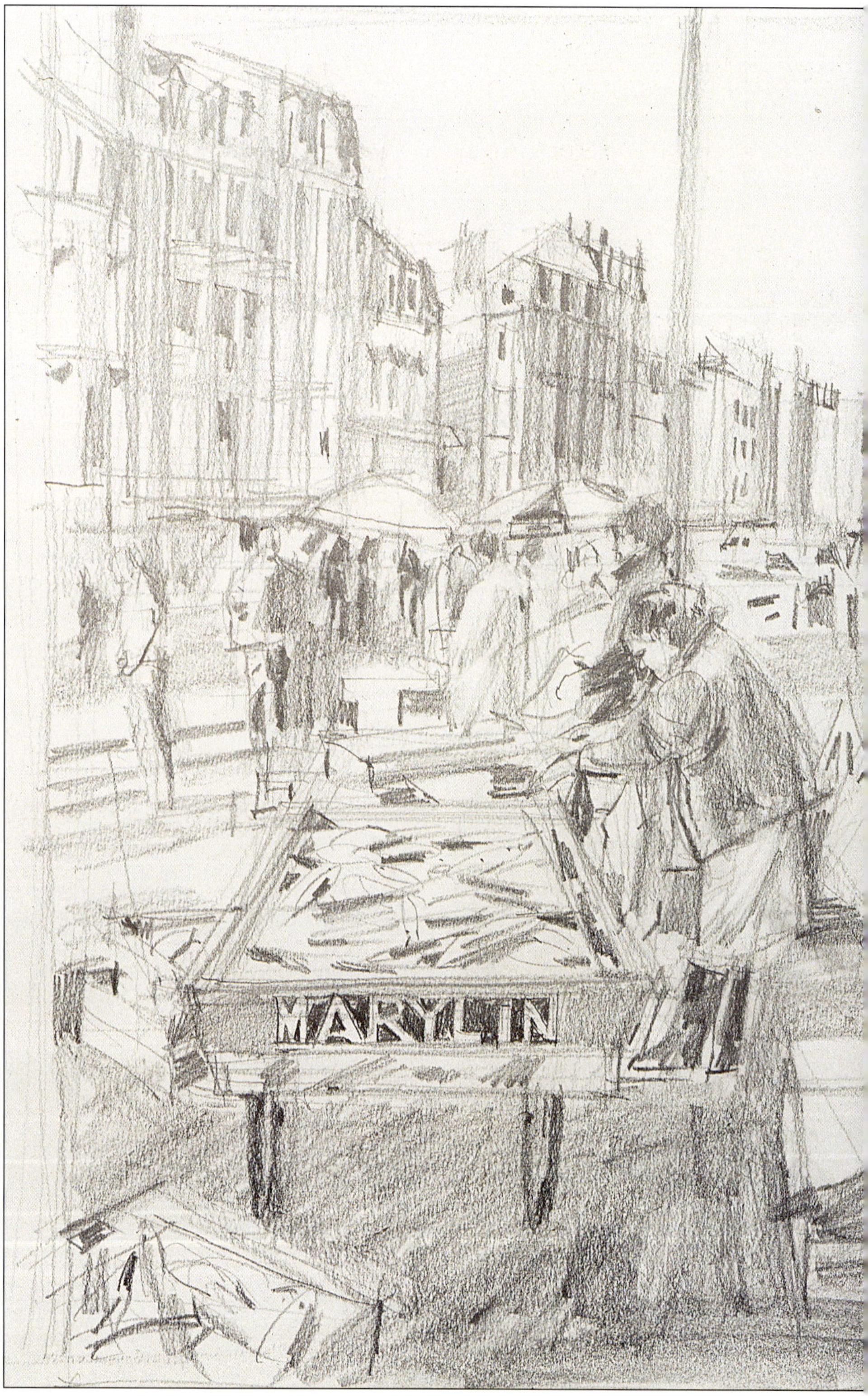

Markets are always full of life, with interesting characters manning stalls and a variety of produce on display, making them an inspiring subject for a drawing. As there is constant movement in a market, make a few sketches on the spot first or take some photographs to capture the scene, then work from these later at home.

A broad medium

Graphite sticks are useful drawing tools for this type of subject, in which an overall impression of the hustle and bustle is more important than fine detail. These chunky sticks are made of compressed and bonded graphite, and produce broad lines and bold shading, ideal for sketching the shapes of figures in a crowd or suggesting distant buildings' features. If they are well sharpened, they can also be used to add the odd detail.

▶ Lively marks and loose blocks of tone made with graphite sticks give this drawing a spontaneous, sketchy quality.

USING THE PUSH-DOWN LEAD PENCIL

Graphite sticks can be rather messy to take with you when you are sketching outdoors. For preliminary sketches, try using a push-down lead pencil (right). The lead pencil (right). The lead can be retracted when not in use and the clip allows you to simply pop it into your pocket. Try to get into the habit of carrying it around so you can practise your drawing in free moments.

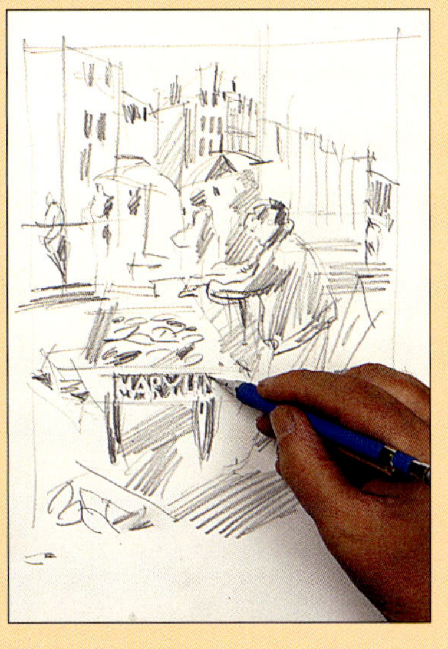

YOU WILL NEED

- Piece of cartridge paper
- 2 graphite sticks: 9B and 4B
- Pencil sharpener
- Glasspaper
- Putty rubber

▶ **Graphite sticks come in various grades and shapes. Some have a casing to protect your hands. They can be sharpened with a pencil sharpener or by rubbing the tip on glasspaper.**

FIRST STEPS

1 ▶ Set the scene Using a 9B graphite stick, draw the verticals of the buildings in the background and the tall lamp-post in front of them. Then put in the roof line. Sketch in the main activity in the midground and foreground – the woman and her stall, some of the passers-by and the parasols. Outline the boxes of fish on the road.

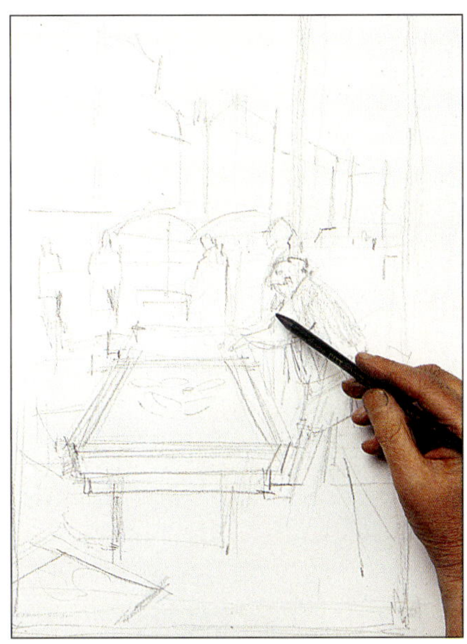

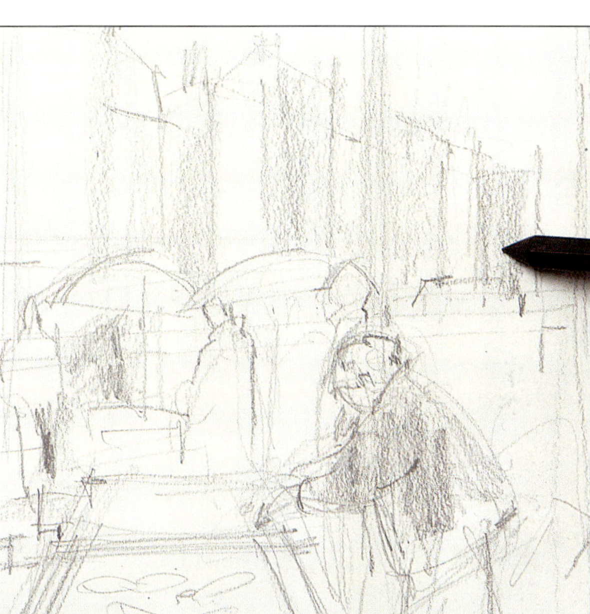

2 ▲ Fill in some tone Change to a 4B graphite stick and block in some medium tone on the stallholder's jacket. Very loosely, scribble in a little tone to indicate the dark clothing of the passers-by. Use long, light strokes to shade the walls of the buildings.

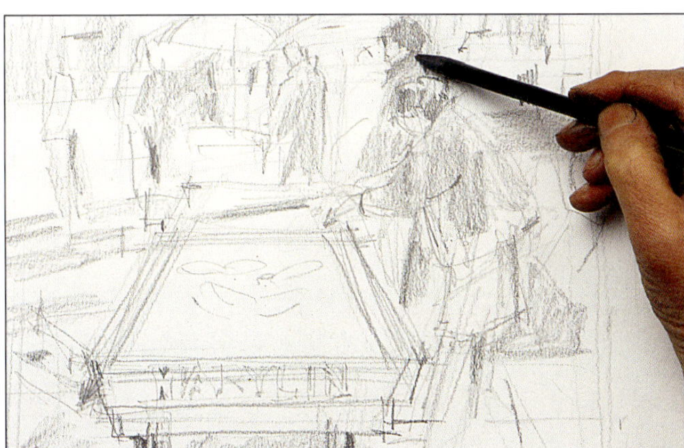

3 ▲ Continue shading Block in the shadows cast on the road by the stall and by the figures on the left. With the 9B graphite stick, work across all the figures, shading in dark tones on their clothing and hair. Use heavy strokes to draw the legs of the stall, then rough in the lettering on the side.

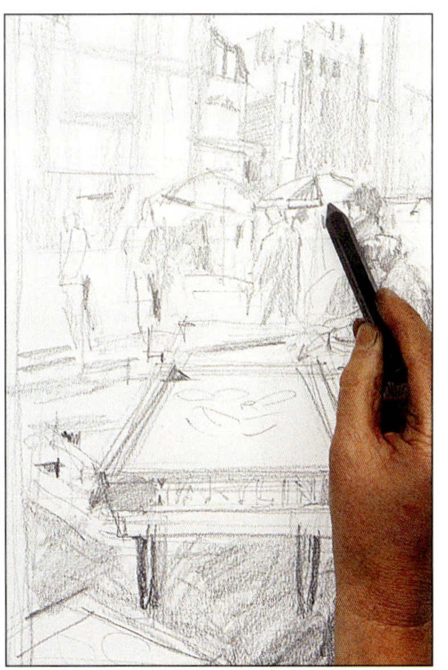

4 ◀ Work across the picture Using the tip of the 4B graphite stick side-on, block in the dark area of road on the right (see Expert Advice, next page). Begin shading some of the roofs and windows of the buildings, and suggest the windows on the left with a grid of lines. Fill in light tone on either side of the lettering on the stall, then shade in the parasol's dark stripes.

GIVING THE SCENE CHARACTER

Once the main outlines and tonal areas have been established, start adding character to the scene. Develop the people and the buildings with loose strokes, keeping any slightly more detailed work for the fish stall and traders in the foreground.

5 ▶ Put in some detail Build up tone on the hair and clothing of the figures in the middle ground. Darken the stallholder's boots and jacket with heavy black tone. Suggest the fish on the stall and in the box with dashes of the 4B graphite stick – this is a shorthand way of describing the pattern they form.

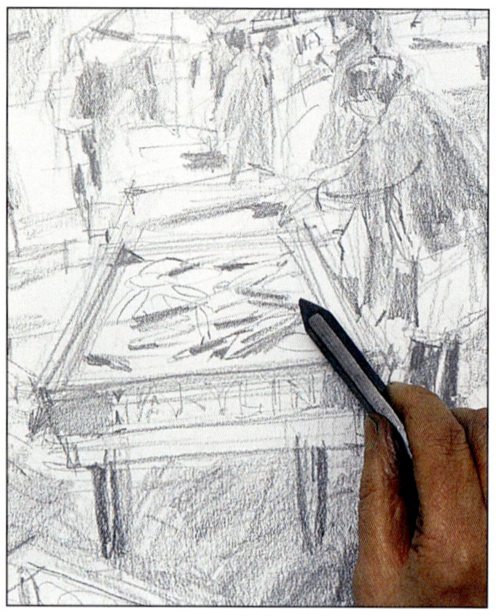

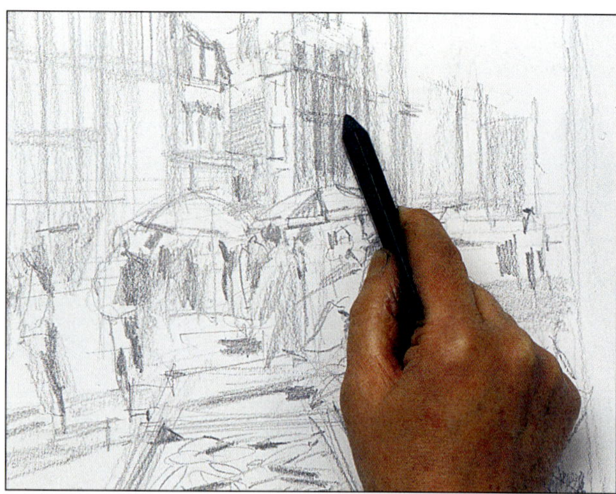

6 ▲ Develop the buildings Pick out the architectural features of the buildings in slightly more detail, but keep the overall effect simple so that you don't detract from the action in the foreground. Outline more windows with simple crossing lines and shade in the dark areas on the roofs. Draw the canopies over the windows of the hotel in the centre.

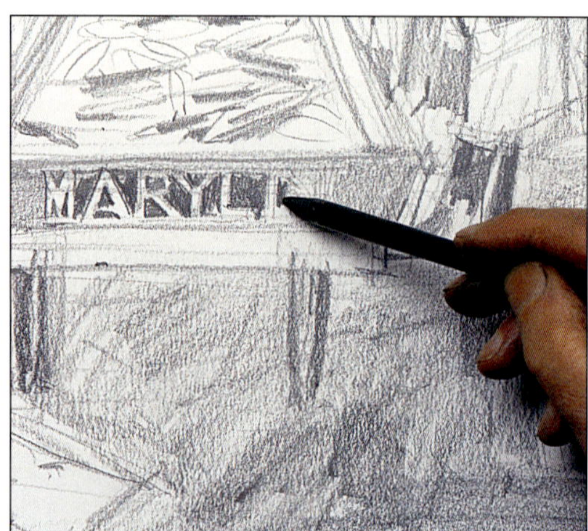

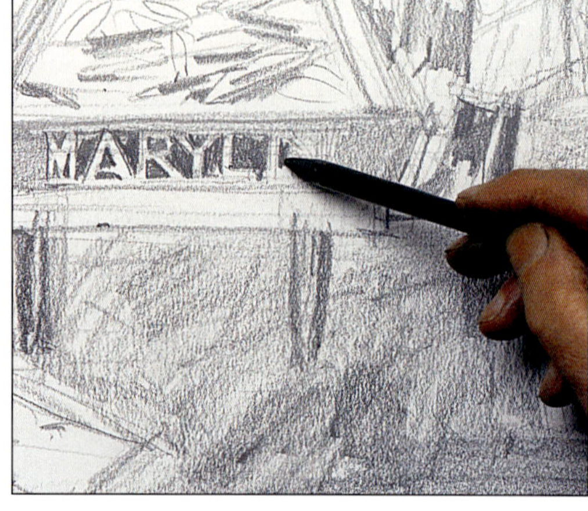

7 ◀ Work on the lettering Change to the narrow 9B graphite stick for this detailed work. Fill in around the outlines of the letters, so that they show up as white against a dark background – press hard with the stick to make a good, dense black.

EXPERT ADVICE
Blocking in large areas

The chunky tip of a graphite stick used side-on is ideal for filling in large areas of tone quickly. Each sweep of the stick will make a broad rectangular mark, and you can layer these to build up texture and tone in the drawing.

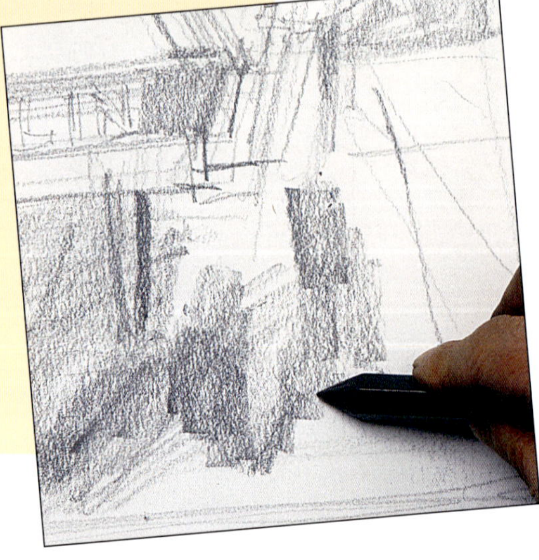

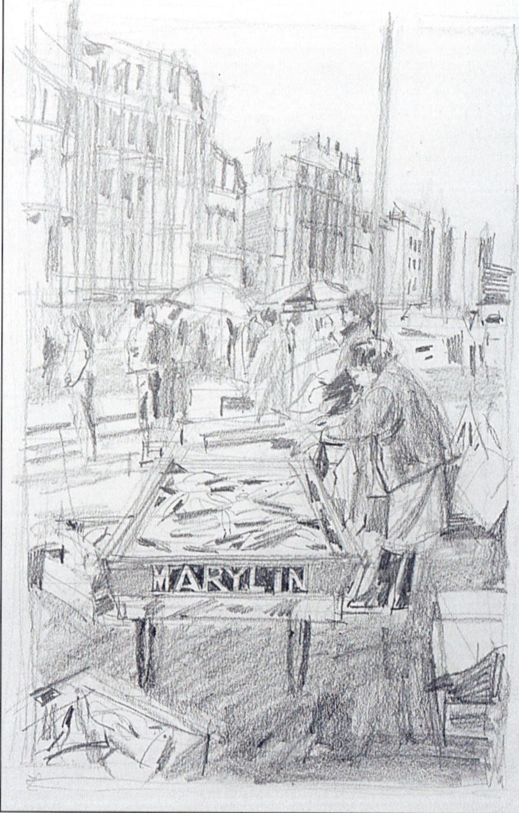

8 ▲ Add overall definition Sharpen the profile of the stallholder by darkening the clothing of the woman behind her, then add some linear details to her jacket. Dash in short vertical lines for the windows on the distant buildings, then indicate some of the balconies. Check the tones of the buildings, darkening them where necessary. Add more fish to the left-hand box and draw the plastic sheet in the box on the right.

A FEW STEPS FURTHER

There is always room for a little more detail in a busy scene such as this – the thinner graphite stick will produce quite fine lines.

9 ▶ Refine the details Give more character to the two figures in the foreground by outlining their profiles with a well-sharpened 9B graphite stick. Darken a few of the windows with heavy strokes.

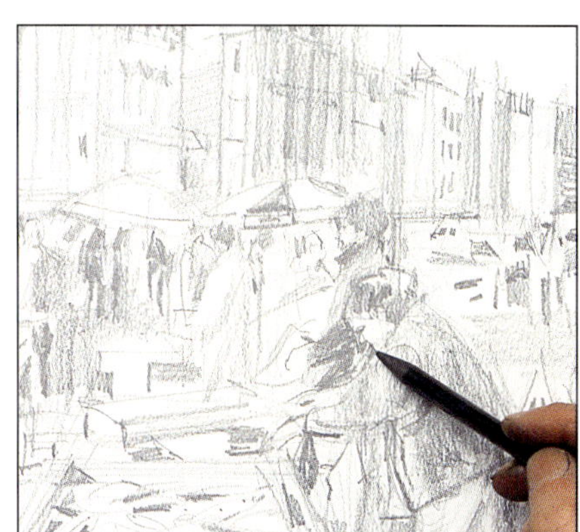

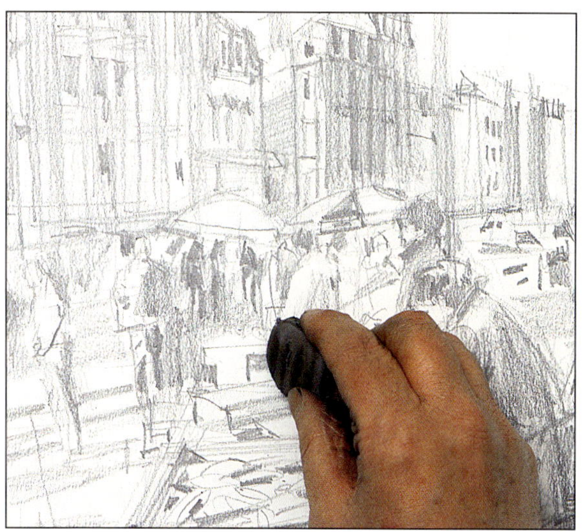

10 ▲ Lift out tone Check the tones over the whole drawing. If you want to lighten any previously shaded areas – for example, the white coat – you can lift off the graphite by using a putty rubber.

THE FINISHED PICTURE

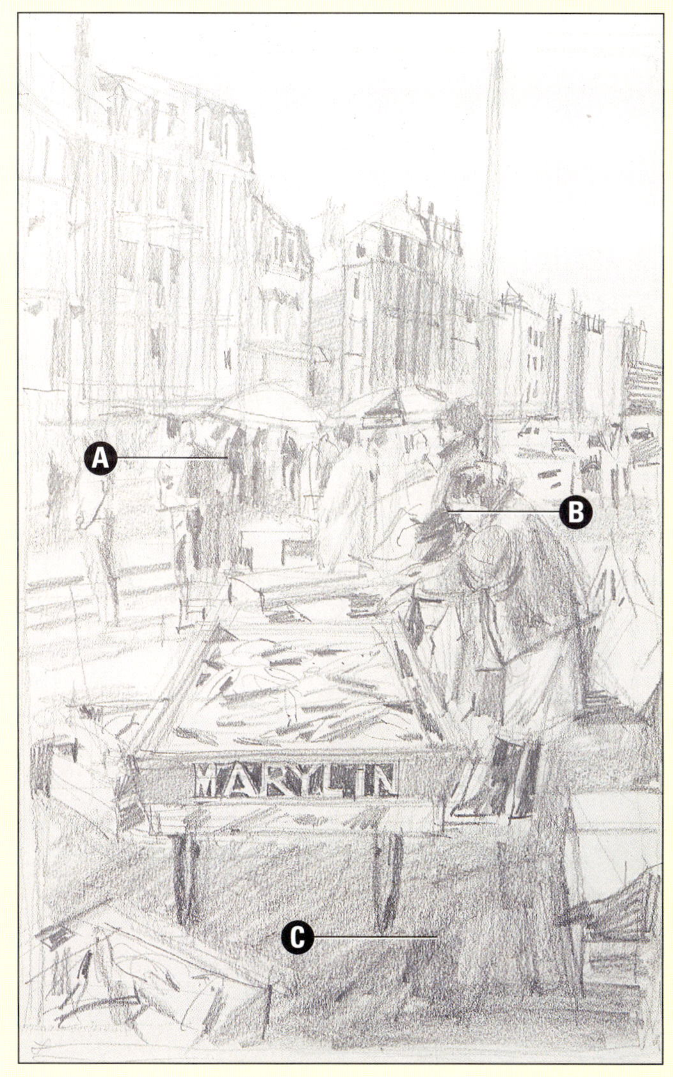

A Groups of people
The clusters of figures in the middle ground were suggested with simple, sketchy marks that indicated just the rough shapes of the bodies.

B Facial detail
Although basically a broad medium, a graphite stick was sharpened finely enough here to give a precise outline to the woman's profile.

C Quick shading
Large areas of tone, such as the dark road in the foreground, were quickly and easily rendered with a graphite stick by using the tip on its side.

Oil pastels

If you like drawing with bold, vigorous strokes, you will enjoy the effects you can achieve with the lively medium of oil pastels, which are available in a range of bright rainbow colours.

Oil pastels are tough, bright and bold – altogether different from the crumbling sticks of chalky pigment that we know as traditional pastels. Pure pastels are chosen for their soft, velvety colours, whereas oil pastels are much harder and produce thick, waxy lines. In fact, their very name is misleading because oil pastels are not actually pastels at all, having far more in common with oil paints and wax crayons than with pure pastels.

A perfect sketching medium

Oil pastels call for a bold, confident approach. They are excellent for quick colour sketches and drawings in which movement and expressive strokes are more important than a very realistic finish. In fact, because of their chunky nature, oil pastels are not particularly well suited to fine, detailed work. Artists who work on a small scale or with subtle colours are likely to find oil pastels too bright and broad for their purpose, although the pastels can be sharpened with a knife to achieve a finer line.

For an immediate effect and for lively, on-the-spot colour sketching, however, oil pastels are second to none. Unlike most drawing materials, they enable you to work quickly on a large scale in colours that are both bright and strong. In this respect, oil pastels have

▶ Oil pastels produce dense, waxy marks and come in a range of intense colours. Unlike soft pastels, they contain wax and oil and do not break easily or crumble.

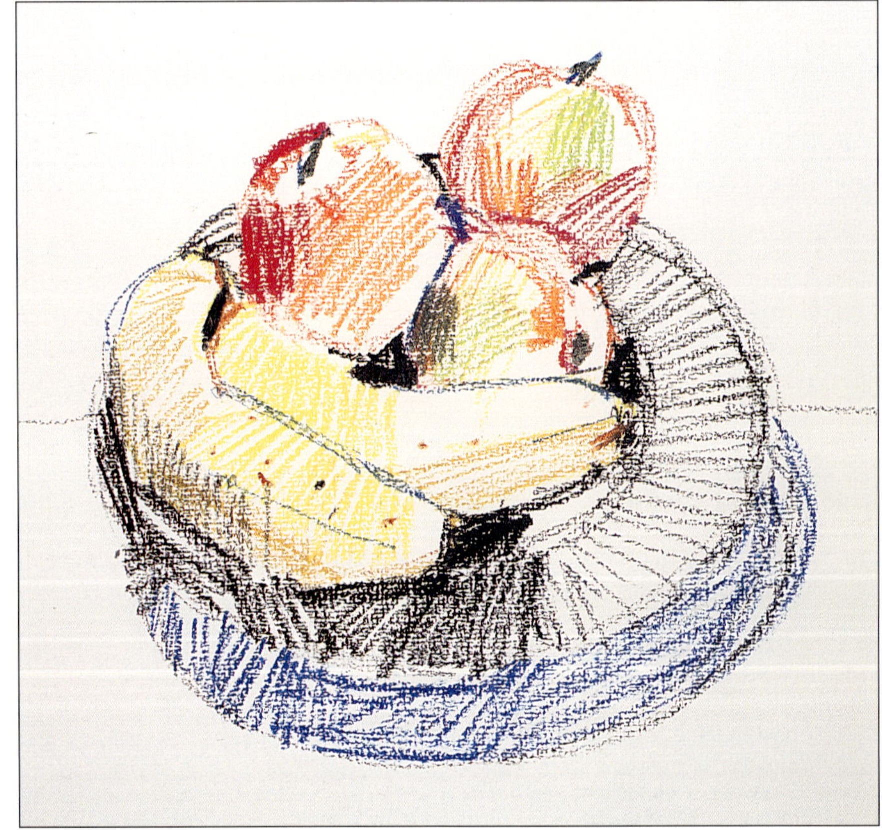

▶ Oil pastel proved to be the perfect medium for this bold, colourful still-life sketch. These pastels are at their best when applied in strong, loose strokes.

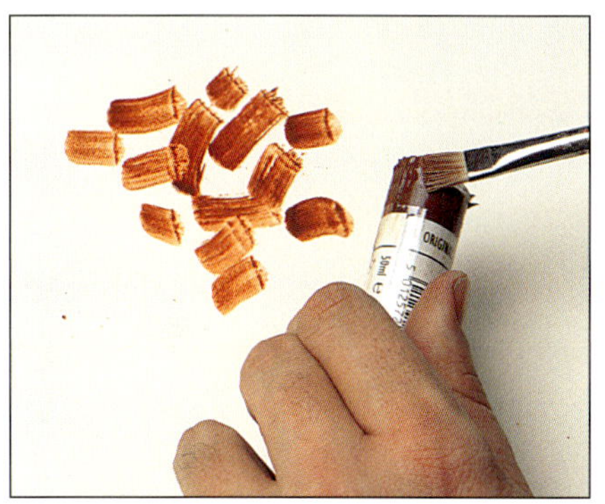

▲ **Oil sticks can be used for painting as well as for drawing. This is done by dissolving the colour with turpentine and applying it to the support with a brush.**

all the advantages of oil paint, but with the added bonus that they are more portable and more convenient.

For working outdoors, simply slip a sketch book and a few oil pastels into your pocket and you are equipped and ready to go. The pastels can be used without any liquid medium and may be applied directly to sturdy paper, oil paper or primed canvas.

Colour blending

Their hard, waxy nature means that oil pastel colours are not easy to blend unless dissolved with a thinner such as white spirit or turpentine. This is normally done on the drawing, so you must first apply the oil pastels to the support. You can then blend the colours with a brush, tissue or finger dipped in the thinner.

An alternative method is to dampen the support with thinner before applying the pastel to it, as shown below left. Note that when blending with thinner, you should work on oil paper or primed canvas; other papers are too absorbent.

As a general rule, blending is more effective when used on a few selected areas of a drawing, or when combined with vigorous, textural strokes. Too

BLENDING OIL PASTELS

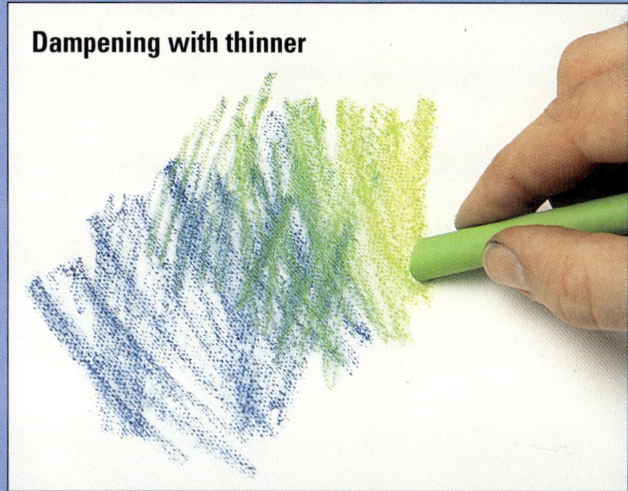

Instead of blending oil pastels once they are on the paper, you can wet the support with turpentine or white spirit first, then apply the pastel to the dampened area.

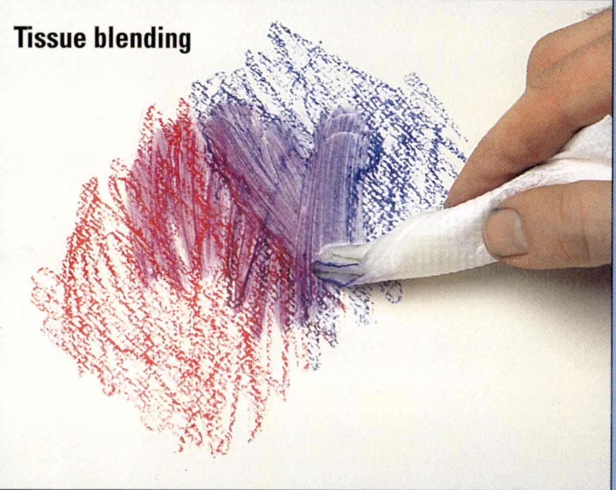

Roughly apply two colours so that they overlap, then blend these together with a rolled-up piece of tissue or kitchen towel dipped in turpentine or white spirit.

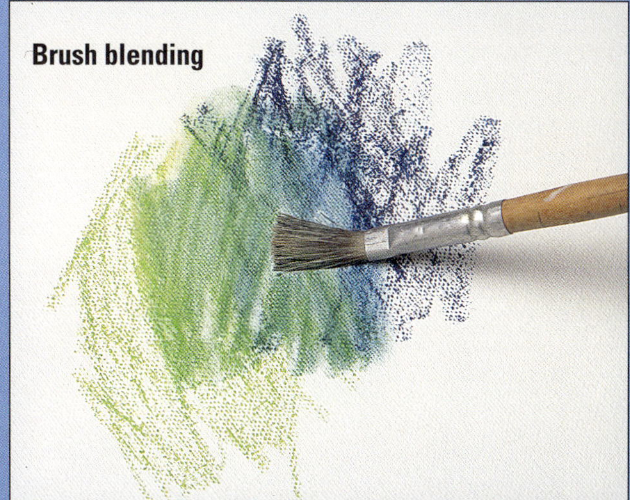

Use a brush dipped in solvent for blending two or more colours together. An oil-painting brush is stiffer and blends much more effectively than a soft brush.

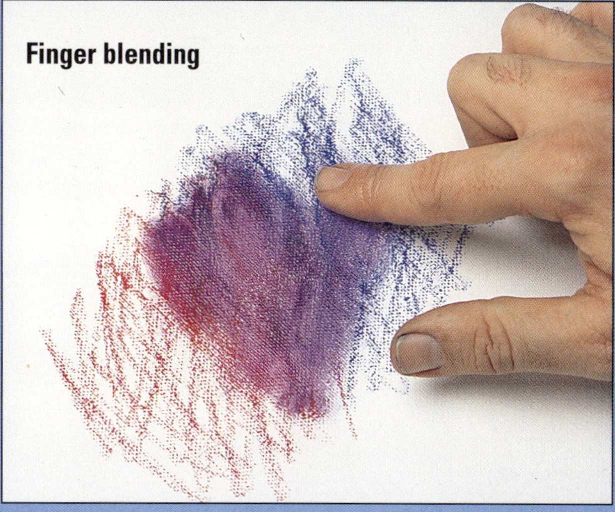

Many artists instinctively use a finger to blend dissolved colours quickly. If you like working in this way, make sure you wash your hands immediately afterwards, as some pigments are toxic.

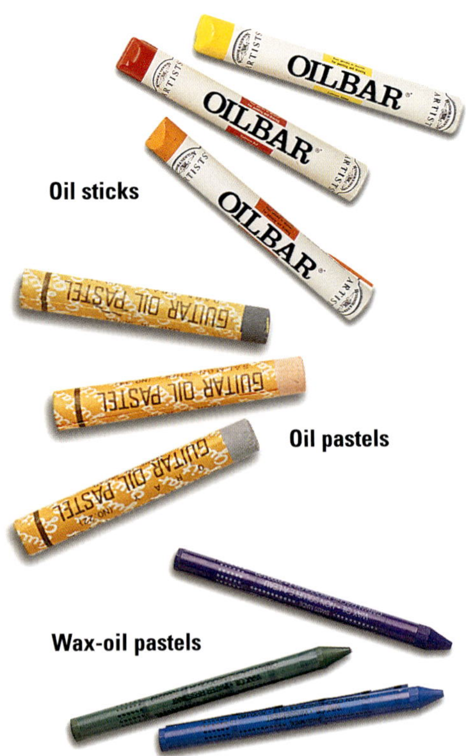

▲ **Depending on the brand, pastels contain varying amounts of wax and oil. The higher the wax content, the harder the pastel.**

much blending can destroy the direct, spontaneous quality of the medium and your picture might start to look smooth and rubbery. An alternative approach is to wait until the blended colours have dried, then to apply bold textural strokes on top of the blended areas.

Overlaid colour

As with all pastels, oil pastel colours can be mixed on the paper by overlaying two or more colours. For example, if you apply yellow over blue, you will create the impression of green. Even though the colours are not actually mixed, they appear to be. Remember, the top colour is the dominant one, so blue on top of yellow produces a bluer green than the other way round.

Oil pastel with oil paint

Oil pastels are compatible with oil paints. Not only can they be used for the initial drawing prior to starting an oil painting, but they are also effective for adding texture and linear detail to the finished painting.

For a softer effect than that given by oil pastels, try oil sticks. The consistency of the fat sticks of colour comes between oil pastels and oil paint – harder than paint, but more malleable than pastels. Oil sticks (sometimes called oil bars) are quite a new invention and, like oil pastels, are excellent for making broad, chunky drawings. Alternatively, you can use oil sticks as a painting medium by dipping a brush in turpentine or white spirit, and taking the dissolved colour from the top of the stick.

Oil and water do not mix

An opposite approach to that of using oil pastels with oil paint is to actively exploit the incompatibility of oil and water. First the oil pastel is laid down, then a water-soluble colour such as watercolour, gouache, coloured ink or even thin acrylic is painted over it. The oily marks repel the water-soluble colour, leaving the coloured pastel marks showing through.

This technique, which is known as resist, can be used to create a variety of marks and textures. It is an exciting way of using oil pastels because the results are sometimes unexpected.

Building up texture

Oil pastels are essentially a drawing material, good for making lively line drawings, with the bold strokes providing texture and colour. If you build them up thickly, however, oil pastels create a dense layer of solid colour and the result is rather like an oil painting.

Once this solid colour has been established, you can then scratch into the waxy surface. Use a scalpel blade or any other sharp instrument to make textures and patterns by revealing the white paper underneath. Another variation of the same technique, known as sgraffito, is to apply one colour over another. By scratching the top layer, you will reveal the colour underneath.

Although they can be used alongside so many other materials, oil pastels are very much a medium in their own right. They provide a powerful means of expression and encourage a bold, overall approach, which is excellent for the less experienced artist who wishes to branch out and experiment. With oil pastels, there can be little subtlety, but you will be pleasantly surprised at the results you will be able to achieve.

MORE TECHNIQUES

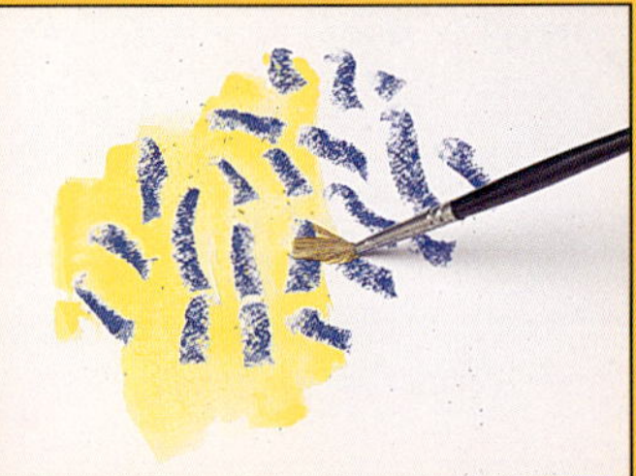

Resist Try painting watercolour or other water-soluble colour over an area of oil pastel. The waxy marks repel the paint and show through the painted colour.

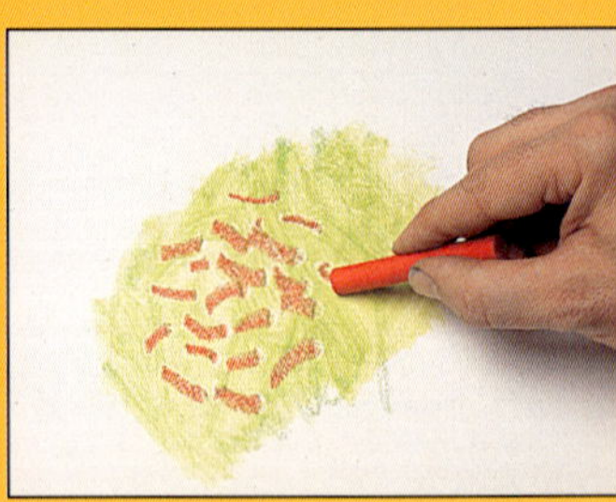

Added texture Small strokes of oil pastel applied on top of a blended area of colour can lend contrasting texture to a smooth, flat surface.

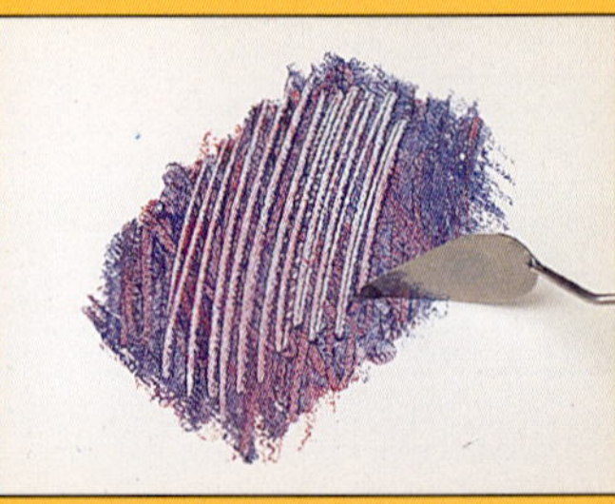

Sgraffito Use a painting knife, scalpel or other sharp implement to scratch pattern and texture into layers of thick colour.

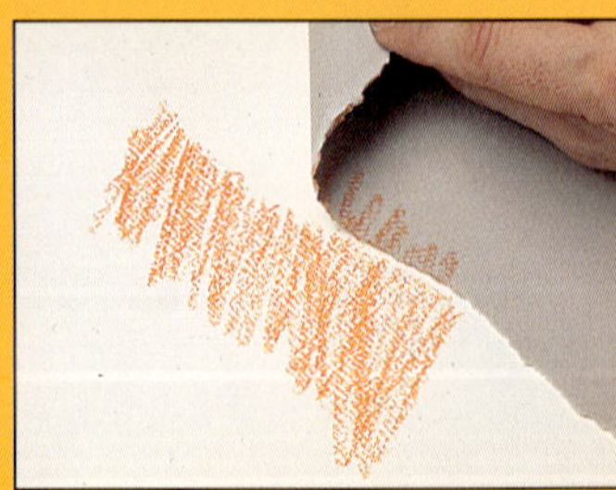

Masking Apply colour roughly over the torn or cut edge of a piece of sturdy paper or thin card to give a crisply defined edge to an area of oil pastel strokes.

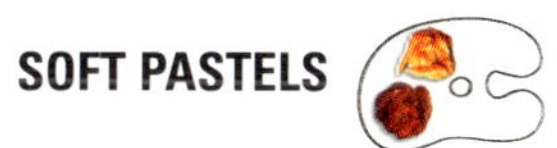

Soft pastels

Working with pastels is highly rewarding – they are extremely versatile and produce a rich depth of colour not found in other media.

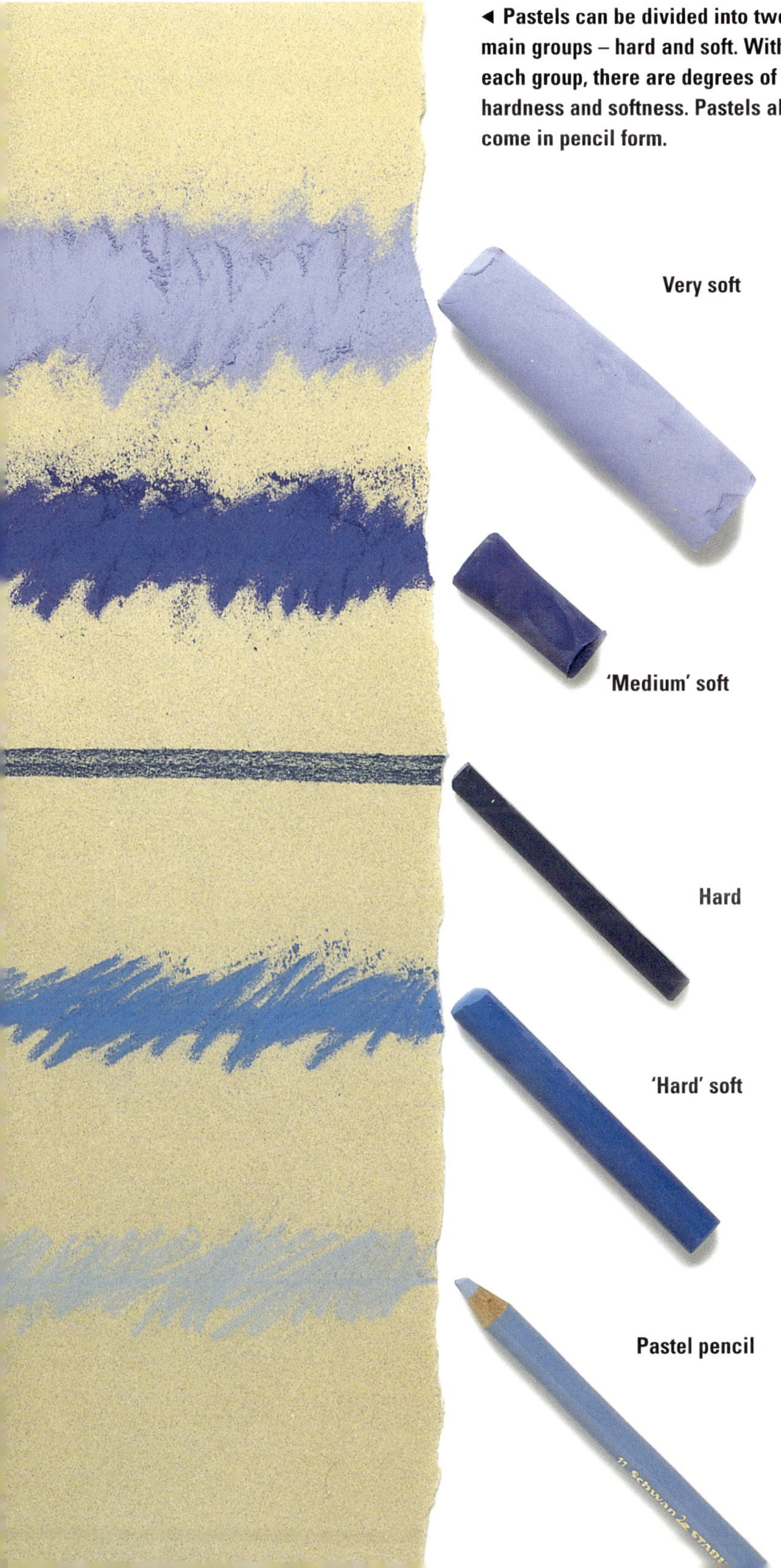

◀ Pastels can be divided into two main groups – hard and soft. Within each group, there are degrees of hardness and softness. Pastels also come in pencil form.

Very soft

'Medium' soft

Hard

'Hard' soft

Pastel pencil

Soft pastels produce matt, velvety colours that range from the intensely brilliant to the palest of pale pastel shades. The most vibrantly coloured sticks are made from pure pigment; lighter tones are made by adding chalk or white pigment to the main colour. Whether you choose pale lemon or deep, resonant gold, however, the powdery pastel pigments will give you a richly dense colour that cannot be matched by any other medium.

Soft pastels are generally thought of as drawing materials because they come in stick form. But they are far more than simply coloured drawing sticks. Pastels are also a versatile and effective 'colouring' medium – excellent for laying down areas of colour, tone and texture, as well as for drawing lines. Used in this way, soft pastels are more like paints than pencils, and this is why pastel pictures are often referred to as paintings rather than drawings.

Soft pastels also have one very important advantage over paints: when working with pastels, you do not have to wait for one colour to dry before applying the next. The powdery colours cannot run, so you can apply each pastel colour when and where you want it, even overlapping or directly adjacent to another colour.

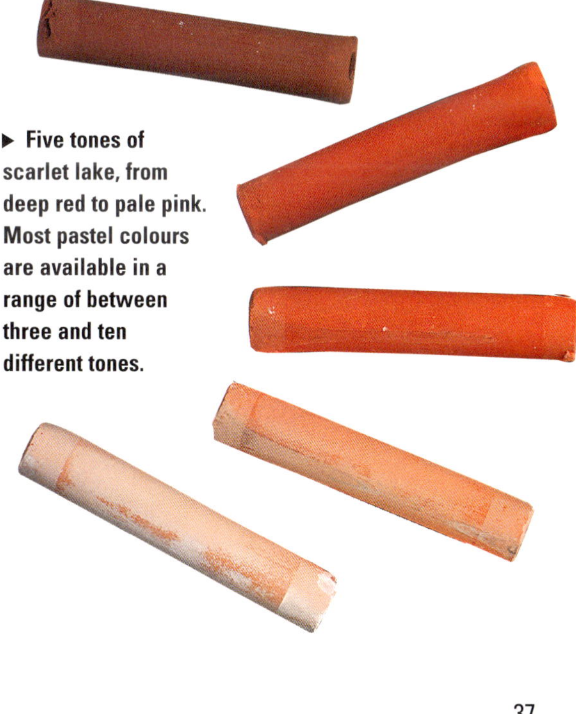

▶ Five tones of scarlet lake, from deep red to pale pink. Most pastel colours are available in a range of between three and ten different tones.

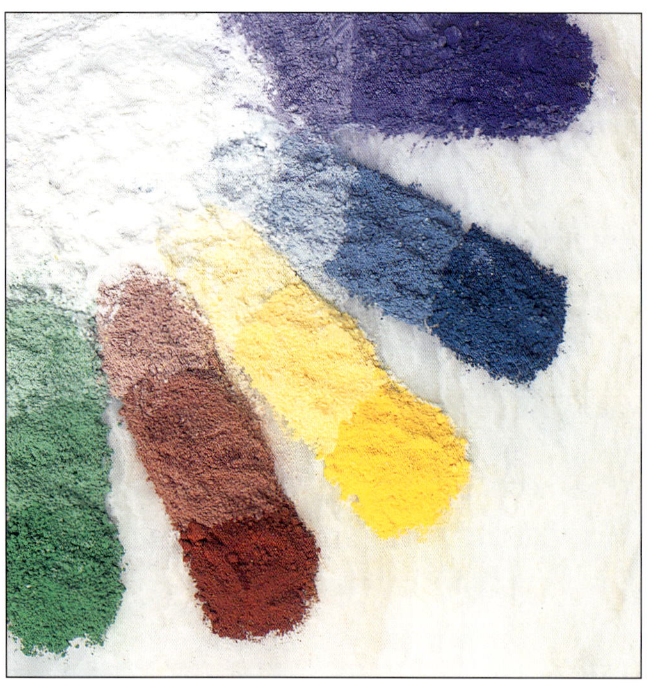

▲ **The more chalk that is added to the pure pigment, the lighter the tone of the soft pastel. A huge variety of shades of the same colour can be achieved in this way.**

Making pastels

Soft pastels have been in use since the early eighteenth century. Until that time their nearest equivalents were hard crayons, usually bound with wax and available in only a few muted colours such as earthy reds, browns and blacks.

Although soft pastels contain exactly the same pigments as paints and other artists' materials, they are a dry medium, requiring no water or any other liquid. Soft pastels are made by mixing the powdered ingredients with enough binder to hold them together. The mixture is then rolled or moulded into sticks and left to dry.

The most usual binders are gum, resin or starch. However, some pigments need a more powerful binding agent than others. For instance, chalky pale shades may be held together with nothing stronger than skimmed milk, whereas others such as cadmium red require a stronger binder. It is the strength and quality of the binding agent that determines how soft or hard a pastel will be.

Hard, soft and very soft

For the sake of simplicity, all artists' pastels can be divided into two main groups – hard and soft. Soft pastels are characteristically chunky and crumbly, and are the most popular of the various types of pastel. However, it is worth

BLENDING SOFT PASTELS

You can use a paint brush to blend two pastel colours together. Brush gently, as a harsh movement will remove the pigment altogether.

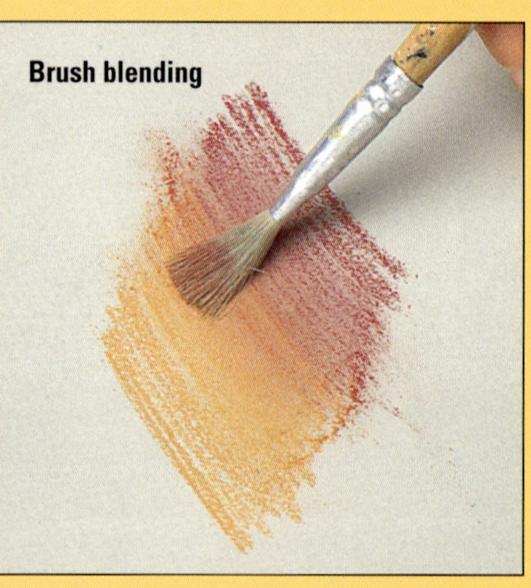

For large areas of colour, a soft tissue or paper kitchen towel blends different shades of pastel quickly and effectively.

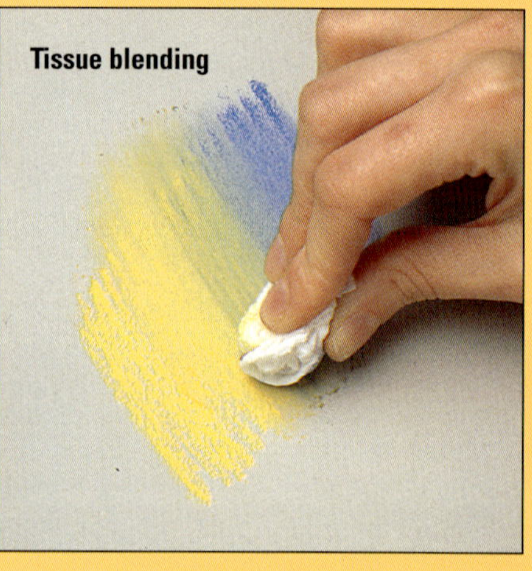

The quickest and easiest way to blend two areas of pastel colour is simply to rub them together with a clean fingertip.

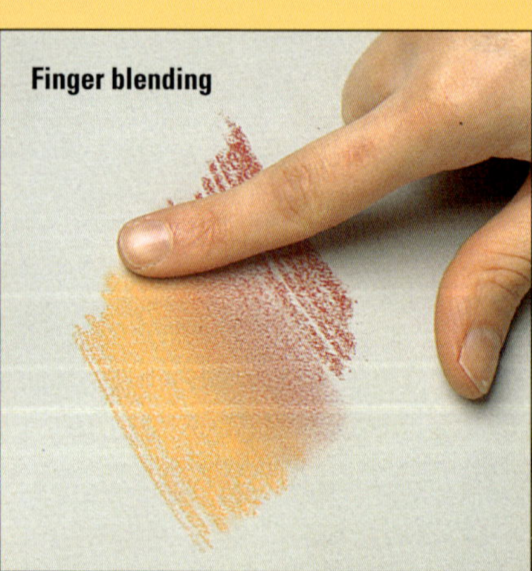

The pointed end of a torchon, a stump of tightly rolled white paper available from art shops, is ideal for blending small, precise areas of pastel colour.

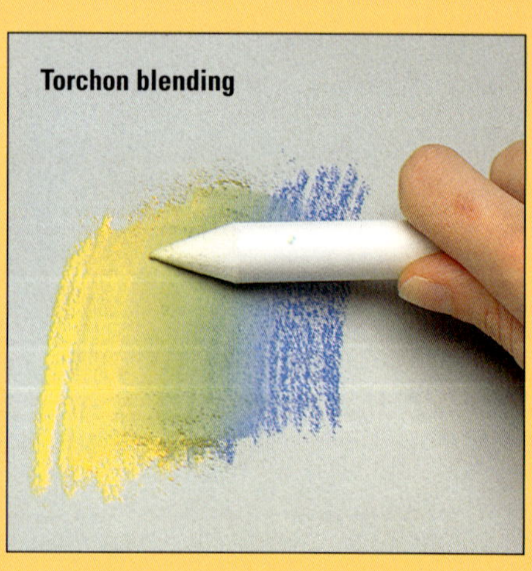

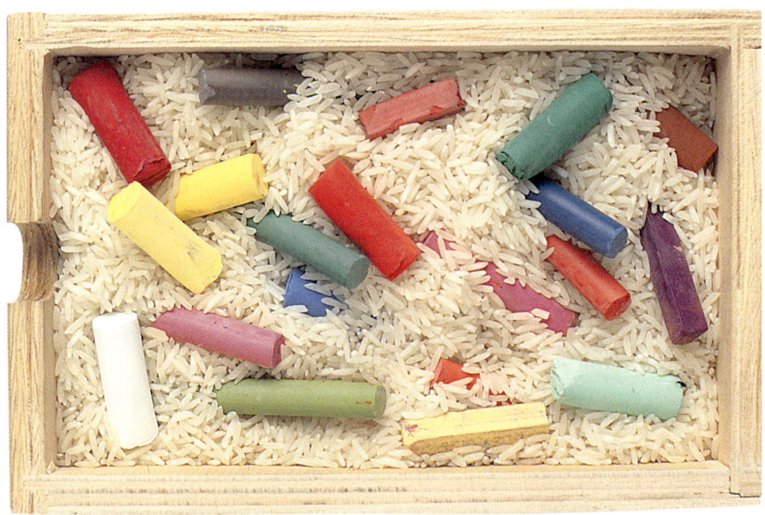

▲ **Keep your pastels clean by storing them in a box of dry rice. The dirt and loose pigment particles on the pastels will rub off on the grains of rice instead of on each other.**

remembering that, even within the category of 'soft' pastels, there are varying degrees of softness. Very soft pastels include those made by Unison, Sennelier and Schminke, the latter being the softest of all. Winsor & Newton's soft pastels and the Talens' Rembrandt range are slightly harder.

Hard pastels come in the form of compressed sticks, often rectangular in shape. The best known of these is the Conté range, although most manufacturers now have their own product on the market. Hard pastels contain more gum than soft pastels, and the colours are usually less intense.

Colour mixing

Unlike paints, soft pastel colours cannot be easily mixed. You will need a different pastel not only for every colour you wish to use in a painting, but also for every shade of that particular colour. This is why most pastel ranges are so extensive. Some manufacturers offer as many as 500 different pastels, including several versions of each colour.

Depending on the make, a range of soft pastels can include up to 10 versions of any one colour, from very light to very dark. The tonal range is often indicated by a number, although the system varies from one brand to another. For example, in the Winsor & Newton range, Scarlet Lake 1 is very pale pink and Scarlet Lake 5 is a much deeper, richer colour.

Although soft pastels are used by many professional artists, their enormous colour range makes them an excellent medium for the beginner. Freed from the worry of mixing colours, the artist is at liberty to concentrate on other aspects of the work. In other words, when you use soft pastels, the manufacturer does most of the colour mixing, not you!

Surfaces

The right surface is important. Papers and boards made specifically for soft pastel work have a definite texture, sometimes referred to as the 'tooth', which may be either coarse or velvety.

On a smooth paper, which has no tooth, soft pastels will simply slide around and produce unsatisfactory, weak patches of colour. However, on the correct surface with the right amount of tooth, the pastel dust will fill the holes gradually, enabling you to build up several layers of matt, impastoed colour. You will know when your paper has reached its limit because it becomes difficult to make the colours adhere and the loose pigment remains on the surface of the paper.

Fixing

Soft pastels smudge very easily and your finished picture will be vulnerable until it has been sprayed with fixative. Fixative may slightly darken the colours, so use the spray sparingly. Hold the can about a foot away from the vertical painting and spray slowly and evenly from side to side until the whole surface has been treated.

Care of pastels

Soft pastels are extremely fragile and will easily become damaged if they are not properly cared for. If you drop pastel sticks on the floor or press too hard with them on the paper, they may break, and you can end up with short stubs that are difficult to hold and fiddly to use.

Piles of much-used pastels get very grubby because they pick up pigments from your hands and from each other. Before long, it can become difficult to see which colour is which. An excellent way of avoiding this is to put the pastels into a tray of dry rice when not in immediate use. In this way, the grains of rice get dirty and the pastels stay clean.

When you have finished a session, put the pastels back in their box. If this is not possible, store the sticks between sheets of corrugated cardboard.

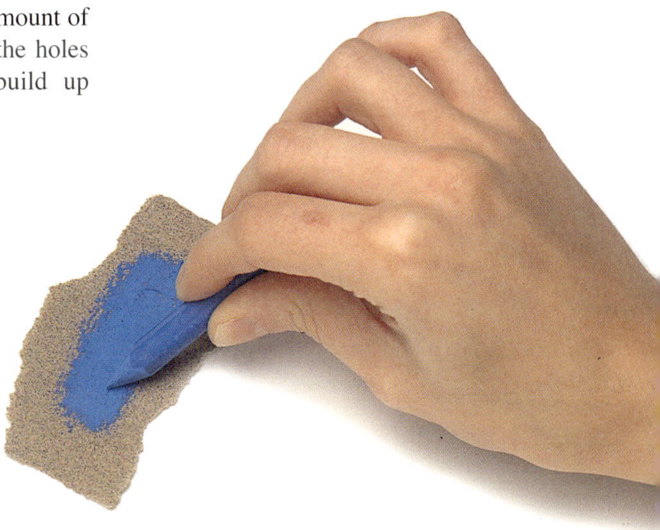

► **Keep a sheet of sandpaper to hand for maintaining a point on soft pastels. To achieve an even point, apply a little pressure as you turn the pastel slowly.**

Experimenting with textured papers

The paper you use will have a huge effect on your finished work. Try drawing on a whole range of textured surfaces to see which ones you like best.

Paper surfaces come in a wide range of interesting textures from coarse and craggy to slippery and smooth. Paper can be hard and gritty or, at the other extreme, it can feel velvety soft to the touch. When planning a piece of work, you might choose a handmade paper with an irregular texture, or you may prefer to use the even, mechanical surface of one of the many machine-made papers – it all depends on the medium you are using and the final effect you wish to achieve.

Get to know your surfaces

Whether you are using pencil, pastel, ink, or any other drawing medium, the texture of the paper makes an enormous difference to the work. You can have great fun experimenting to discover which effects you like best.

Textured papers have tiny indents on the surface known as the 'tooth'; the bigger the indents, the rougher and more pitted the paper will feel. The colour of textured paper is important, as drawn or painted marks tend to sit on the paper surface, leaving the little indents visible as paper-coloured flecks.

This flecked look is most pronounced on the very coarse papers, and the colour of these tiny flecks directly affects the colours you work with. For instance, when drawing or painting in blue on a textured yellow paper, the yellow flecks make the blue appear green. Similarly, red over yellow will produce orange, and so on.

The 'wet and dry' rule

As an initial guide, drawing materials can be divided into two very broad categories – 'wet' and 'dry'. The 'dry' drawing materials, including pastel, charcoal and coloured pencils, are not very effective on an extremely

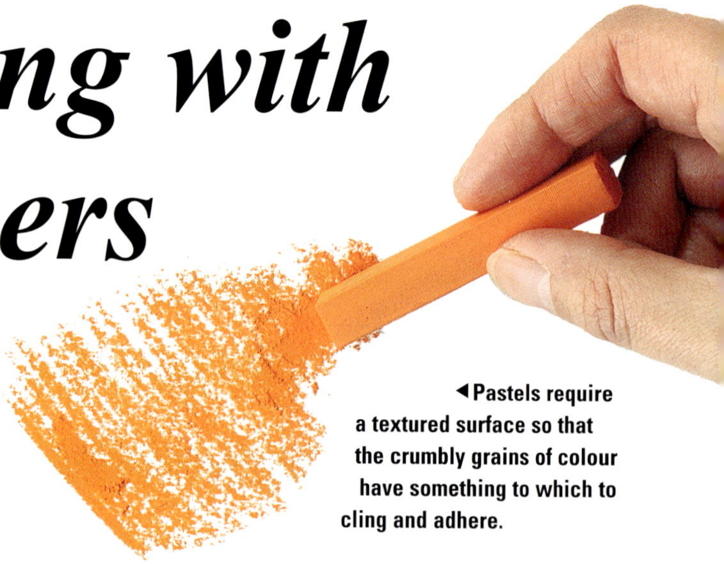

◀ **Pastels require a textured surface so that the crumbly grains of colour have something to which to cling and adhere.**

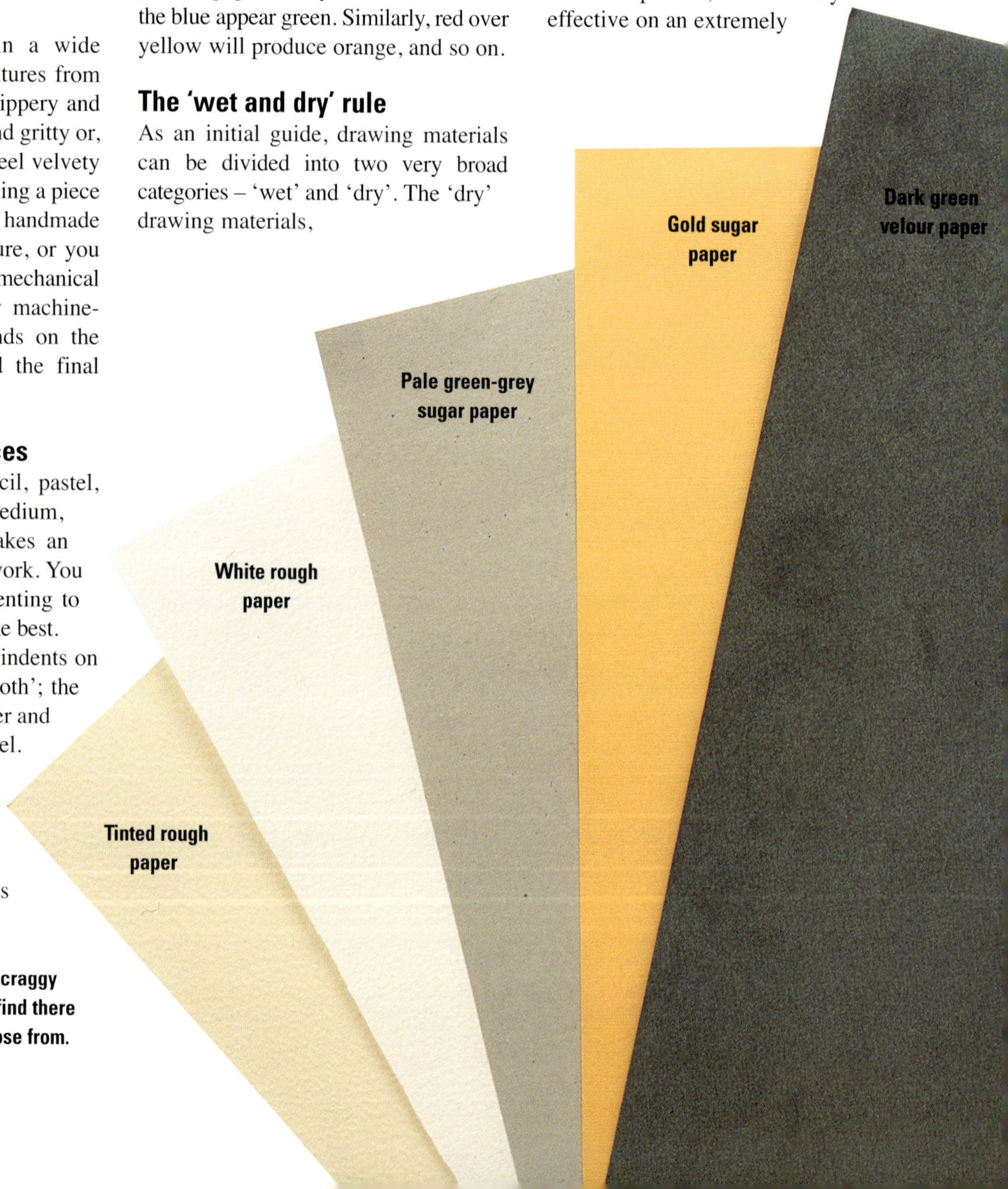

Dark green velour paper

Gold sugar paper

Pale green-grey sugar paper

White rough paper

Tinted rough paper

▶ **From smooth velour paper to craggy and toothed rough paper, you'll find there are a wealth of surfaces to choose from.**

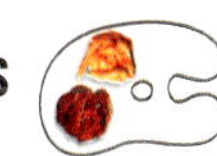

smooth surface because they simply slide around and leave a rather feeble mark. Conversely, most 'wet' drawing materials, such as pen and ink and felt tips, are excellent on smooth surfaces. In fact, 'wet' drawing materials can be quite difficult to use on a very toothy surface because the texture of the paper interferes with the flowing lines. This is especially true of fine-nibbed pens, which tend to catch on the toothy surface.

Most papers are targeted at a single market – watercolour papers for use with watercolour paints, pastel papers for pastel work, and so on. But you should never feel restricted by this. For example, watercolour papers are excellent for pastel, pencil and coloured pencil work, while pastel papers are good with drawing pencils and coloured pencils.

Improvised surfaces

Although watercolour paints require a heavy or stretched paper to prevent cockling, most drawing materials are far less exacting. It is useful to practise drawing on any number of inexpensive papers to see what results you can get. A roll of lining paper is good value for large sketches in chunky charcoal or pastel, and dressmakers' stiffening paper can be used effectively with pastels and paints.

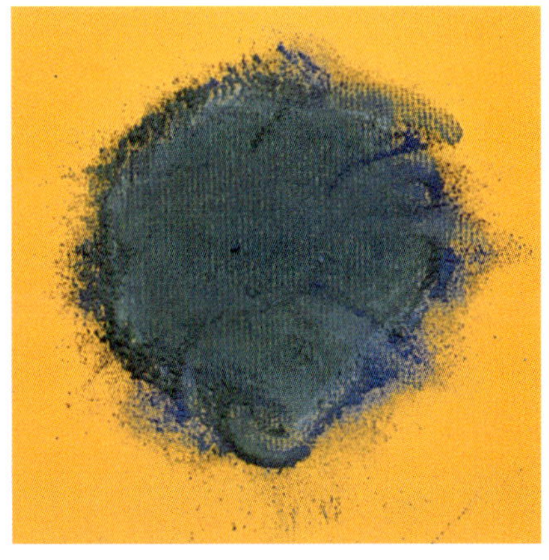

▶ This thick application of green and blue soft pastels shows how they break down into tiny crumbs. Only textured papers provide a sufficiently rugged surface to allow the colour to be built up in layers.

Watercolour papers

Choose watercolour papers for drawing according to the type of effect you want to create. Hot-pressed (HP) papers are smooth and work well with pen and ink and hard pencils. Not ('not' hot-pressed) paper is good used with most drawing materials and lends a slightly granular feel to the work. Rough paper is excellent for bold drawings and sketches, but the effect is definitely rugged, and you will not be able to draw detail.

Pastel papers

Pastels are soft and crumbly to use and the right sort of paper is crucial. There are lots to choose from, but initially it is a good idea to buy papers specially made for pastel work. These have a definite tooth which holds the crumbs of pastel dust and allows you to build up colours.

When the pastel is drawn lightly over the surface, the underlying coloured paper shows through to give characteristic flecks of broken colour. If, however, you work on a smooth paper, the pastel will slide around and you will get skid marks instead of the beautiful matt colours which can be achieved on the right paper. See the box overleaf for more information on pastel papers.

Exotic papers

There are literally hundreds of different kinds of handmade oriental papers,

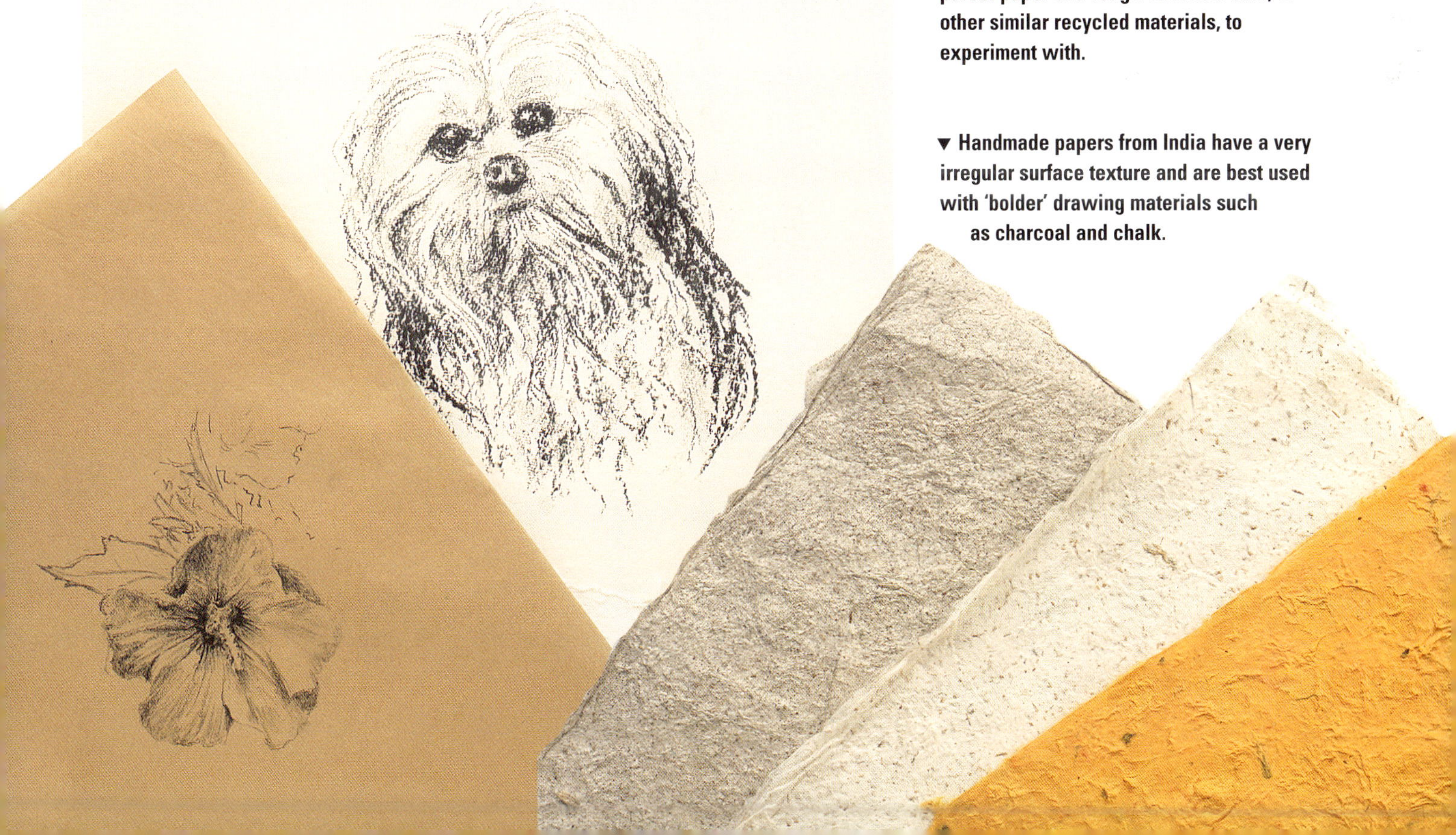

◀ Expensive papers are not a prerequisite for good drawing. Look around your home – you will probably be able to find brown parcel paper and rough-surfaced card, or other similar recycled materials, to experiment with.

▼ Handmade papers from India have a very irregular surface texture and are best used with 'bolder' drawing materials such as charcoal and chalk.

CHOOSING THE RIGHT BACKGROUND

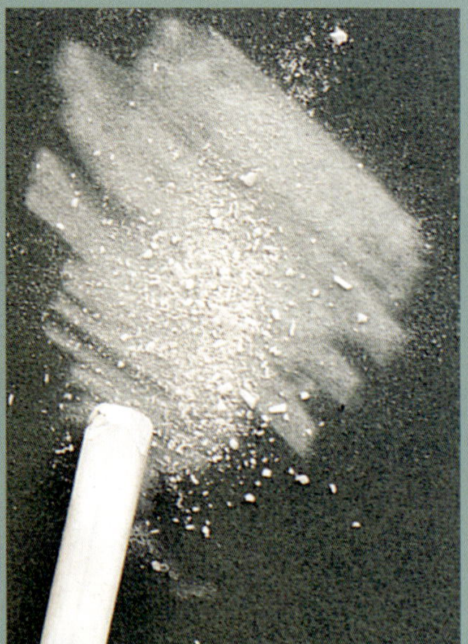

White chalk on black
Chalk isn't used only on a blackboard by teachers – artists also use it to create bold drawings. White chalk glides easily onto black velour paper and makes an obvious impact.

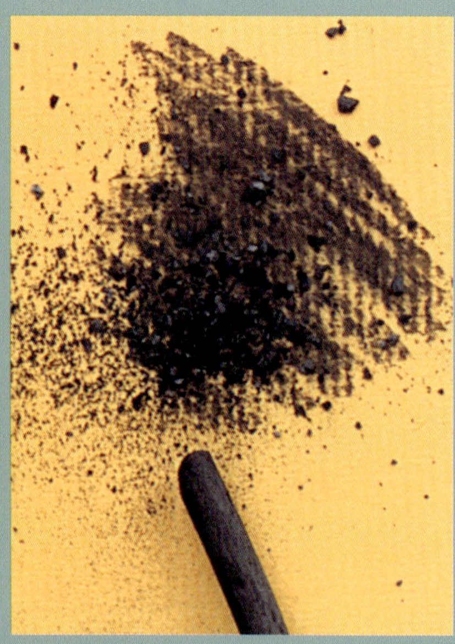

Charcoal stick on gold
Fragile charcoal sticks crumble easily and make a rich dark mark. They look particularly good against the lighter range of backgrounds, such as this gold-coloured sugar paper.

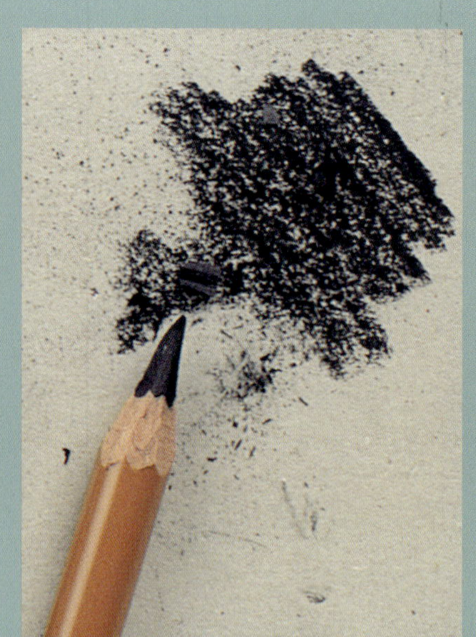

Charcoal pencil on grey
Charcoal pencil also works well on sugar paper. As the charcoal is compressed, marks made with pencils appear harder, cleaner and less crumbly. This is good for more detailed drawing work.

made from bamboo, rice, straw and many other plants and fibres. Some of these will not stand up to vigorous handling, but others make beautiful and unusual drawing papers, so experiment to find out which you like.

Japanese papers are too delicate for robust drawing and rubbing out, but the intricate surface textures look stunning under soft pastel or delicate watercolour washes. Why not try painting on them with a soft brush, or even a bamboo brush? Don't forget to leave plenty of empty spaces in the painting so that you are able to see the paper in between the painted colours.

Indian papers

Indian papers are generally tougher than Japanese ones – more like rough watercolour paper or papier maché.

▶ There are all sorts of plain or tinted papers available for pastel work. Pastels used lightly will allow the paper surface to show through, giving a broken-colour effect. Pastel pressed firmly into the tooth of the paper will give solid patches of colour.

PASTEL PAPERS

Ingres and Canson Mi-Teintes	These are traditional pastel papers, made in a wide range of colours with just the right surfaces for pastel work. The surfaces are similar, allowing flecks of the paper to show through when colour is applied, but try them both to see which you like best. Both also work well with chalk and charcoal.
Velour papers	A velvety surface is the main attraction of these papers. Pastel colours adhere beautifully, allowing you to create such rich, dense areas of colour that little of the velour paper shows through. Try them also with other drawing materials for a soft, broad effect.
Sansfix papers	These have a fine, slightly gritty finish which holds a lot of colour and allows you to build up quite thick layers of pastel. Experiment using them with other drawing materials, too.
Sandpapers	Cabinet paper, flour paper and artists' sand-grain paper are all included in this category. They have a definite gritty tooth which gives a bold, rugged effect to the work. However, these coarse surfaces wear away pastels, chalks, charcoal and pencils surprisingly quickly.

Capturing reflections

The distorted reflections of two houses near Venice help to create a wonderfully vibrant image – perfect for coloured pencils.

Reflections in water are fascinating to draw. Unless the surface of the water is absolutely mirror-still, the reflected image will be distorted.

In this scene, the water has been disturbed by the swell of a passing boat. The reflection of the houses is clearest near the bank, where the water is calmest, but it becomes gradually more distorted by the ripples, especially in the upper window and roof areas.

▼ The low evening sun brings the façades of the waterside houses to life, creating a bold, brightly coloured image.

In the two waves created by the swell, an unusual effect has occurred – two narrow slivers of the reflection can be seen, as though they have broken off the main image. The shapes found in these thin strips of colour are so distorted that the reflections have become an abstract pattern.

Coloured pencils are versatile drawing tools, ideal for capturing watery effects. Use them for linear work and for layering to give a rich depth of colour. Make broken marks where the reflections are distorted to create an impressionistic interplay of different colours.

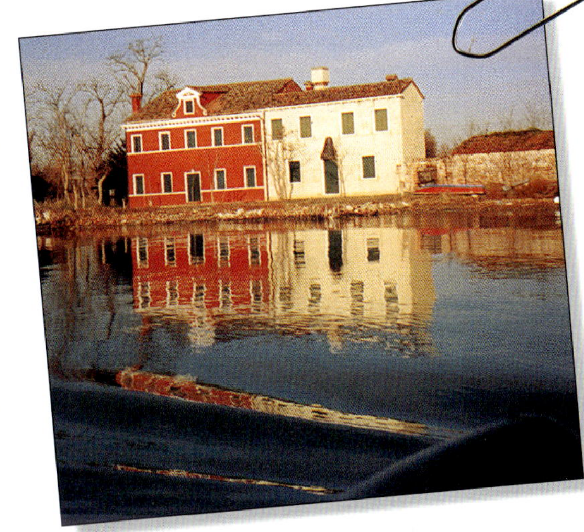

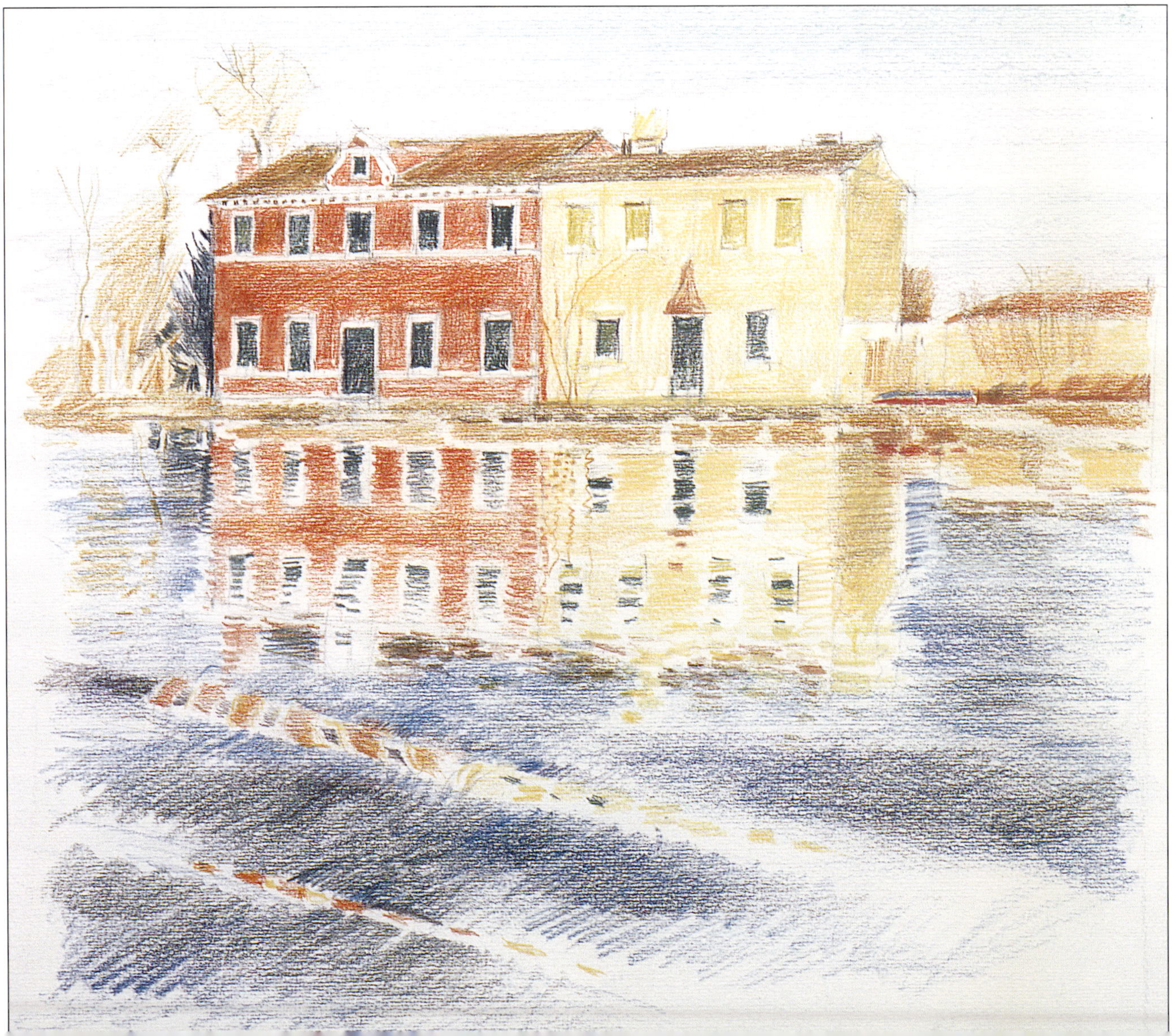

YOU WILL NEED

Piece of textured cartridge paper 43 x 50cm (17 x 19¾in)

19 coloured pencils: mid grey; pale blue; pale lilac; vermilion; Venetian red; orange; cerulean blue; deep olive green; Naples yellow; very pale sap green; Prussian green; dark Prussian green; raw sienna; pale olive green; dark blue-grey; burnt umber; deep rose; cobalt blue; black

Scrap paper

Putty rubber (to erase mistakes)

Craft knife (to sharpen pencils)

FIRST STEPS

1 ▶ Sketch the scene Using a mid grey coloured pencil, put in the line of the bank, then draw the houses and outbuilding. Roughly indicate the trees. Now draw the reflections of the houses and trees directly underneath, describing the reflected windows with zigzag lines. Mark in the diagonals of the boat's wake in the foreground.

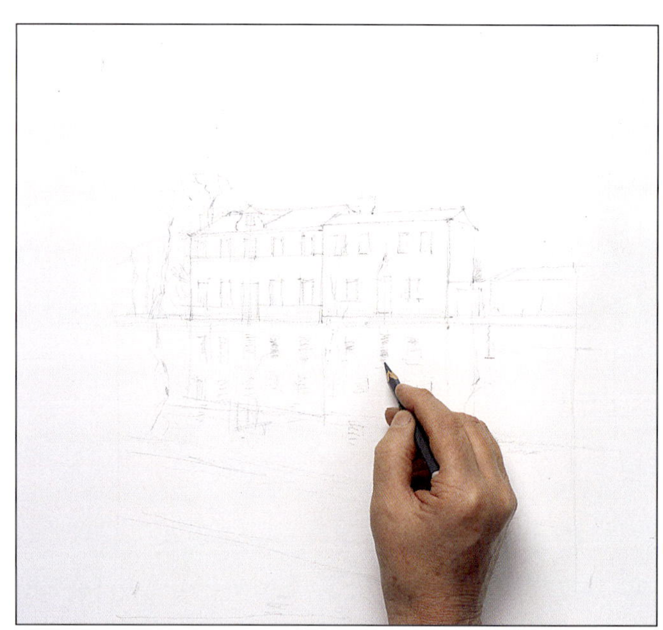

2 ▼ Introduce colour With a pale blue pencil, shade lightly over the sky and down into the water. Change to a pale lilac pencil and work across the sky to suggest clouds. Strengthen the sky above the houses with more pale blue.

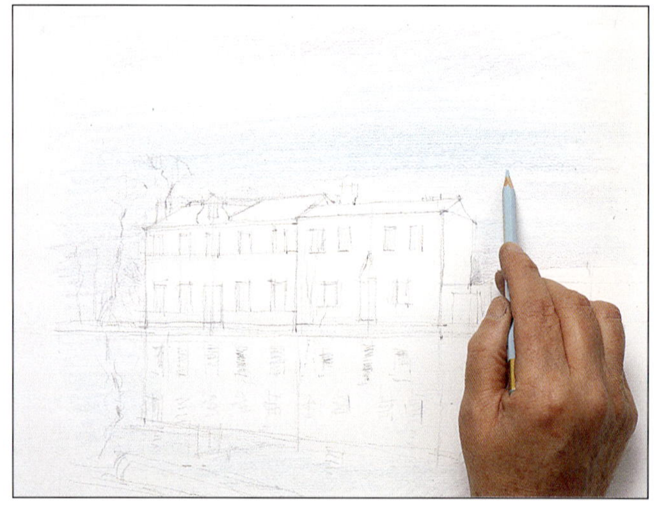

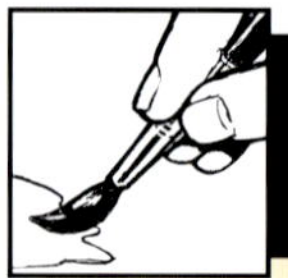

EXPERT ADVICE
Realistic reflections

If a house is set back from the water's edge, only its top part is reflected. Similarly, because the roof slants backwards, only the front edge is visible. Make sure you capture these effects to create a sense of recession.

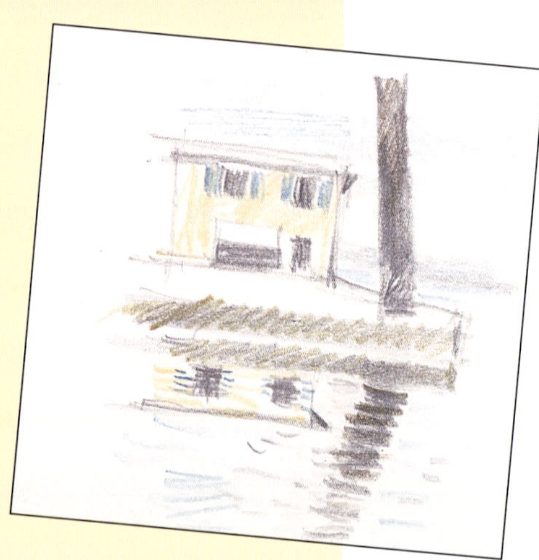

DEVELOPING THE DRAWING

As you begin to add colour, take care to show the differences between the houses and their reflections. In the reflections, the solid colours and firm lines of the façades are broken up, giving a feeling of movement to the water.

3 ▶ Work on the red house Use a vermilion pencil to colour the wall and gable of the red house, working neatly around the windows. Take the same colour down into the reflection of the house, but this time use loose, hatched lines.

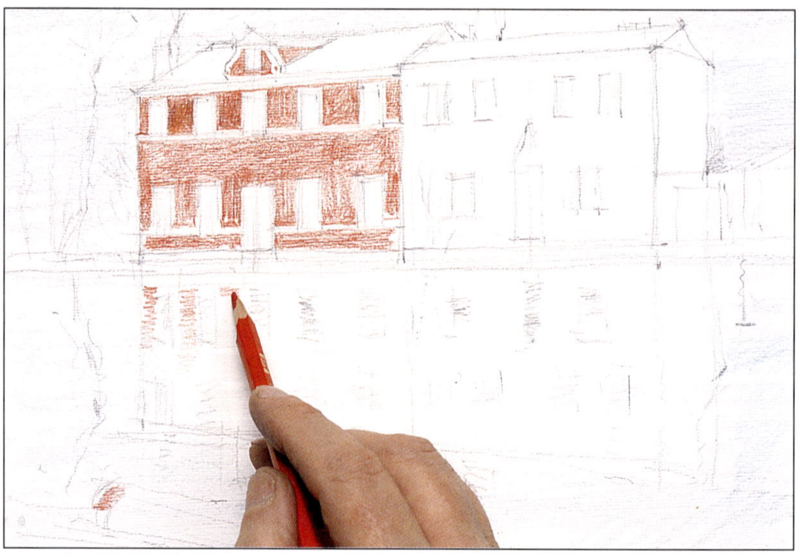

4 ▸ Layer some reds Continue shading the vermilion reflections, including the chimney, making looser marks where ripples of water break up the colour. Work, too, along the sliver of reflection visible in the boat's wake. Now create a more accurate colour for the house wall and its reflection by layering Venetian red, orange, then more Venetian red over the vermilion.

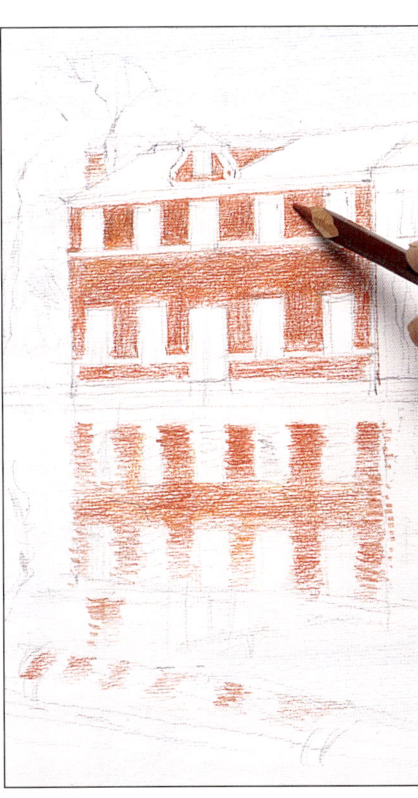

5 ▾ Colour the roofs Darken the water with cerulean blue, making loose, diagonal marks in the foreground. Now use Venetian red and deep olive green for the roof tiles. For their reflections, make broken marks to suggest the disturbed water. Show the tree on the left and the bank with deep olive green, then add their reflections.

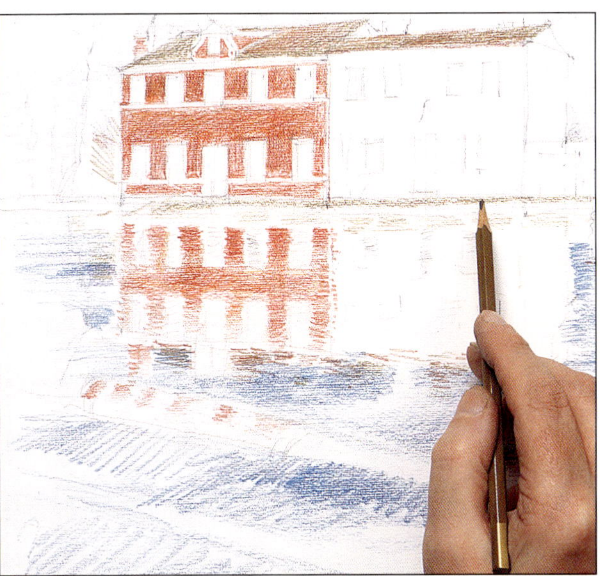

6 ▾ Work on the cream house Shade Naples yellow across the cream house and outbuilding, then layer very pale sap green on top. Work Venetian red on the roof of the outbuilding. Use the same colours for the reflections, making short, horizontal dashes of colour where the moving water distorts the image.

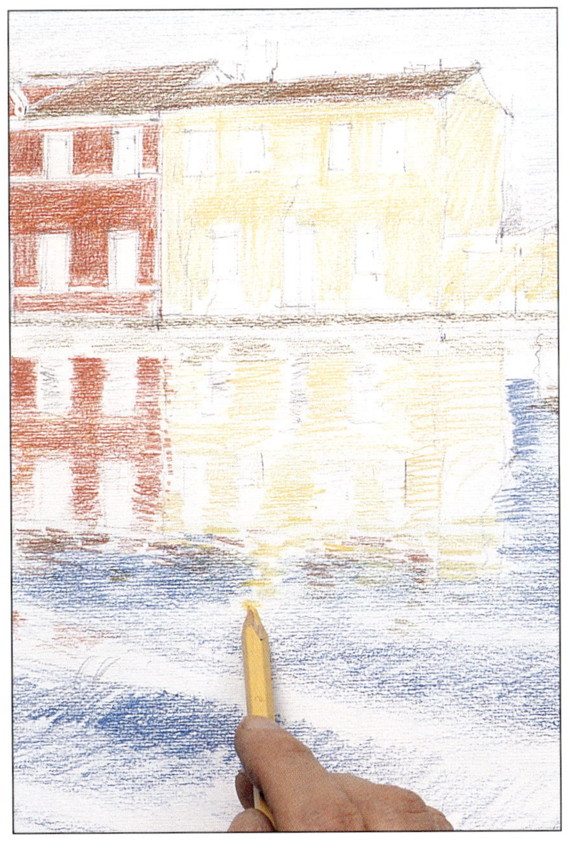

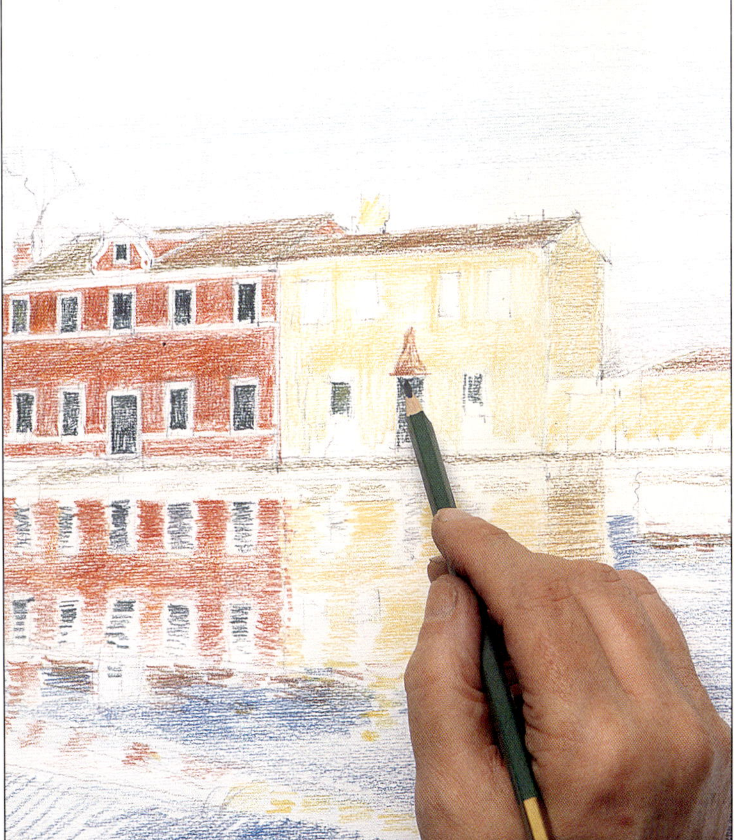

7 ▴ Put in some darks Strengthen the reflection of the cream house with more Naples yellow. Darken the shadowed side and reflection with deep olive green. Blend Prussian green and dark Prussian green to create an almost black shade for the doors and dark windows on both houses – use hatched lines for their reflections. Add a porch roof to the right-hand door with Venetian red.

8 ▶ **Complete the windows** On the right, work up the bank, trees and their reflections in raw sienna. Block in the upper windows of the cream house with pale olive green. Now hatch in the reflections of the lower windows, door and porch, using the two Prussian greens and Venetian red. For the distorted reflections of the upper windows, alternate bands of pale olive green and Prussian green.

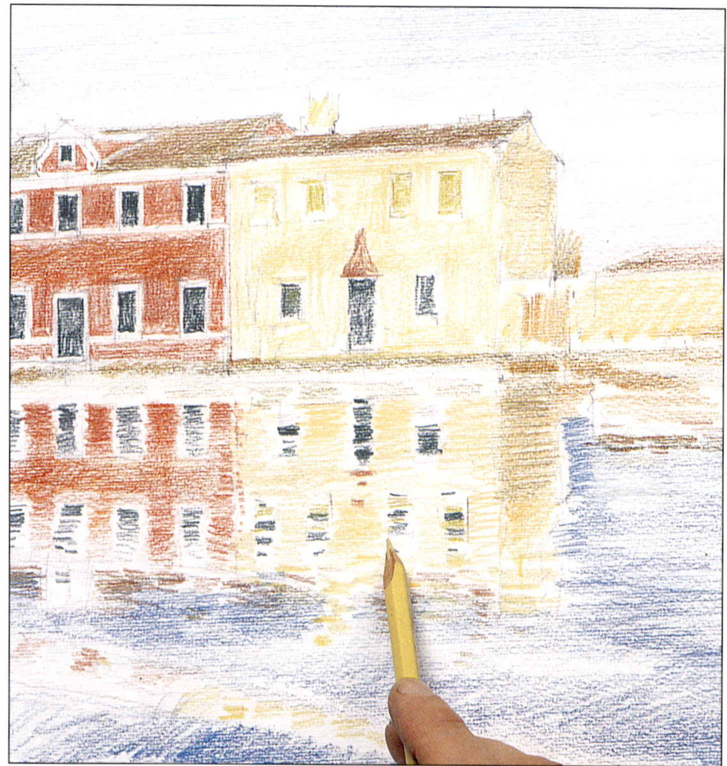

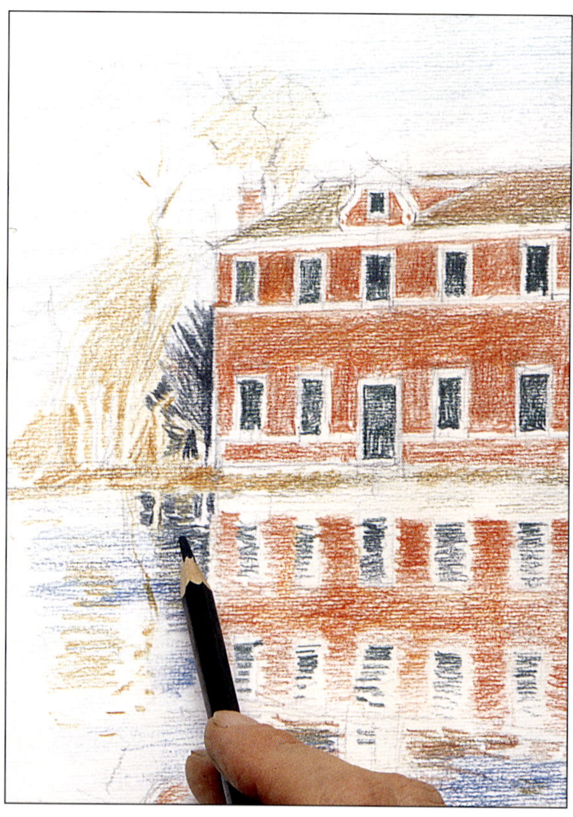

9 ▲ **Define the trees** With raw sienna, roughly indicate the trunks and bare branches of the trees on the far left. Then, using dark Prussian green, draw the diagonal branches of the conifer. Work up the reflections of the trees, using the same colours.

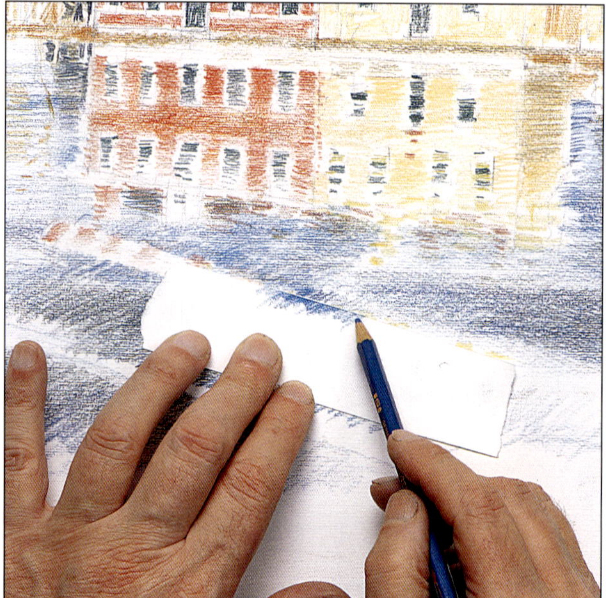

10 ▲ **Darken the water** Shade dark blue-grey across the whole water area. When you reach the boat's wake in the foreground, work over a strip of scrap paper to achieve straight edges along the shadows here. Layer cerulean blue over the dark colour, again using the paper strip along the wake.

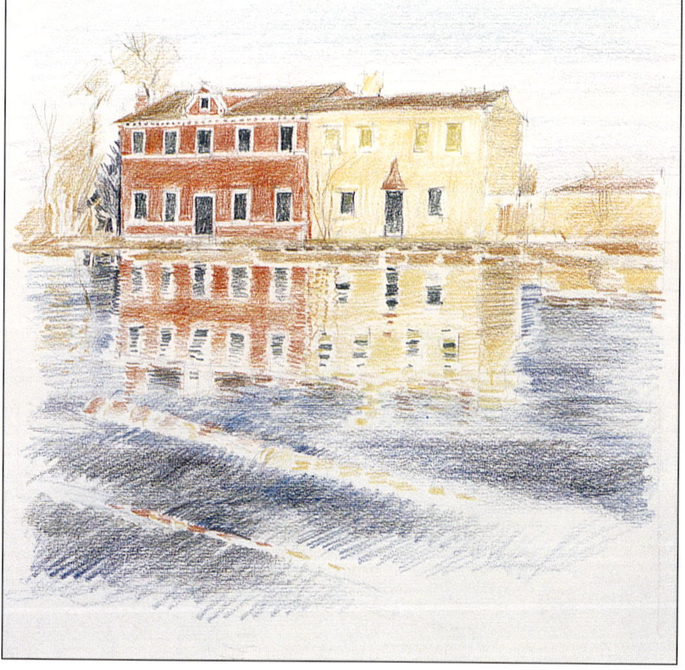

11 ▲ **Add details** Strengthen the reflections along the wake with Naples yellow and vermilion. Edge the bank with burnt umber, using raw sienna for its reflection. Draw a tree in front of the cream house, adding a reflection with dots and wavy lines, then hint at trees in front of the outbuilding with deep olive green. Decorate the eaves of the red house with burnt umber dashes.

A FEW STEPS FURTHER

A few extra colour accents will complete the drawing. Draw the pink-and-blue boat on the bank and add more colour where the houses are reflected along the wake.

12 ▼ Draw the boat Using Venetian red, build up the trees to the right of the house and their reflections. Draw in the boat on the bank, using bands of deep rose and cobalt blue. Mark the boat's reflection with deep rose.

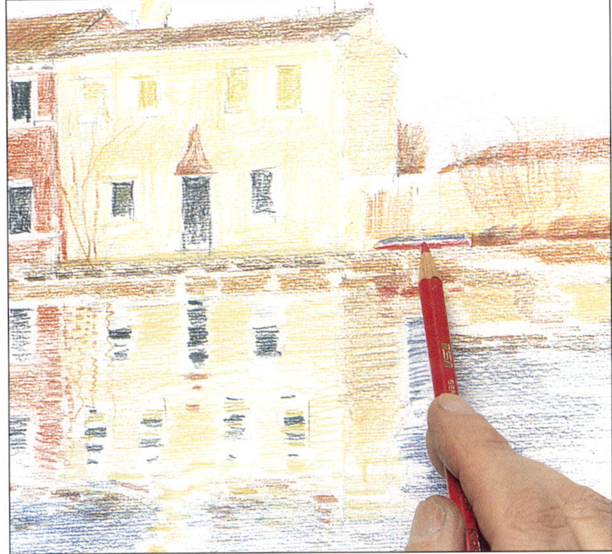

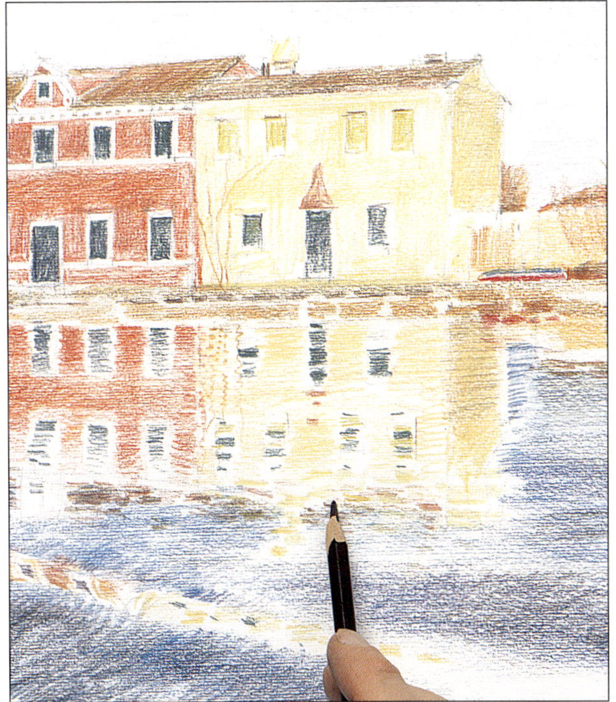

13 ▲ Develop the reflections Shade over the end wall of the cream house with pale olive green, then define the windows and chimney with burnt umber. Work up the slivers of reflection with orange, Venetian red, dark blue-grey and Prussian green. Add touches of black to the broken-up reflection on the right.

THE FINISHED PICTURE

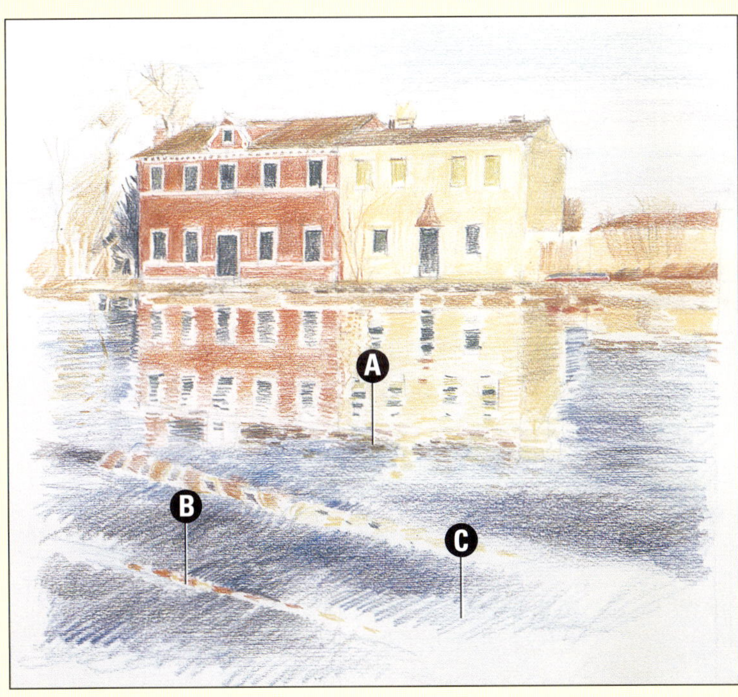

A Rippled surface
Dashed and dotted coloured pencil marks suggest the broken-up reflections of the roofs in the disturbed water.

B Abstract effect
The reflections along the line of the wake have been filled in with patches of colour that form a decorative, abstract pattern.

C Moving water
Diagonal, rather than horizontal, pencil lines in the foreground give the impression of movement in the water.

Drawing with a grid

Make a grid to help you position objects on paper and create a balanced outline. Shade in the composition using a charcoal pencil for a bold effect.

There's no need to go anywhere special to find interesting subjects to draw. It is quite possible simply to stay at home and pick out some of the objects around you in order to create a worthwhile composition.

Mapping size and position

Even experienced artists can have difficulty in accurately mapping the size and proportion of objects. One solution is to stand a sheet of white card with squares drawn on it behind your still life, then to rule a corresponding grid onto your drawing paper. This makes it easier to plot the height and volume of different objects.

Another plus point is that the white backdrop encloses the objects, aiding concentration, while making a clear surface for any shadows to fall on. In this project, however, it is the outline of the objects, their place within the grid and their 3-D form that are important.

Using a charcoal pencil

The outline is drawn using a 2B pencil, which is easy to rub out in case of mistakes; however, the shading for this particular drawing is done with a charcoal pencil, to create strong, dark lines. In fact, because charcoal handles so differently to graphite pencil when it comes to shading, it's a good idea to get a feel for it first.

On a scrap piece of paper, move the pencil freely from side to side. Press lightly at first, then harder, and note the difference in the strength of the impression. Then go over your initial strokes with further strokes in different directions and check the varied textures you create. You will soon find yourself familiar with the way that charcoal pencils work.

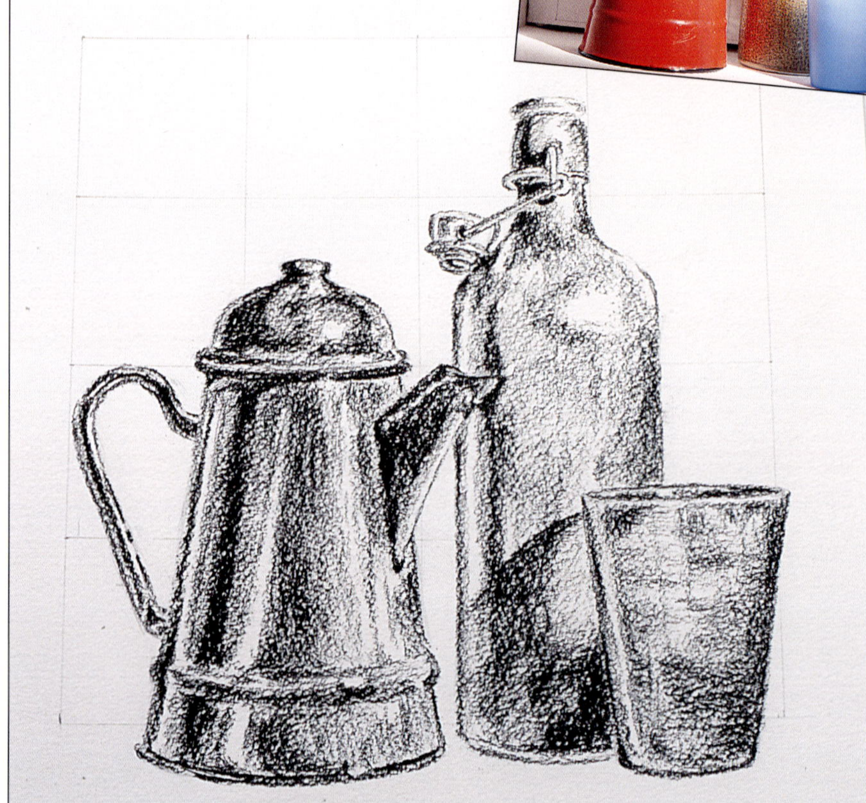

▲ It is much easier to draw a still life if you plot the position of the objects in it against a grid.

YOU WILL NEED

- Piece of white card approx. 43cm (17in) high by 1m (40in) or more
- Masking tape
- Metal ruler
- Rubber
- Pencils: 2B; charcoal
- Scalpel or pencil sharpener
- Large sheet of lightly textured drawing paper

HOW TO MAKE A GRID SCREEN

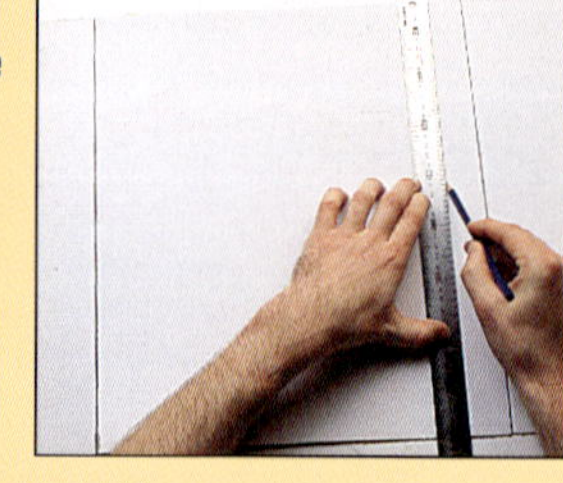

1 Mark a vertical line about 20cm (8in) from each end of the pliable white card. Cut along these lines, then tape the severed pieces of card back in place with masking tape. This creates the moveable side flaps that will allow the screen to stand upright. Then use a 2B pencil to mark out the limits of the grid, making sure its base is positioned as close as possible to the bottom of the card.

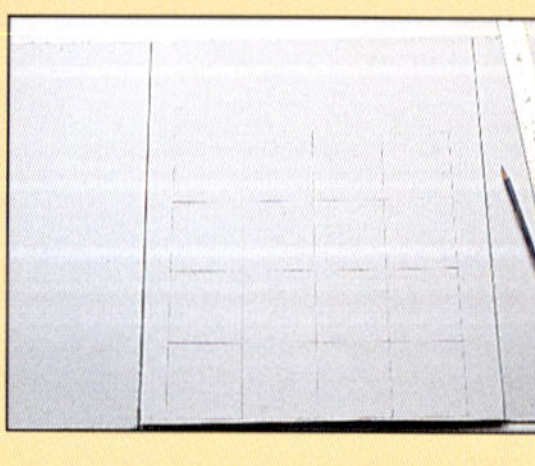

2 Continue ruling horizontal and vertical lines on the card to complete the grid. The version shown here has 16 squares, each 8 x 8cm (3 x 3in) in size. Arrange your still life group at eye level and stand the grid screen behind it. You are now ready to start drawing.

HOW TO USE THE GRID METHOD

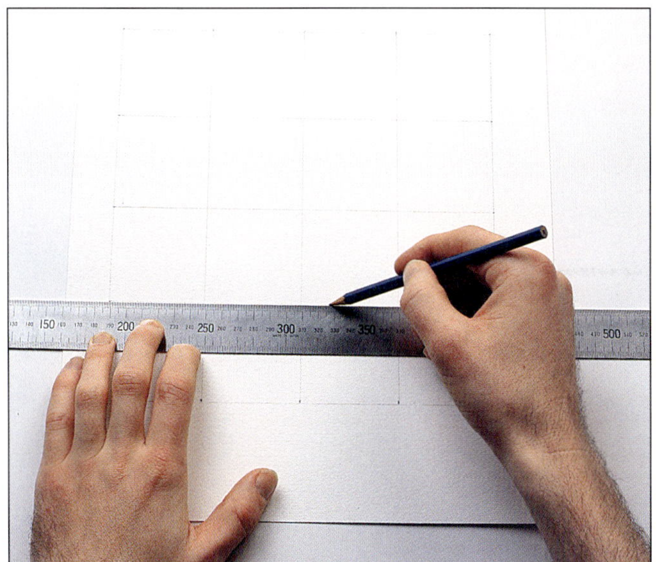

1 ▲ **Draw a corresponding grid onto your paper** Using the 2B pencil, draw another grid onto the drawing paper. You will need to divide it up into the same number of squares as appear on the card screen – although they do not have to be the same size as those you drew previously. The squares shown here measure 6 x 6cm (2.5 x 2.5in).

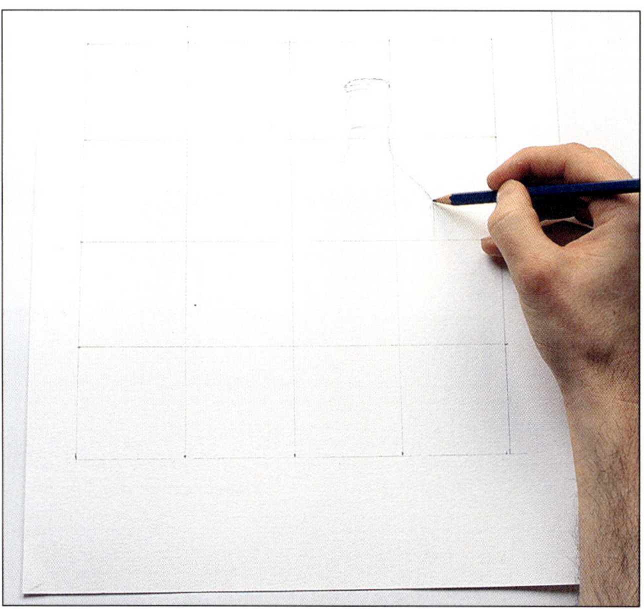

2 ▲ **Start drawing the bottle outline** Start with the bottle, as it is the tallest object in the group. Study where and how its outline crosses the squares on the grid behind it. Then start drawing in the bottle's outline using the 2B pencil. Make sure that you place each individual line in the corresponding grid square on your piece of paper as you draw.

3 ▶ **Check as you draw** Continue drawing the bottle, including its stopper, referring frequently to the grid lines behind the object. Use a series of small strokes rather than a single line.

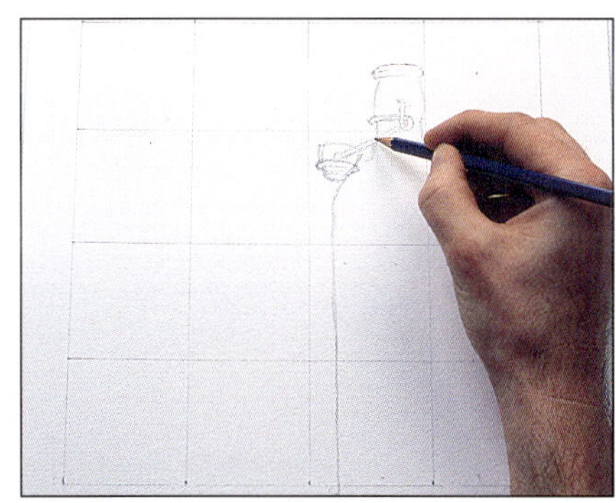

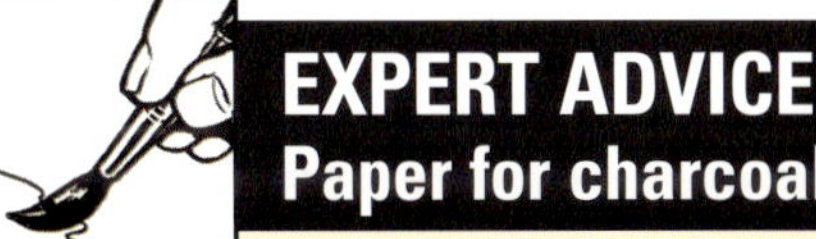

EXPERT ADVICE
Paper for charcoal

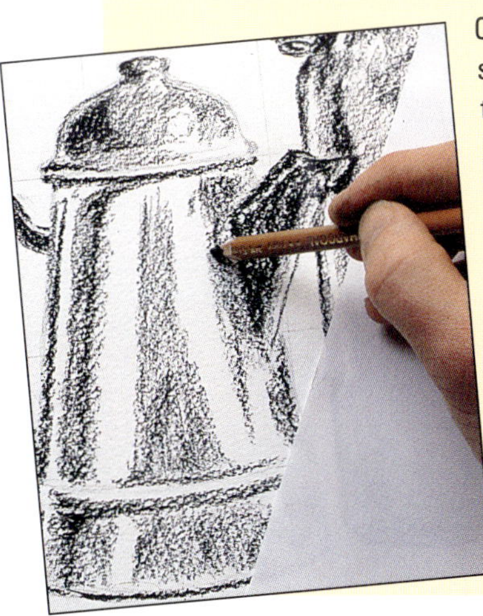

Charcoal, being a powdery substance, works best on slightly textured paper, which gives it something to 'grip' on to. If you use smooth or shiny paper, you will see the charcoal slide all over the place. Once you are familiar with how it handles, you can try using charcoal on paper with a highly textured surface. As the grain on this type of paper is prominent, it adds a distinctive character to the drawing.

ADD IN THE OTHER ITEMS IN THE GROUP

Once you have established the position of the first object in your still life – in this case, the bottle – you can add the other items around it. By continuing to follow the grid lines, you ensure that the objects relate to each other as in the original.

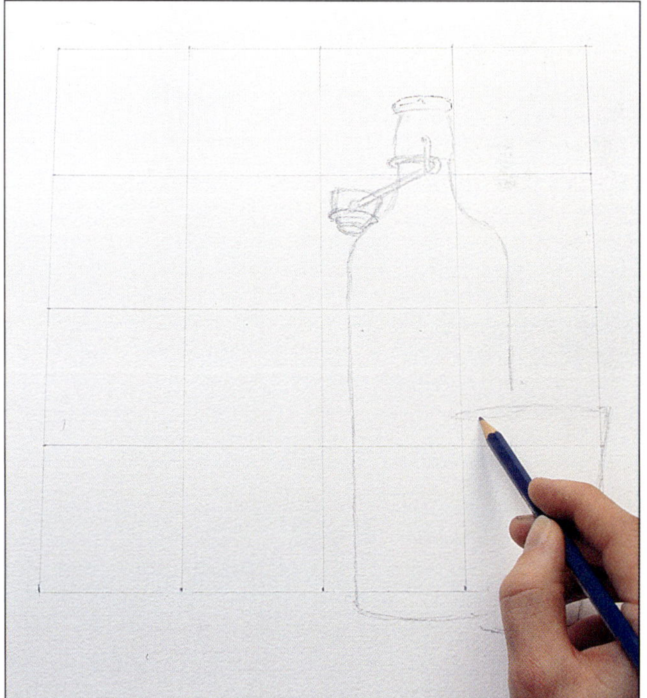

4 ▲ **Sketch the outline of the glass** Again using the grid lines for reference, draw in the outline of the glass. The glass is positioned just in front of the bottle, so it appears slightly 'lower' in relation to the bottle's rounded base.

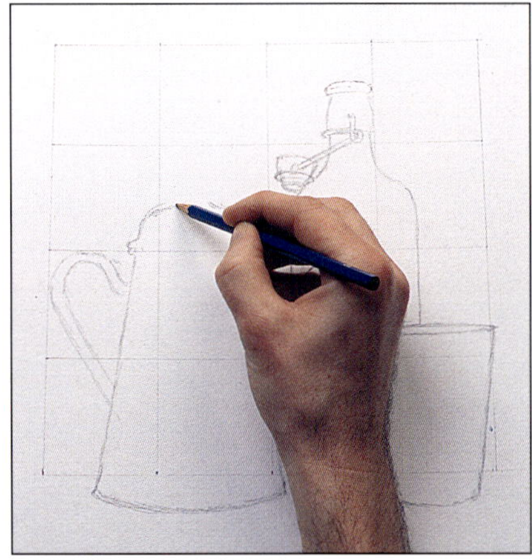

5 ▲ **Draw the coffee pot** Next, sketch the outline of the coffee pot, once again following the grid lines. Study the shape carefully and thicken up the lines slightly where the contours seem more intense – for example, on each side of the lid. If you use the rubber to correct any errors, you are likely to rub out the grid lines as well. Make sure to pencil these back in.

6 ▶ **Complete the pencil sketch** Add the details on the coffee pot. You have now achieved your initial sketch – a well-proportioned group of objects ready for developing with the charcoal pencil.

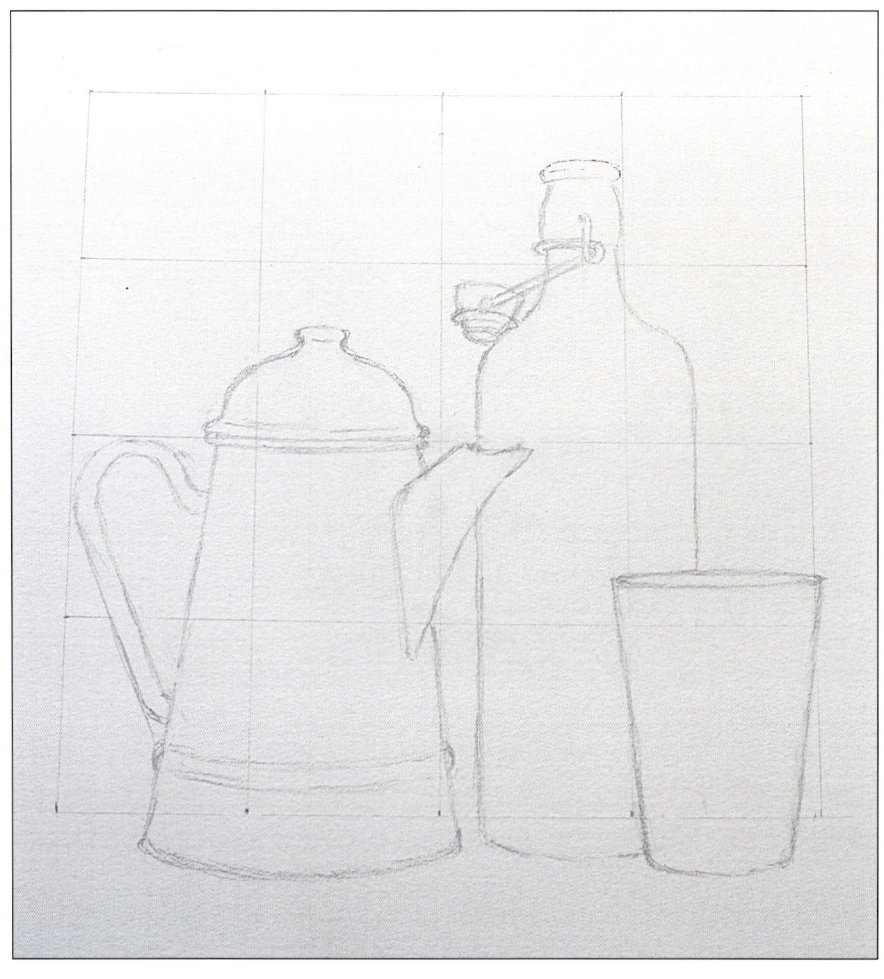

A FEW STEPS FURTHER

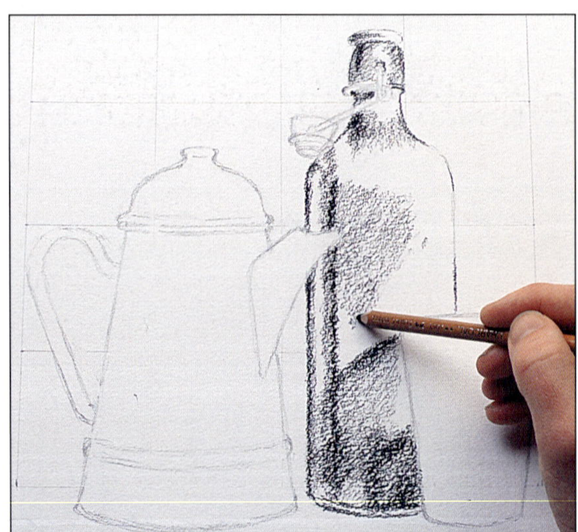

7 ▲ **Shade the bottle** Study how the light falls on the group of objects that you have just been drawing. Then use the sharp charcoal pencil and a combination of intense and lighter strokes to shade the bottle, building up areas of light and dark tones, and leaving the highlights bare.

8 ▶ **Give form to the glass** Use the sharp point of the pencil to give form to the bottle's stopper. Then turn to the glass. Use heavy strokes to create the shaded areas along its right-hand edge and around the lower half, then use medium strokes to give form to the other areas. Leave the highlights on the left and near the top of the glass untouched so that the white paper shows through.

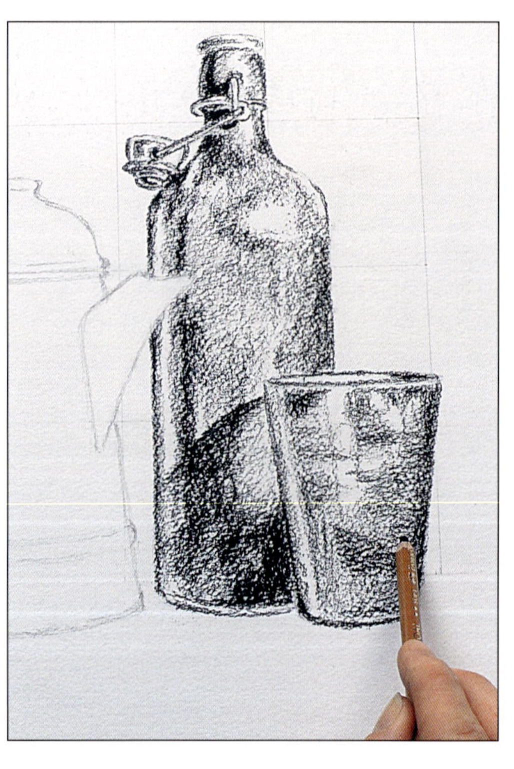

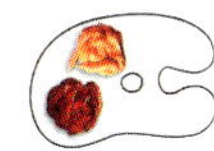

9 ▸ Work on the coffee pot Place a sheet of paper over the finished parts of the drawing to prevent them smudging as you work. Then start to shade the coffee pot, leaving the main highlights as wide vertical strips.

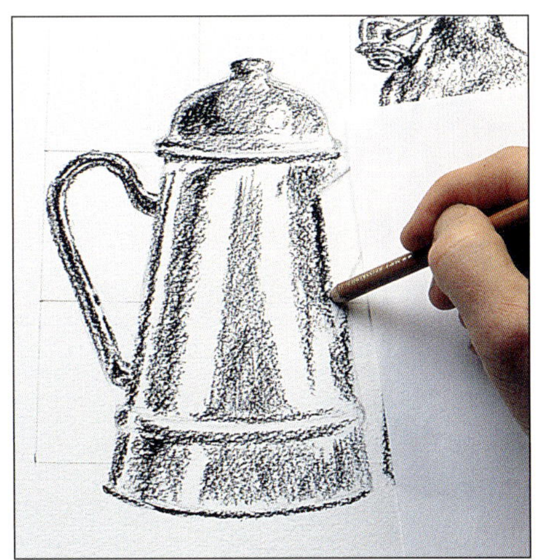

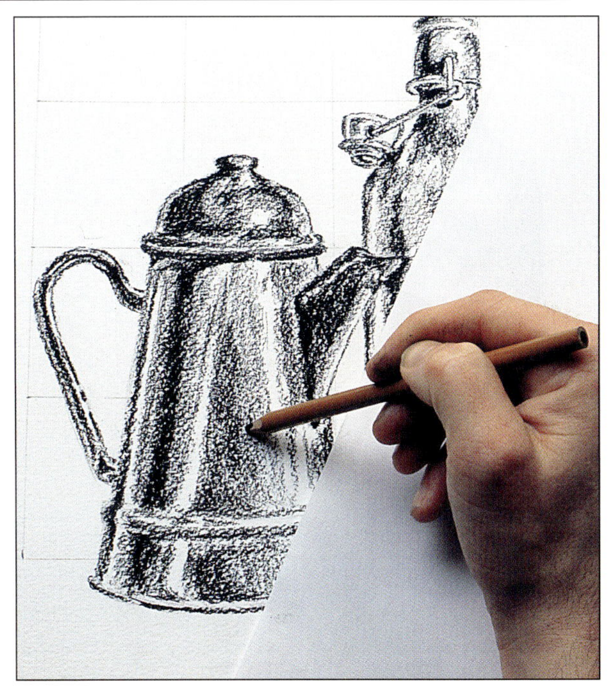

10 ▸ Build up the tones on the coffee pot Gradually work up and darken the shading on the coffee pot. Reduce the main highlights to a few narrow bands, where the light bounces most intensely off the shiny, curved surface of the object.

THE FINISHED PICTURE

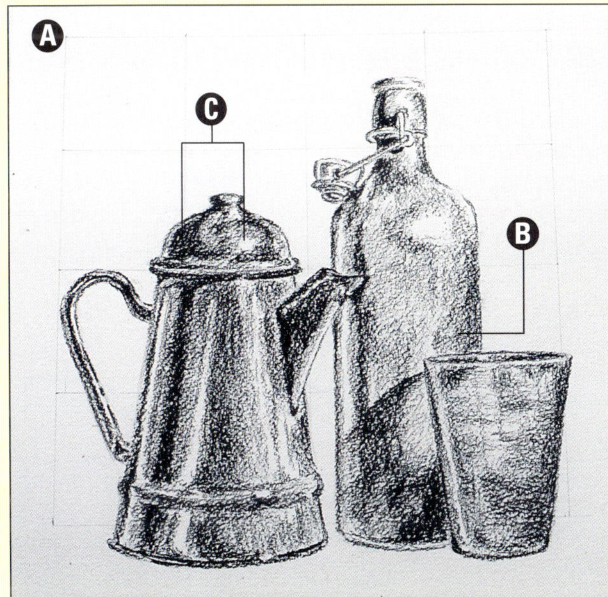

A The grid
The way the objects in the picture relate to their surrounding grid lines should mirror the way in which the original still life is positioned against the grid on the card screen. You can rub out the grid on the paper to complete the picture.

B Use of charcoal
The lines made with the 2B pencil, which was used to create the initial sketch in case of error, are completely hidden by the subsequent shading with the charcoal pencil. The charcoal produces darker tones and gives a softer finish.

C 3-D form
Once the shapes and arrangement of the three objects in the still life had been established on the grid, the artist then created the 3-D quality of their curved surfaces. This was achieved by the use of shading, and by creating highlights.

USING WATER-SOLUBLE COLOURED PENCILS

If you would like to introduce colour into your still life, you can achieve a very different effect from a charcoal drawing by using water-soluble coloured pencils. These are extremely versatile, as you can first draw your subject with them, then add water with a brush to soften the outlines and blend the colours. The final result is similar to a watercolour painting. You can then add more pencil strokes over the top of the blended areas once the paper is completely dry.

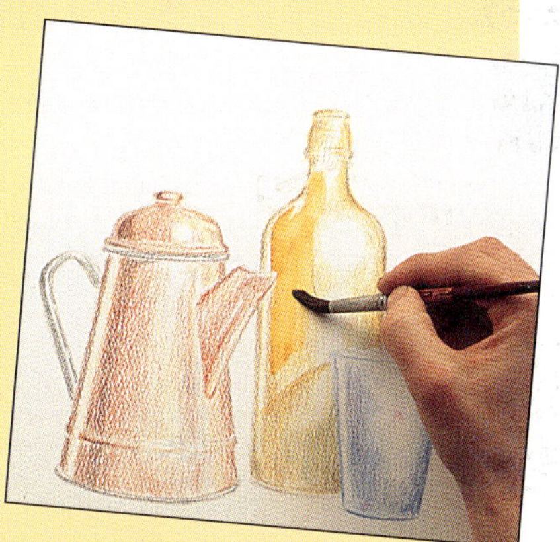

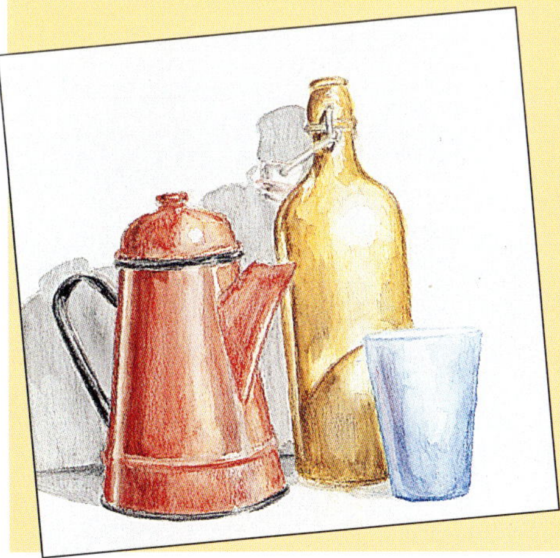

Choosing the best palette

Essential to creating good paintings is colour mixing – and, to do this successfully, you first need to have the right palette.

Artists' palettes are made from a variety of materials and come in an enormous range of shapes and sizes. Your choice depends largely on the paints you are intending to use. For example, you will need a flat palette for oils and acrylics, and deeper mixing dishes for watercolours.

It is important to work with a palette that is big enough to accommodate all the colours you are likely to need. There is nothing more frustrating than trying to mix on a cramped surface – either you tend not to use enough of each colour or the mixes overlap, creating muddy colours.

Oil paints

The kidney-shaped wooden palette with a hole for the thumb is traditionally used for oil paints. This design has been in use since the advent of the medium in the early fifteenth century. The best wooden palettes are made from mahogany or mahogany veneer, but there are now cheaper options, including plywood and other wood composites.

When choosing a wooden palette, try it out for size, weight and comfort. The ideal palette can easily be held in a horizontal position – usually by using the forearm as support. A badly designed one will be difficult to hold up and will soon make your thumb and wrist ache.

Before using your palette for the first time, seal the wood by rubbing it with linseed oil. Doing this helps to prevent the palette from absorbing oil from the paint, causing the colours to dry out. After one or two painting sessions, the palette ceases to be as absorbent and provides an excellent paint-mixing surface. If cared for properly, a good wooden palette will last a lifetime.

Acrylic paints

For acrylics, use a plastic or plastic-laminate palette. Acrylic paint dries quickly and, if left for several hours or overnight, the paint turns first rubbery, then hard. On a wooden palette the colours will stick fast to the slightly irregular, pitted surface and will be difficult to remove. However, the smooth surface of a plastic palette provides no key for the paint, which can be removed easily by soaking, then peeling it off.

A special 'wet' palette designed to keep the colours moist for as long as possible is also available for use with acrylics. The palette works on the principle of osmosis. It consists of a shallow plastic tray with a sheet of absorbent wet tissue placed in the bottom under a thin membrane paper. When the acrylic paint colours are laid out on the membrane, the moisture from the wet tissue is drawn through, so preventing the paints from drying out.

Alternatively, you can make your own wet palette from a plastic or foil dish and some sheets of wetted kitchen paper, with a sheet of greaseproof paper for the membrane.

Watercolour and gouache

Palettes for mixing watercolour or gouache must be deep enough to hold watery mixtures without the colours running together. They are available in a range of shapes and sizes from small round dishes, known as tinting saucers, to much larger, more complex palette trays which have 24 or more recesses for mixing colour.

Watercolour palettes are usually made of ceramic, plastic or enamelled metal. Plastic palettes are light, tough and inexpensive – excellent for painting expeditions and for working outdoors. However, the plastic surface has a slightly repellent effect on water and the paint tends to break up into globules rather than forming even

INTEGRAL PALETTES

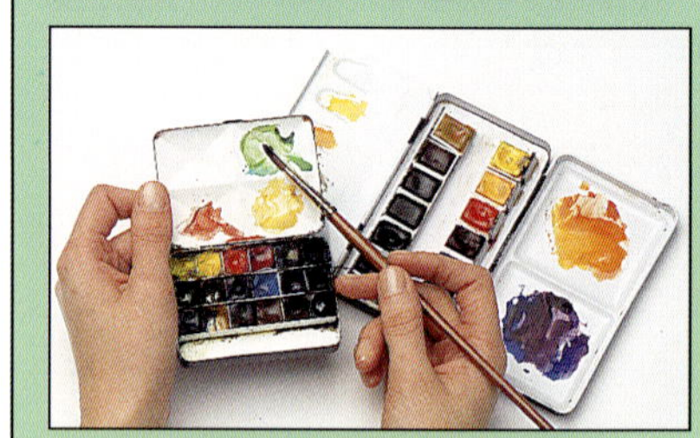

Most enamelled watercolour boxes have lids that open out to form a small palette. They are often divided into two or more recesses and sometimes unfold to provide a larger mixing area. These boxes are particularly handy for outdoor work and sketching.

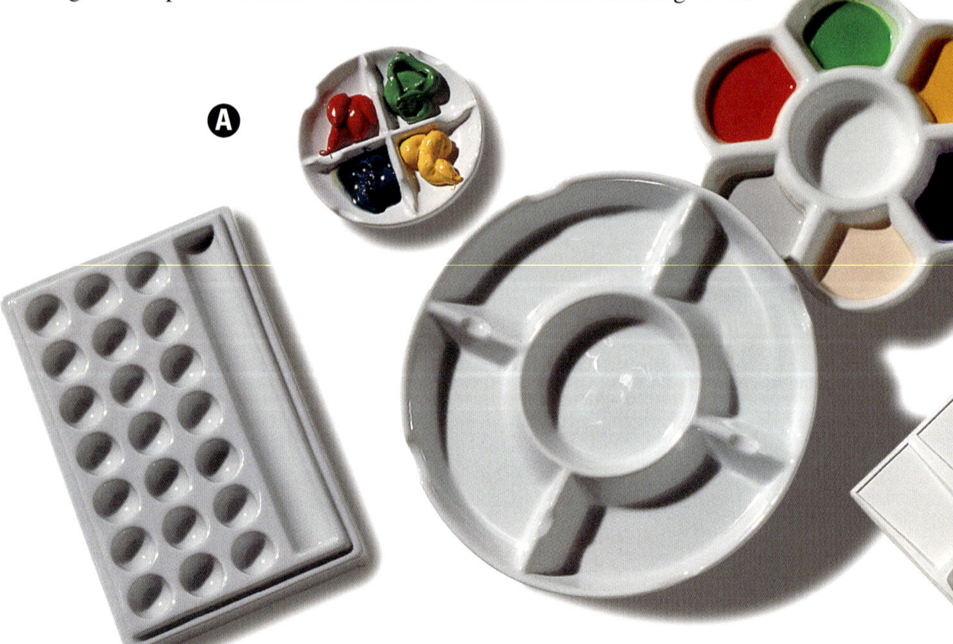

pools. This makes no difference to the colours, but it can be irritating and makes it difficult to judge how much colour you have mixed. In addition, some plastics stain easily and soon lose their whiteness. For these reasons, many artists prefer to use ceramic palettes.

Improvised palettes

Lack of a proper palette need not prevent you from painting. For oils and acrylics, you could always improvise with a sheet of plastic, Perspex, laminate or glass. The latter can be made safe by binding the sharp edges with tape. One great advantage of a home-made palette is that you can choose a size and shape to suit your needs. It can be as large as you like, perhaps even cut to fit a particular table top.

Other alternative palettes for oils and acrylics are greaseproof paper, old plates and other discarded kitchenware. You can also buy disposable paper palettes in tear-off pads. For watercolour, use old dishes and saucers.

Cleaning an oil palette

To clean your oil palette, you need a knife and some diluent – for example, white spirit or turpentine left over in a dipper after a painting.

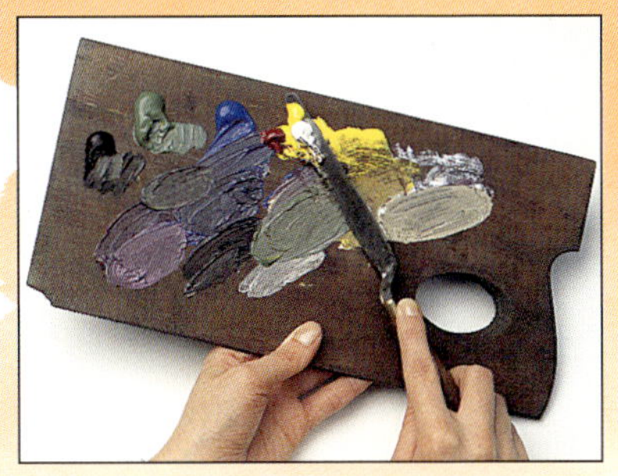

1 ▲ **Remove excess paint** Scrape off leftover colours with a knife while the paint is still wet.

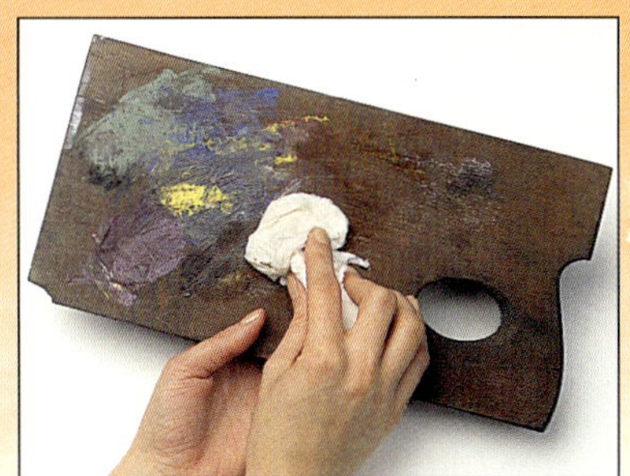

2 ▲ **Wipe the palette** Dip a rag in diluent and wipe the remaining paint off the palette.

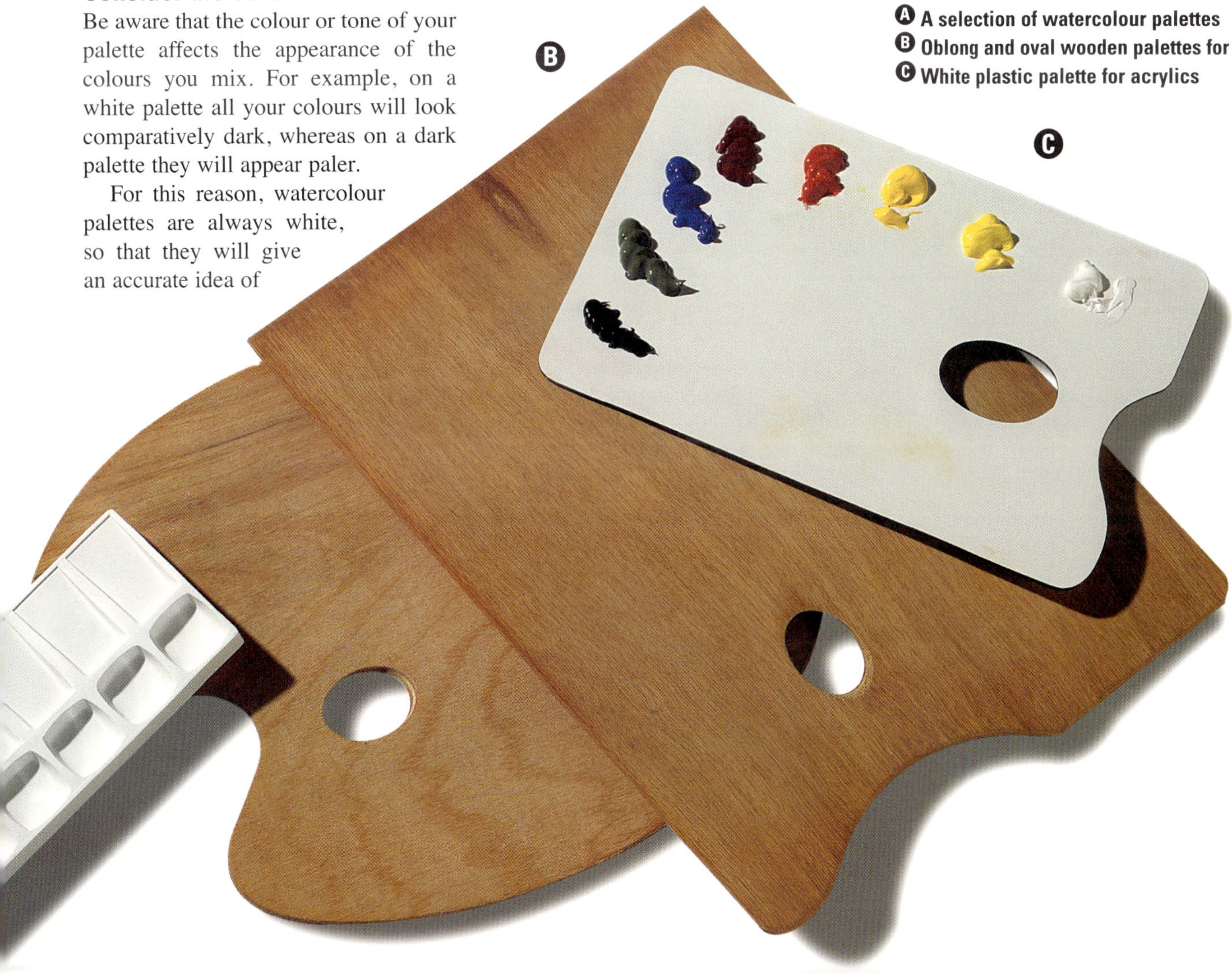

Consider the colour

Be aware that the colour or tone of your palette affects the appearance of the colours you mix. For example, on a white palette all your colours will look comparatively dark, whereas on a dark palette they will appear paler.

For this reason, watercolour palettes are always white, so that they will give an accurate idea of how the colours will appear on white paper. Most oil paintings, on the other hand, are executed in a darker tonal range, and the artist often blocks out the bright white canvas in the early stages of a painting. For the oil painter, therefore, a wooden palette provides a better idea of how the mixed colours will look in the finished painting.

Some artists like to use a sheet of clear plastic or glass as a palette. They can then put a sheet of coloured paper underneath, matching the paper they are using as a support.

A A selection of watercolour palettes
B Oblong and oval wooden palettes for oils
C White plastic palette for acrylics

Brushes

It's worth building up a collection of different brushes as they will help you achieve a wide range of exciting paint effects.

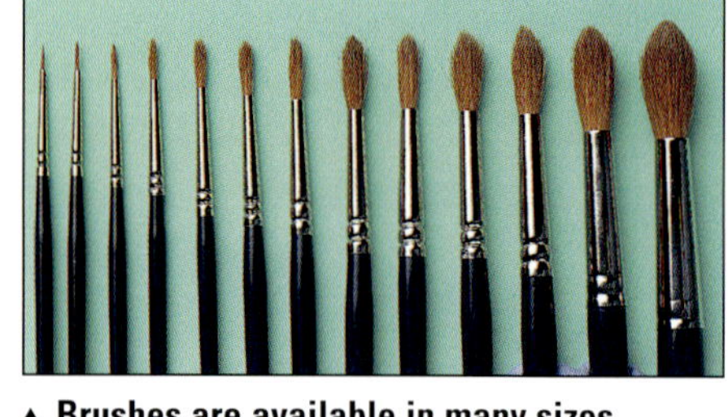

▲ **Brushes are available in many sizes. These sable rounds range in size from the finest No. 0000 to the much larger No. 20.**

Artists' brushes are available in an enormous range of shapes and sizes, corresponding to the various purposes they are intended for. They may be made from several different kinds of natural bristles or from synthetic fibre, and the difference in price between the different types of bristle can be considerable. The choice is wide, but in the end the decision as to which to buy and use is a personal one, often depending on trial and error. Initially, it is a good idea to experiment with one or two brushes at a time to see how you get on.

WHAT TO LOOK FOR

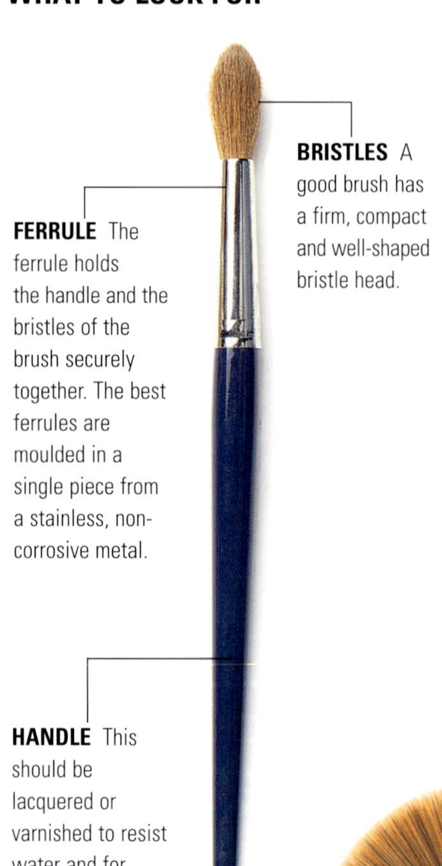

Small and large

Most artists' brushes come in a range of sizes, usually numbered. For example, a standard watercolour brush range can start with a tiny No. 0000, used only for the very finest work, going up to No. 20 and even larger. However, it is worth remembering that each brush manufacturer has a slightly different system. Hence a No. 2 brush made by one manufacturer is not necessarily exactly the same size as a No. 2 brush produced by another. The size of some flat brushes may be expressed in terms of total bristle width instead of numbers – 25mm (1in), 51mm (2in) and so on.

Types of brush

Each type of brush is designed to make a specific kind of mark. Choosing a brush depends very much on the effect you want to achieve, but if you have one or two of the following basic brush types they will be all you need to begin with.

Round This is a brush with a rounded ferrule, and it is a popular, general-purpose brush with a full bristle head that holds a lot of paint. Large rounds are useful for laying washes and wide expanses of colour. The point can be used for painting lines and detail.

Flat or chisel-headed This type of brush has a flattened ferrule with a square-cut bristle head. The wide bristles are good for applying paint in short dabs and for laying flat areas of colour, while the narrow edge of the bristles is useful for making thinner lines. A flat with very short bristles is sometimes referred to as a 'bright'.

Filbert Somewhere between a flat and a round, a filbert has a flattened ferrule but with tapered bristles. It is a popular and versatile brush, combining the functions of other brush types.

Fan The attractively shaped fan brush, or blender, as it is also sometimes known, has widely splayed bristles and is used primarily for blending colours together smoothly.

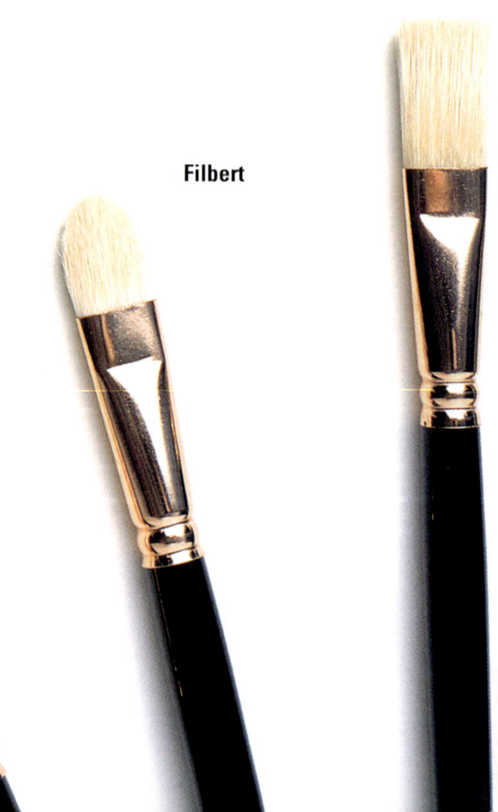

gger

ble rounds

ynthetic
ushes

Mop

Watercolour brushes

Watercolour brushes are usually softer than those used with oil and acrylics. The very best-quality watercolour brushes to be found are sable brushes. These are made from only the tail-end hairs of the sable, a small, fur-bearing animal that is found in certain regions in Siberia. This is why pure sable brushes are so expensive. To reduce cost, manufacturers sometimes mix sable with other natural hair. This is usually ox or squirrel hair, but occasionally goat, camel or even mongoose hair is used.

Why are sable brushes so good to work with? For a start, they combine strength with suppleness, and this allows you to paint in a lively yet controlled way. They also wear well, and will keep their shape. If properly cared for, a sable brush can last a lifetime.

However, manufactured bristles have improved in quality in recent years. They fall into two main categories. Soft brushes are made especially for water-colour paints and have a texture and pliancy which aim to match the qualities of natural hair. Stiffer, general-purpose nylon brushes are made mainly for use with oil and acrylics, but are occasionally used by watercolourists to give a textured surface.

Caring for watercolour brushes

Each time you use a brush, rinse it in water. Either hold your brushes in your free hand while you work, or lay them down on a flat surface. Never leave them standing head down in water because this will bend the bristles. Once this has happened, it can be difficult to restore a brush to its proper state.

At the end of a painting session, wash each brush thoroughly in warm soapy water, then rinse well under running water. Gently shake the bristle head back into its natural shape. If necessary, reshape the bristles with your thumb and index finger. Store brushes upright with the handle end downwards.

Special brushes

You may come across various eye-catching and exotic-looking brushes in the art shop. Though they may appear unusual and have intriguing names – rigger, oriental, mop and spotter – these brushes are very practical and invaluable for creating specific effects.

Rigger So-called because it was originally used to paint fine ship's rigging in marine paintings, the rigger has long, tapering bristles. Today it is used more generally for all linear work, but especially for lettering, poster writing and also calligraphy.

Oriental brushes Recognizable by their cane or bamboo handles, these brushes produce the characteristic, flowing lines which give Japanese and Chinese paintings their distinctive quality. The bristles taper to a fine point, and the brushes can be used for painting fine lines, as well as for creating broad strokes and laying washes.

Spotter Miniature paintings and all fine detail can be executed with a retouching brush, or spotter. The spotter is a small round brush with short bristles, good for all precise work.

Wash brushes There are several large brushes designed specifically for laying flat washes. Most artists use a soft, flat brush; others prefer a large round, or a mop. The mop brush has a large, rounded head and is especially good for laying textured washes such as sea and sky.

Brushes for oil and acrylic

Brushes made for oil and acrylic paints are stiffer than those used for watercolour painting. However, watercolour brushes can also be used with oils and acrylics, especially if you are painting areas of thin colour or painting detail. Oil-painting

WATERCOLOUR BRUSH MARKS

Rigger

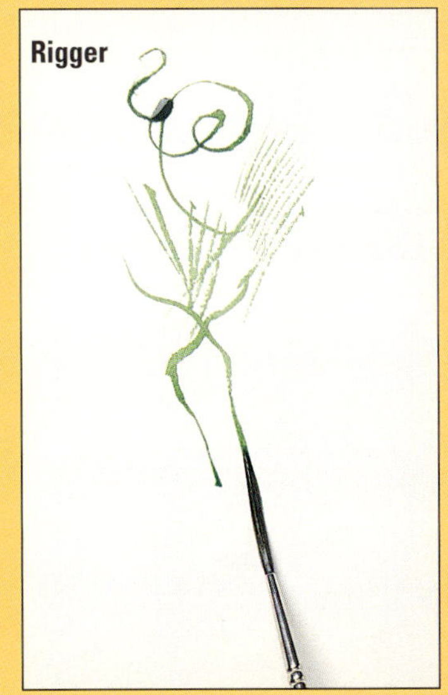

The long bristles of a rigger are designed for linear work.

Flat or chisel-headed

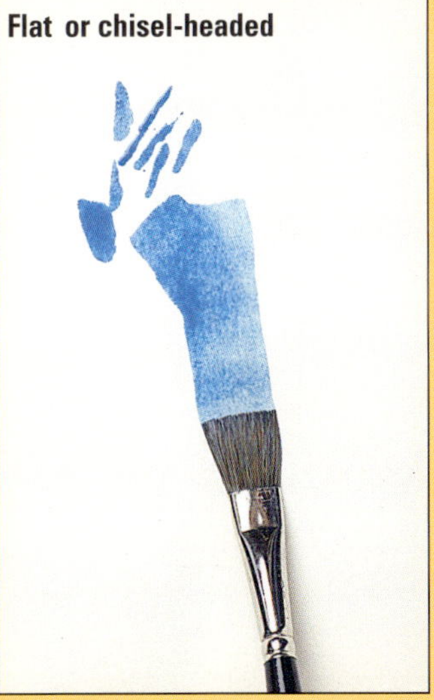

A flat brush can give broad or narrow lines of paint.

Round

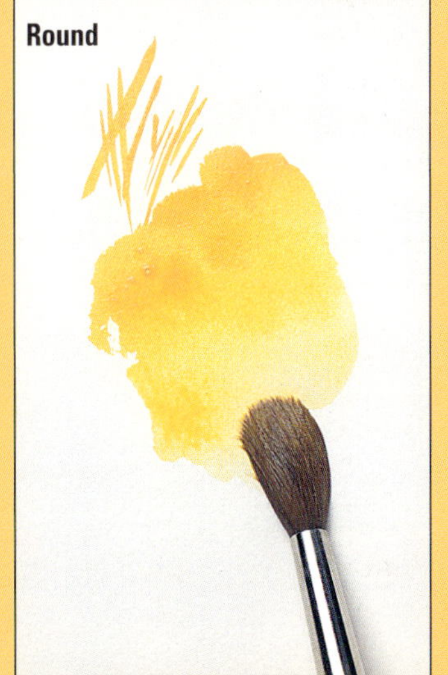

Use the whole brush for painting large areas, and the tip for details.

ACRYLIC BRUSHMARKS

Round

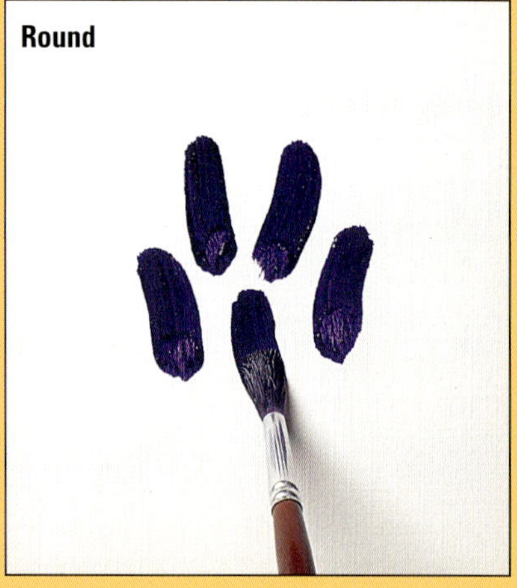

The oval marks made by a round brush echo the shape of the bristle head.

Flat or chisel headed

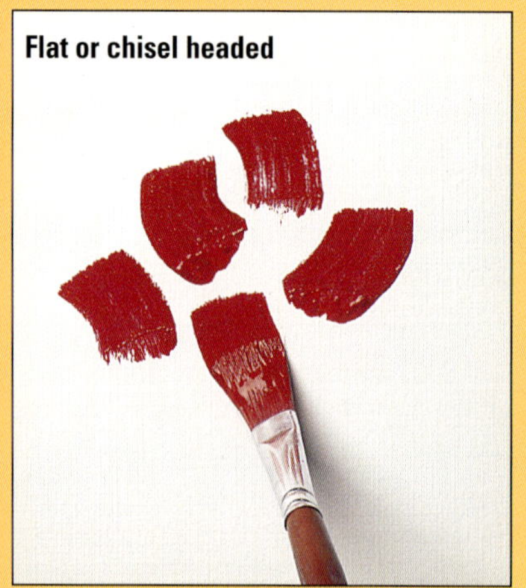

The rectangular profile of a flat brush produces regular dabs of acrylic colour.

Filbert

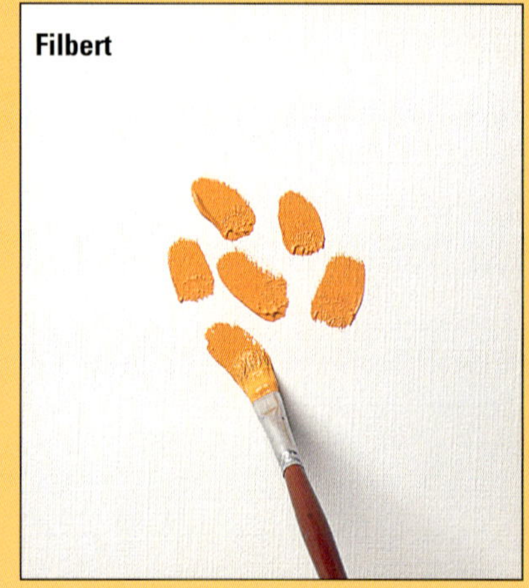

Filbert bristles curve gently to a point and give strong, tapering strokes.

Fan

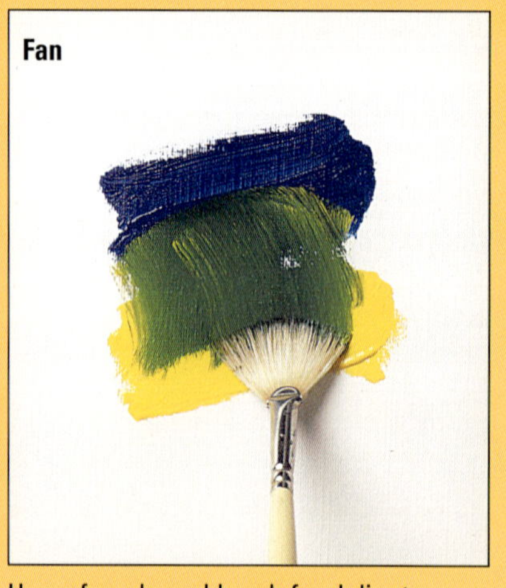

Use a fan-shaped brush for delicate blending effects with acrylics.

brushes are traditionally made from a natural bristle, usually hog's hair. There are also excellent synthetic brushes now available and some artists actually prefer to use these, finding them easier to clean and harder-wearing.

Certain synthetic brushes have been specially developed for use with acrylic paints, but, as a general rule, both natural bristle and synthetic brushes can be used with either oil or acrylic paints. A word of warning, however: oil and water do not mix. Brushes which you have already used with oil paints should be carefully cleaned before you go on to use them with acrylics, which are water-soluble.

Care and cleaning

Whether you are using oils or acrylics, paint should never be allowed to dry on the brush. At the end of every painting session, clean your brushes carefully by first wiping off excess paint with paper or kitchen roll. Brushes used with oil paint should then be rinsed in turpentine or white spirit, wiped clean and washed in warm water and household soap. Rub the soapy brush in the palm of your hand to loosen the paint that has accumulated round the ferrule. Rinse the brush well, then shake it to remove the water. If necessary, carefully reshape the bristles then leave the brush to dry in a jar, with the bristle end up.

Acrylic brushes should be cleaned only in warm water and soap. As acrylic paint dries so quickly, it is a good idea to keep brushes moist during the painting session when you are not using them. Do this by laying brushes in a dish of water with the handles resting on the side of the dish.

If you let acrylic paint dry on the brush accidentally, you can rescue the brush by soaking the bristles overnight in methylated spirits. This will soften the paint, which can then usually be washed off with soap and warm water.

Other handy brushes

Once you have finished experimenting with the range of recognized artists' brushes, you might like to try other kinds. Small house-decorating brushes are excellent for painting flat areas of colour and can save time if you like working on a large scale. Avoid very cheap ones – they tend to moult and you may end up wasting any time you would have saved picking loose bristles off your painting. The very best decorating brush is still much cheaper than the equivalent artists' brush. Other useful brushes include a stencilling brush with a flat end to create stippled colour; a sash brush for painting large areas; and an old toothbrush for spattered effects. A fitch is a cheaper alternative to a sash brush.

Synthetic

Hog's ha

Sash

Fitch

Stencilling

Decorating

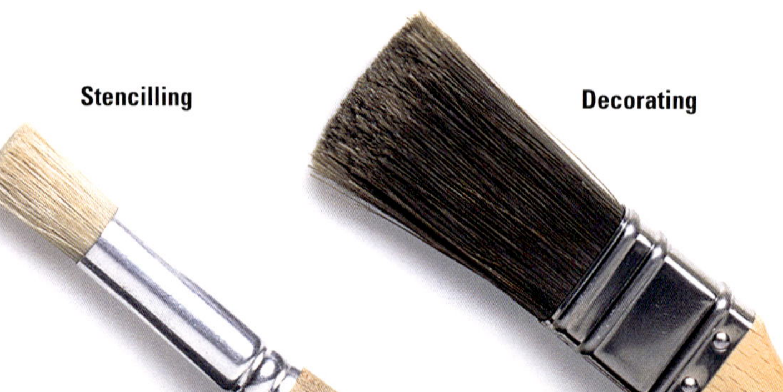

Using oil mediums

For centuries, artists have used traditional natural materials to dilute their oil paints, and these are just as popular today. In addition, there are now other mediums that make painting in oils easier and more versatile.

Oil paint is wonderfully stiff and buttery when you squeeze it from the tube – perfect for textured effects, but too thick for most other purposes. Fortunately, oils are easily diluted. The traditional method is to use a combination of oil and turpentine. You can also try oil mediums, which can be added to the paints to alter their consistency and give exciting effects.

Oil and turpentine

Real turpentine comes from pine trees and is one of the oldest solvents for diluting oil paints. Because the solvent thins the oil in the paint, the colours dry with a matt finish; if a lot of solvent is used, it tends to dull the colours. For this reason, turpentine is usually used in conjunction with an oil to replace the lost sheen. Linseed oil is the most popular, although there are alternatives to both linseed oil and traditional turpentine.

Ideally, use a double dipper such as the one below for the oil and turpentine. This small container clips on to the edge of the palette and is designed to minimize the risk of spills. Mix the colour on the palette, adding turpentine and oil with a brush until you have the consistency you want. If you need a large amount of diluted colour, mix it separately in a jar rather than on the palette.

Note: it is important to avoid using a turpentine substitute or white spirit as an inexpensive alternative to real turpentine for thinning paint. Both these solvents tend to deaden the colours of your paints and produce a cloudy patina on the paint surface.

Painting 'fat over lean'

Oils should be applied 'fat over lean'. In other words, start by blocking in the subject with very thin colour diluted with turpentine. Gradually add more oil colour and less turpentine to the paint as the picture progresses.

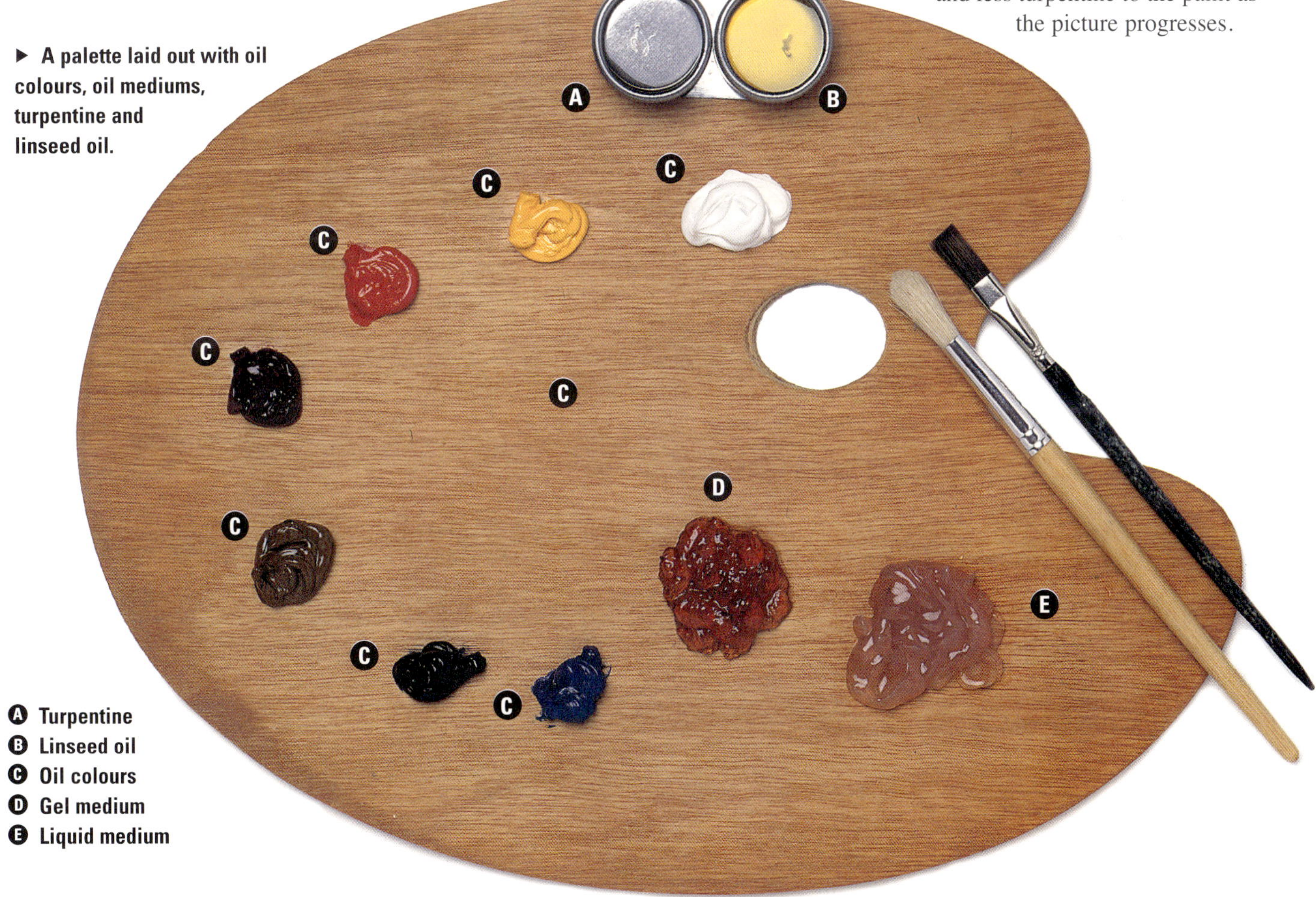

▶ **A palette laid out with oil colours, oil mediums, turpentine and linseed oil.**

A Turpentine
B Linseed oil
C Oil colours
D Gel medium
E Liquid medium

MIXING OIL MEDIUMS WITH PAINT

TURPENTINE AND LINSEED OIL

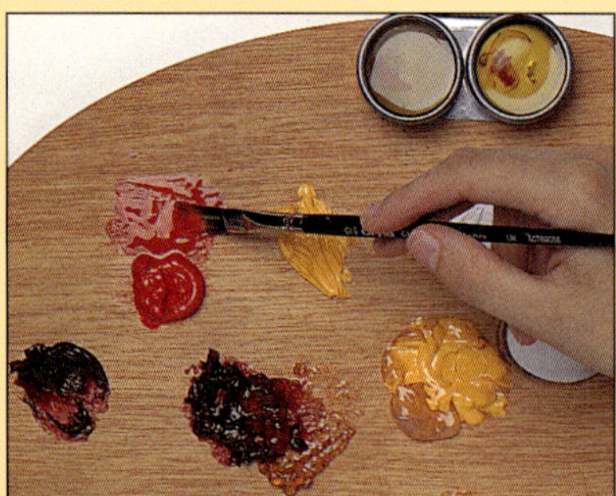

Use a double clip-on dipper for the oil and turpentine. Dilute the colour by loading the brush from the dipper and adding to the paint.

GEL MEDIUM

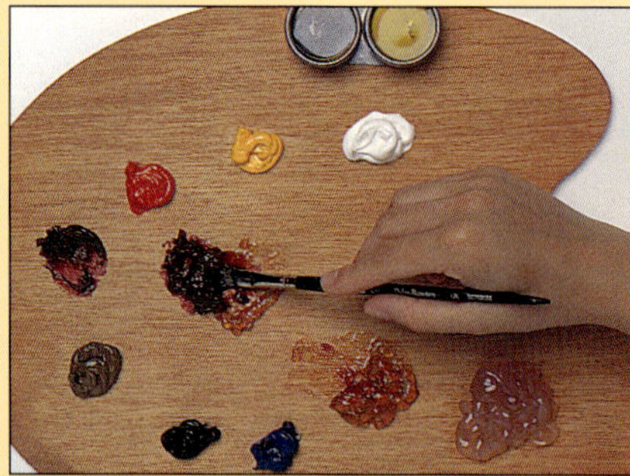

Squeeze gel mediums directly on to the palette. Mix in the colour using a knife or a stiff brush. The mixture generally becomes stiffer if left to stand.

LIQUID MEDIUM

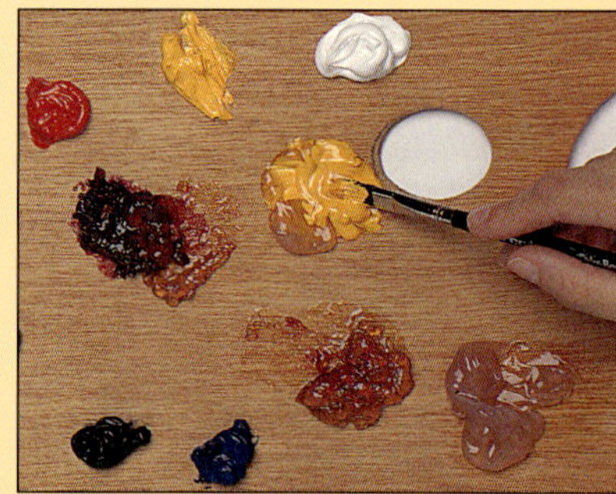

Pour the liquid medium on to the palette or into a container. Many mediums dry quickly, so don't use too much. Add to the colour, mixing with a knife or brush.

Using this method, the underpainting dries quickly without holding up the rest of the work, and the finished surface has a rich, glossy colour.

Other mediums

There are various specialist mediums designed to alter the paint for specific purposes. Depending on the product, a medium can make oil colours thicker or thinner, improve the flow, create a matt finish, or speed up the drying time of the paint. Some mediums are simply ready-mixed versions of traditional ingredients; others contain synthetic materials.

Colour thickeners

Thick mediums come in tubes, in gel or paste form. They can be squeezed on to the palette alongside the colours and added to the paint as required. For a very thick consistency, use a paste, but gels are best used where expressive brushwork is required. Mix the paint with the gel or paste, and leave to stiffen before use. These mediums can also be mixed with a solvent to make paint flow more easily.

Liquid mediums

Oil paint diluted with turpentine alone dries with a dull, matt finish, but if you add a little liquid medium, the paint will dry with a smooth, shiny surface. Most liquid mediums are also suitable for glazing – they dilute the colour to make it more transparent without affecting the glossy nature of the paint. Alternatively, buy a glazing medium made specifically for the purpose.

Despite their name, 'liquid' mediums are not necessarily completely liquid in consistency. Although some are quite runny, others are more like jelly. Small amounts of the latter can be poured directly on to the painting palette, but very liquid mediums are best kept in a separate container.

Trying out the mediums

If too much of any medium is added to an oil colour, it will inevitably alter the opacity and strength of the colour. Only by trial and error with a particular product will you find out exactly how much of the medium you can introduce without spoiling the particular result you are aiming to achieve.

Also, it is important to bear in mind that mediums are essentially additives which change the nature and chemistry of the paint. If you overdo their use, you might reduce the durability of the completed painting.

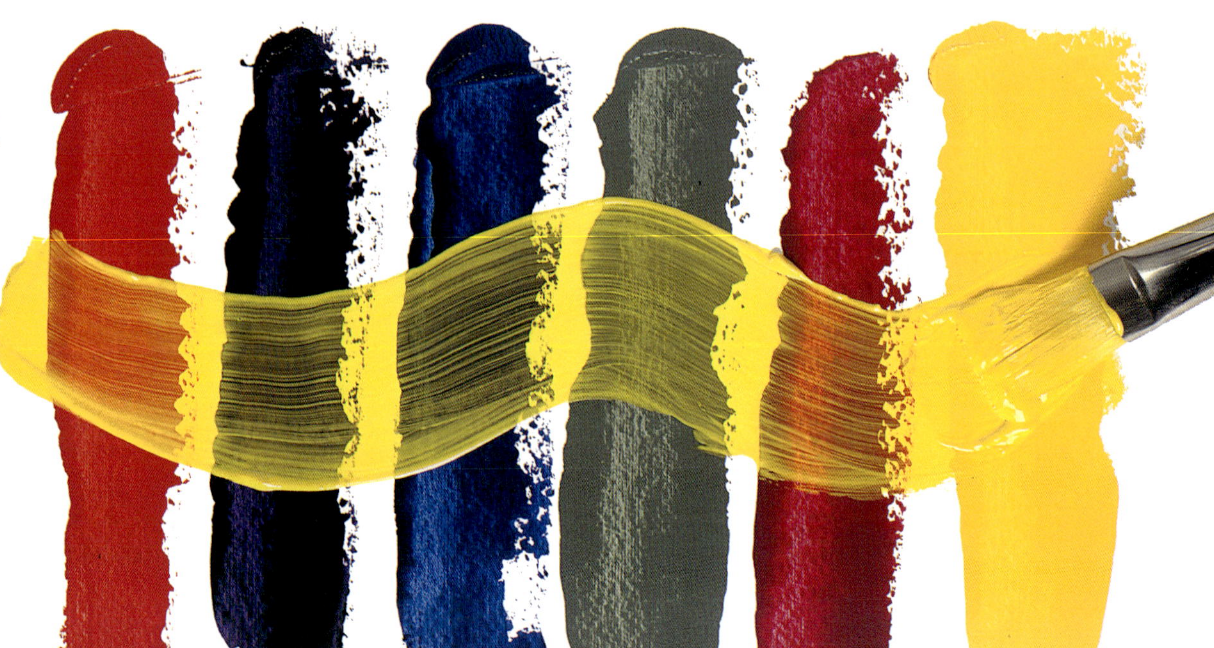

▸ **GLAZING Mix the paint and glazing medium to the consistency of single cream and apply this to a dry undercolour. Some colours, such as lemon yellow, are naturally transparent and work particularly well in glaze mixtures.**

Using acrylic mediums

Adding mediums to your acrylic colours can completely change the look of your pictures. You can make your paints glossy or transparent – or even create textured and sculptural effects.

▼ Thoroughly mix the medium and paint using a clean, stiff brush. If you are working with a palette, the mixing can be done on the flat surface, using either a brush or knife.

Used on their own, acrylics are opaque and can dry with a rather dull finish. However, there are a number of mediums that will alter the appearance and character of the paint, making it glossy, matt, transparent, textural or flat. These mediums are usually added to the wet colour before it is applied to the painting, although one or two can also be used to prime the support and to protect the surface of the finished picture.

Mediums appear cloudy in the pot or tube, but when they dry they become completely transparent and do not therefore affect your colours. However, too much of any medium will make a colour so transparent that the colour underneath shows through. On white paper, for example, a colour mixed with a lot of medium will appear paler.

Retarder and flow improver

If you find the quick-drying nature of acrylics difficult to handle, the answer could well be a retarder, which slows down the drying time of the colours by several hours. Remember, this medium is effective only if you paint fairly thickly – very diluted colours will dry quickly however much retarder you add to them. Use flow improver to help the paint spread more evenly and smoothly. This is particularly good for hard-edge painting when you are using masking tape, as the flowing colour remains thick enough not to run under the edge of the tape.

Gloss and matt

Gloss medium gives colours a shiny finish; matt medium produces a flat, unreflective surface. You can buy both in either fluid or gel form – the fluids improve the flow and make the paint easier to apply, and the gels create slightly thicker colour. Both fluid and gel mediums increase the paint's transparency without making it thin and watery.

Fluid-type mediums are excellent for mixing glazes – for applying a layer of transparent colour over another colour so that the undercolour shows through. Depending on the effect you want, mix the gloss or matt medium with the glazing colour in a ratio of up to 10:1. Gloss medium is the general favourite for glazing, as it produces particularly luminous, brilliant colours.

An alternative to varnishing

Fluid mediums can also be used to seal the canvas or paper prior to painting and used instead of a varnish to protect the surface of a completed painting. In both cases, apply the medium carefully

Making paint

Mixing your own acrylic paint is straightforward and should be done just before you start work. If you end up with more paint than you need, you can keep the mixture for a short time in a plastic airtight container.

1 ▶ Mix with powder Using a palette knife, mix dry powder pigment well with either gloss or matt medium to create your own painting colours.

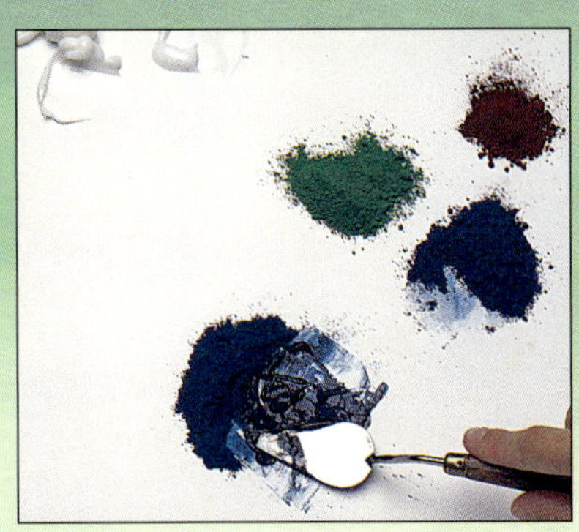

2 ▶ Use it or lose it The mixed colours are ready to use immediately. Like manufactured paints, these colours dry fairly quickly – so mix only as much as you need for one painting session.

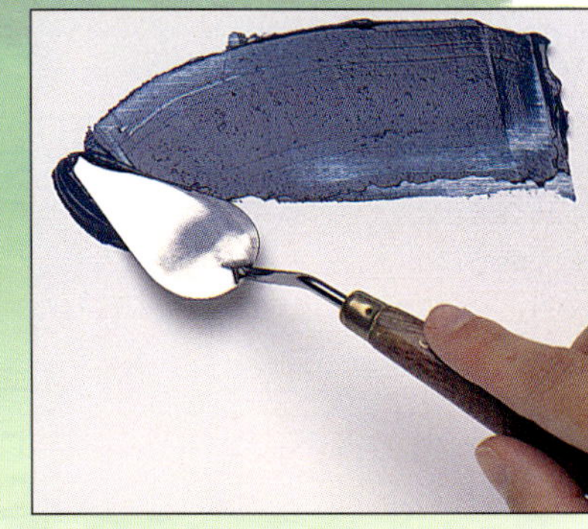

Adding textures

Here are some of the textures you can make by adding various grains and particles to acrylic medium. The adhesive medium binds the texture-making substances, which can be left in either their natural state or painted.

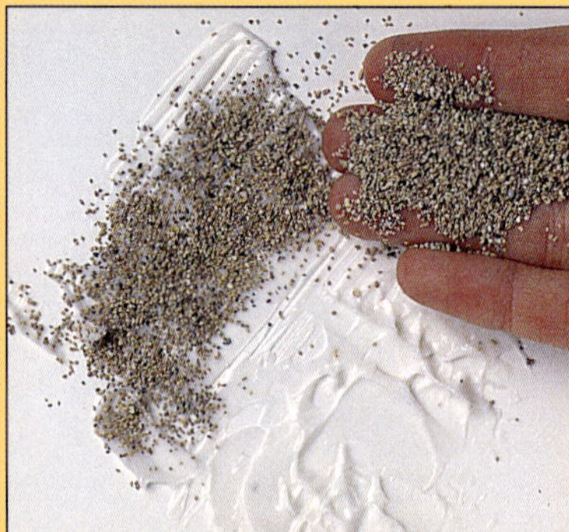

Dry sand Scatter this on modelling paste for a medium-textured effect.

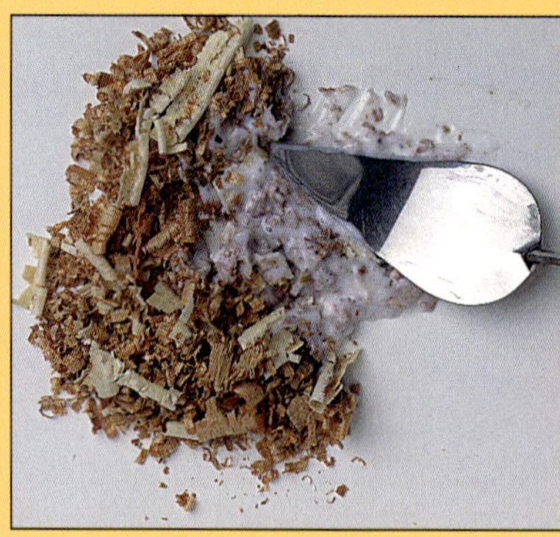

Sawdust and wood shavings Mix with gel medium for a soft, complex texture.

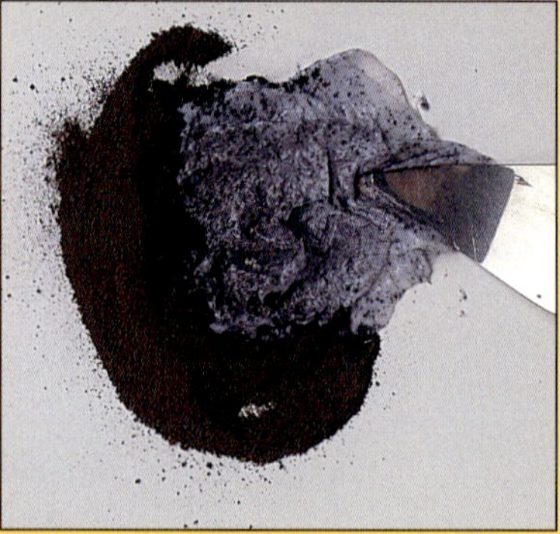

Fired clay Mix this with gel medium for a fine-textured result.

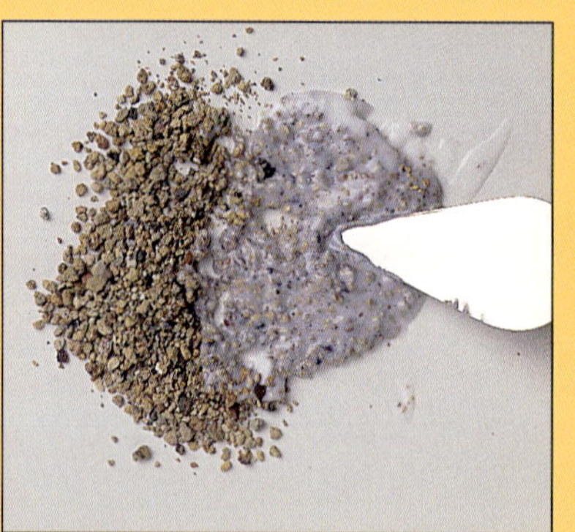

Grit and gravel Gel medium mixed with these will create a really rough effect.

with a large brush, using smooth parallel strokes. Take care not to do too much brushing, as you'll produce tiny air bubbles that affect the dried surface.

Impasto effects

Although paint thickened with gel medium to some extent retains the shape of the brush marks, this will produce only a moderately textured surface. For a more dramatic textured effect you will need to mix the colour with acrylic impasto medium – especially good for knife painting and for covering areas with thick colour quickly.

For a really pronounced impasto, try using modelling, or texture, paste. This can be applied to build almost sculptural swathes of colour, which can then be sanded or even carved when dry. Mix the paste with colour prior to painting or, alternatively, apply the paste on its own, then paint it when dry. Unlike other mediums, modelling paste is white and opaque, and might slightly lighten the colour, so you should remember to make allowances for this.

A word of warning: thickly applied modelling paste is not wholly flexible and can crack if used on a non-rigid surface such as canvas. Counteract this risk by mixing the paste with equal parts of gel medium. Also, the risk of cracking is reduced if you build up the paste in layers, allowing each layer to dry before applying the next, instead of working in thick wedges.

Making textures

Some mediums contain tiny particles of various inert substances to create specific instant textures. These include sand, flint, pumice and even tiny glass beads. The glass beads are often used for creating the effect of frothy air bubbles in water or adding decorative touches to the image.

Special effects

You can easily make your own special-effect mediums by adding gritty or granular materials to any one of the standard mediums (see Adding textures, left). All acrylic mediums are adhesive, so choose one to give the effect you want – gloss medium for a shiny texture, impasto medium or modelling paste for a thickly applied effect.

For example, to capture the effect of a sandy beach in a seascape, you might mix real sand with a little matt medium. You could then go on to experiment with sawdust, particles of clay and dust, or any other materials you can think of. You will be amazed at the difference a few creative textures will make to your finished pictures.

Make your own paints

There are some acrylic artists who never use manufactured paint, preferring instead the more direct approach of mixing powdered pigment with gloss or matt medium. As the mediums have no colour of their own, the pigment retains its full strength and intensity in the painting. The mediums are also flexible when dry, so your home-made paints can be used on canvas or paper.

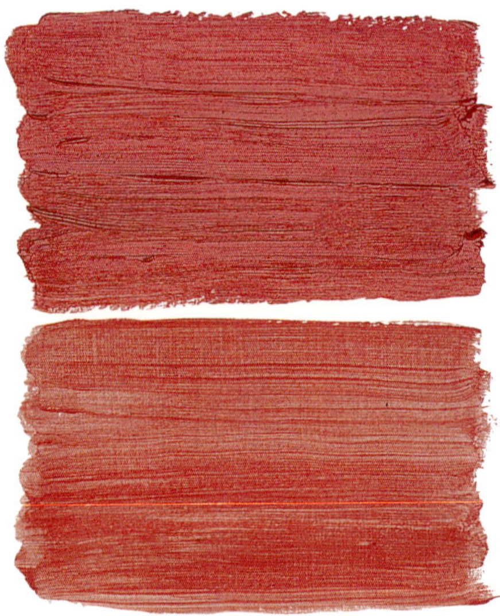

▲ **GLOSS AND MATT**
For a shiny paint surface, add a little gloss medium to your acrylic colour (top). Matt medium mixed with the paint (bottom) will produce a more non-reflective surface.

Using mixed media

Once you feel confident using a range of drawing and painting materials, try combining two or more of them in a single image.

YOU WILL NEED

- Short lengths of tree branch with interesting patterns
- Sheet of rough-textured paper
- 6B pencil
- 5 oil pastels: cadmium yellow; white; flesh tint; light brown; black
- 2 watercolour paints: sepia; ivory black
- Brush: No. 3 round

Certain media, such as pastels and watercolour, or charcoal and chalk, work well together because their different qualities enhance or complement one another. By using a combination of different media and techniques, it is possible to create optical and textural effects that will broaden the range of your work. It is exciting to experiment to see the results that can be achieved and to decide which suit your style.

In the three projects that follow, the aim is not to create finished pictures, but to make a series of quick studies from nature by experimenting with mixed media. You can combine different drawing media, a mixture of painting media, or even a combination of both. The idea is to use your creative imagination to interpret patterns and textures with a range of materials that you feel are compatible with the subject.

PROJECT 1

Making studies of found objects is an absorbing exercise that will develop your powers of observation and your ability to draw well. These tree branches have interesting surface patterns that lend themselves well to a mixed media approach. Try homing in on a small area of the subject and enlarging it on the page.

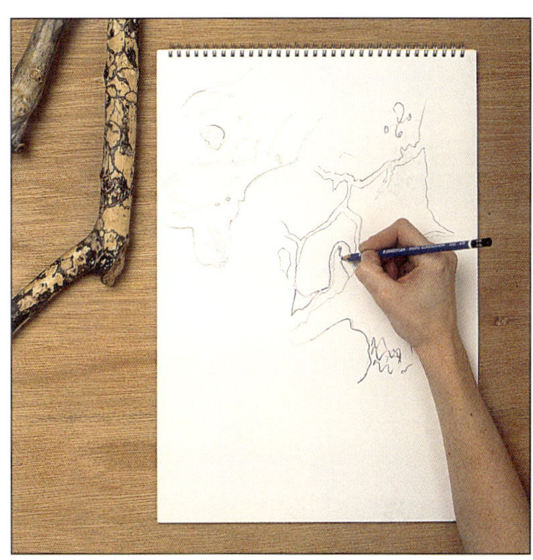

1 ► Draw the outlines Decide which parts of the branches you are going to concentrate on and lightly sketch their outlines using a 6B pencil. Map in the 'snakeskin' pattern on the right-hand branch.

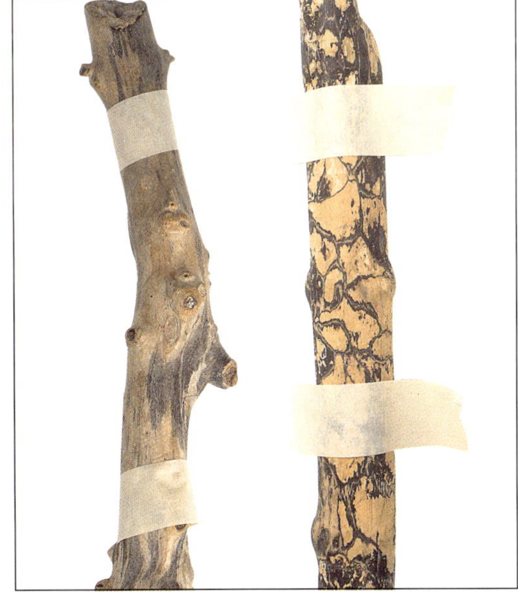

▼ Isolated areas of bark pattern can have a fascinating abstract quality.

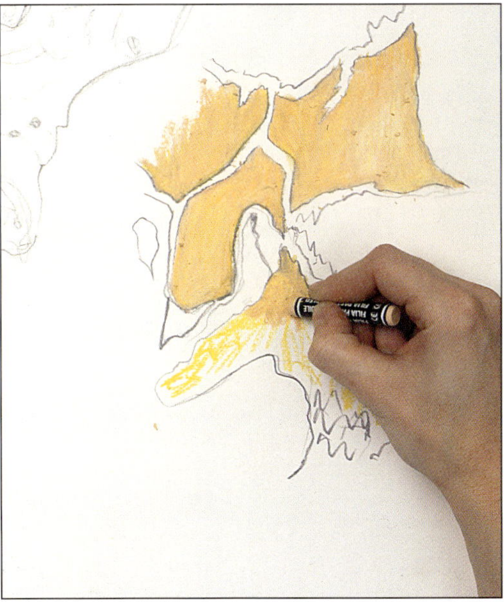

2 ◄ Work on the right-hand branch The base colour of the right-hand branch is a bleached yellowish-white. Re-create this using pastels, applying strokes of cadmium yellow, white and flesh tint on top of each other, then blending them together with your finger to create a thick, even layer of colour. Leave the dark patterns untouched for the moment.

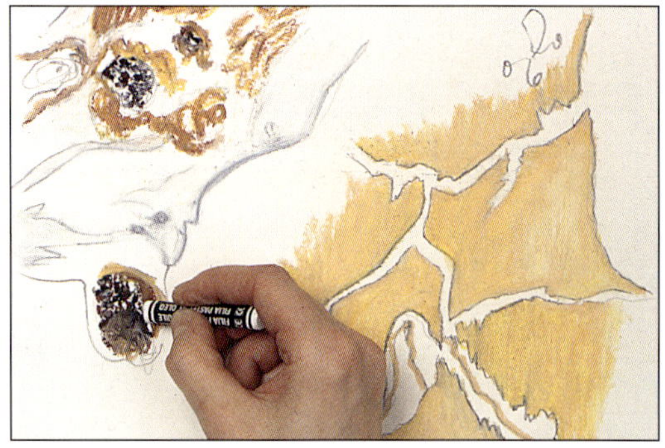

3 ▲ Work on the left-hand branch Add colour to the left-hand branch, using overlaid strokes of flesh tint, cadmium yellow and light brown. Mix light brown with black for the dark areas, and with white for the light areas. Blend white pastel into the pencil outlines to soften them.

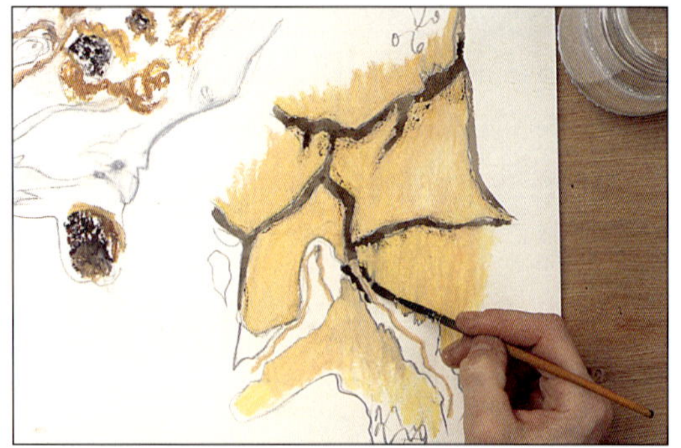

4 ▲ Add lines with watercolour Returning to the right-hand branch, fill in the dark lines with sepia watercolour, using a No. 3 round brush. Go over the edges of the drawn lines slightly – the surrounding pastel resists the paint, which dries in feathery streaks. Use the same method to add small, random marks to the pastel areas between the dark lines. Leave to dry.

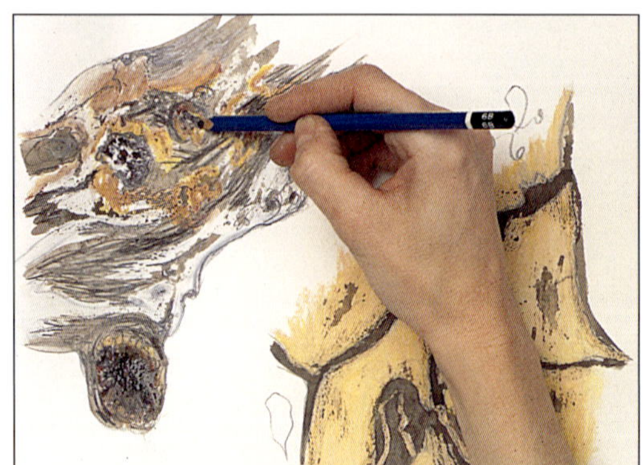

5 ▲ Complete the left-hand branch Return to working on the left-hand branch. Mix a dilute wash of sepia and ivory black, and brush this over parts of the branch, leaving some areas of bare paper to indicate bleached wood. While the paint is still wet, draw lines and whorls with the 6B pencil, pressing quite hard so that the paper is slightly indented.

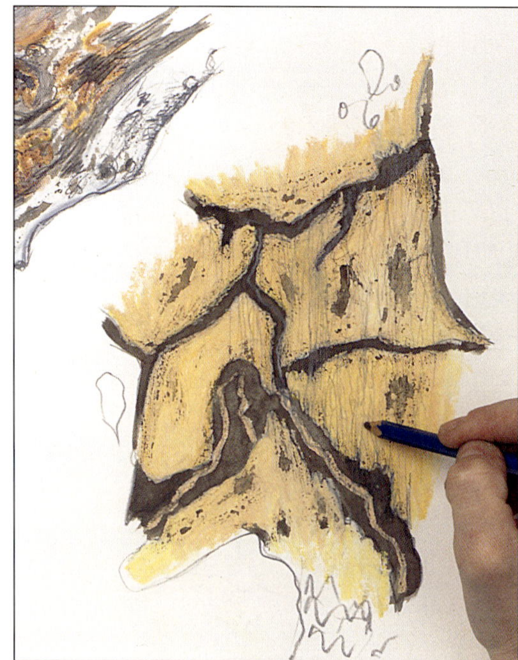

6 ◄ Complete the right-hand branch Close observation of the branch on the right shows long, vertical, slightly wavering lines over the pale areas of bark. Finish off the sketch by drawing these lines over the blended pastel areas with the 6B pencil. This extra definition gives a subtle indication of texture and detail to the bark, making the study more realistic.

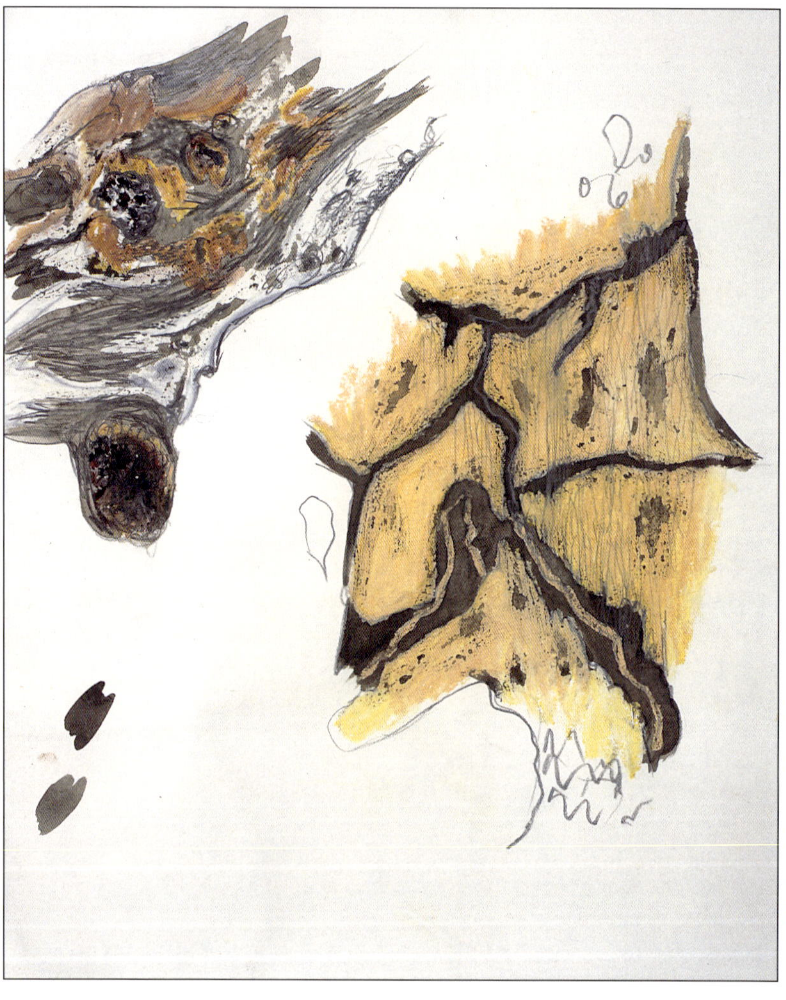

7 ▲ The finished study Although this mixed-media exercise is a study rather than a finished image, it conveys a strong sense of form and pattern, based on direct observation from nature. The use of watercolour with pastels conveys the natural, organic appearance of the bark.

PROJECT 2

An irregular fragment of tree bark with a rough, peeling surface is the inspiration for this study. To create a realistic image, a sheet of paper is first placed over the bark and rubbed gently with a soft graphite stick so that the texture comes through – a technique known as 'frottage'. The image is then built up in colour, using watercolour, soft pastels and coloured and graphite pencils.

▲ **The intricate texture of this bark is re-created using four different media.**

YOU WILL NEED

- Piece of bark
- Sheet of cartridge paper
- 6B graphite stick
- Putty rubber
- 3 watercolour paints: sepia; ivory black; Chinese white
- Brush: No. 12 round
- 2 soft pastels: burnt umber; sap green
- 5 coloured pencils: Van Dyke brown; golden brown; copper beech; scarlet lake; cedar green
- 6B pencil

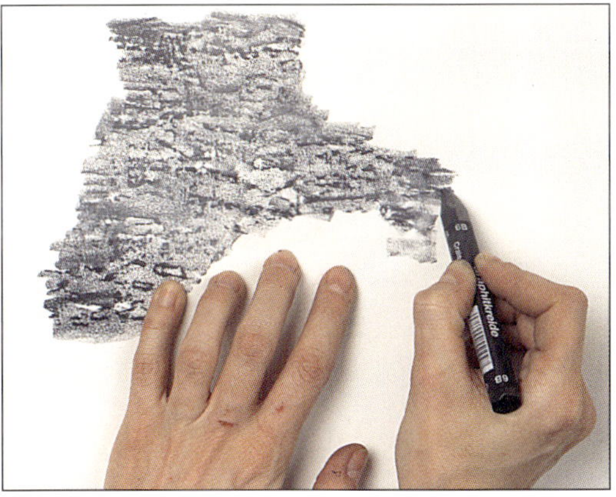

1 ▶ **Use the frottage technique** Lay a sheet of paper over the tree bark and gently shade with a 6B graphite stick until the texture of the bark is revealed. Use small, localized movements with the stick rather than long, sweeping ones, and don't press too hard.

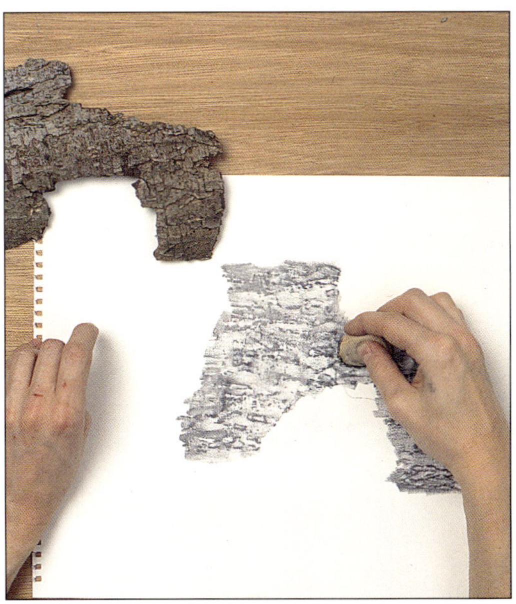

2 ▶ **Soften the marks** Use the corner of a putty rubber to soften the textural marks made in step 1 and lift off some of the graphite so that it doesn't mix with the watercolour wash that is to be applied at the next stage. Do this very gently, with short dabbing motions, so that the texture of the bark is still visible – if you pull the eraser right across the paper, the marks will disappear.

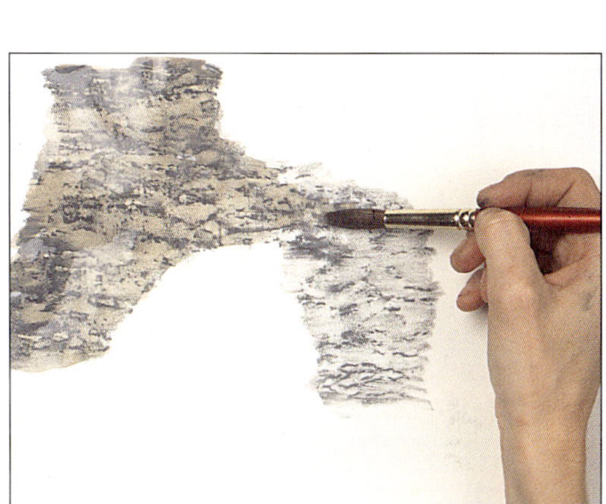

3 ▲ **Add a watercolour wash** Apply a thinly diluted wash of sepia and ivory black watercolour paints over the bark, using a No. 12 round watercolour brush. The bark has a silvery sheen in places – suggest this by applying thin washes of Chinese white to these areas while the previous wash is still slightly damp.

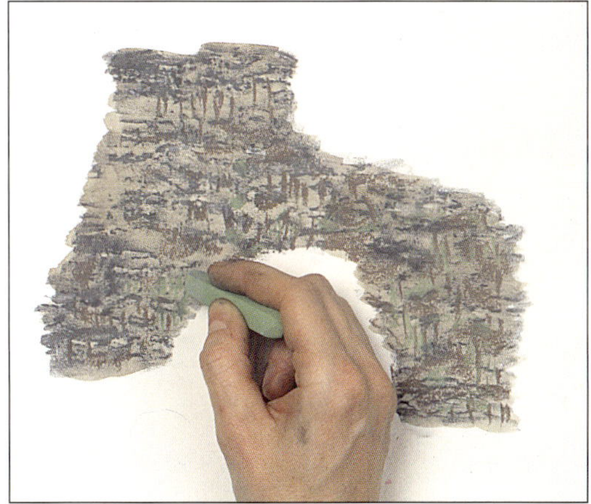

4 ▲ **Start to suggest texture** Define the rough surface of the bark and the warmer brown tones using a pastel stick in burnt umber. Use the tip of the pastel to make short vertical lines and the side of the pastel to make broader, horizontal blocks. Then do the same with a sap green pastel.

5 ▼ **Continue building up the texture** Work on top of the pastel marks, using coloured pencils to add small lines and marks that suggest the cracked and peeling texture of the bark. Here, coloured pencils in Van Dyke brown, golden brown and copper beech (which provide dark, light and medium shades) are being used, along with touches of scarlet lake and cedar green.

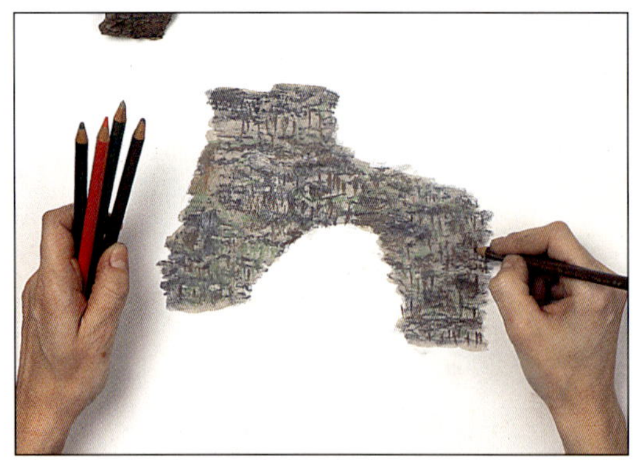

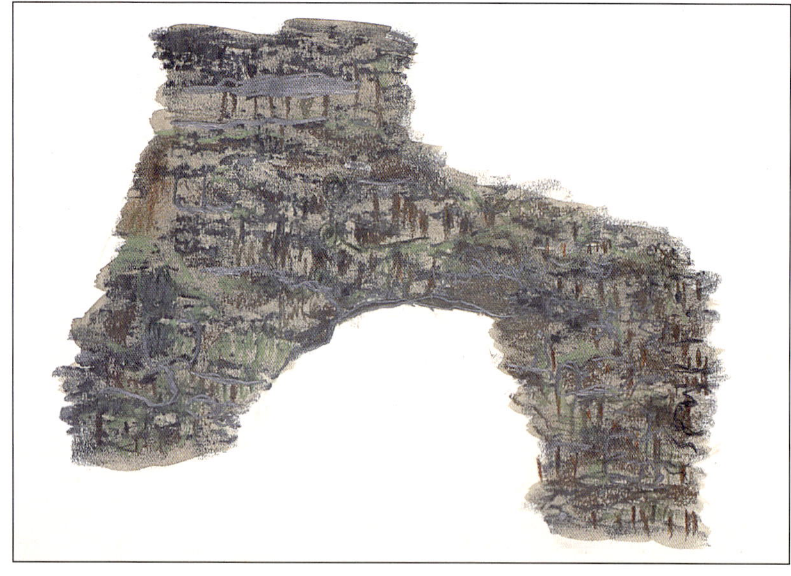

6 ▲ **The finished study** The study is completed by using graphite once again, this time in the form of a 6B pencil. Press hard with the pencil to suggest the edges of the flaking pieces of bark.

PROJECT 3

Using a piece of tree bark once more, this three-dimensional interpretation involves working over a thick layer of PVA glue with pastels and acrylic paint. These bond with the dried surface of the glue to create random, mottled patterns that magically suggest the rough texture of the bark. The final details are added using graphite and coloured pencils.

► **This chunky piece of bark has a tactile, sculptural quality that offers a special challenge.**

YOU WILL NEED

- Piece of bark with interesting texture
- Sheet of thick cartridge paper
- 6B pencil
- 6B graphite stick
- PVA glue
- Large flat hog's hair brush
- 2 soft pastels: burnt umber; raw umber
- 2 coloured pencils: Van Dyke brown; golden brown
- 1 acrylic paint: burnt umber

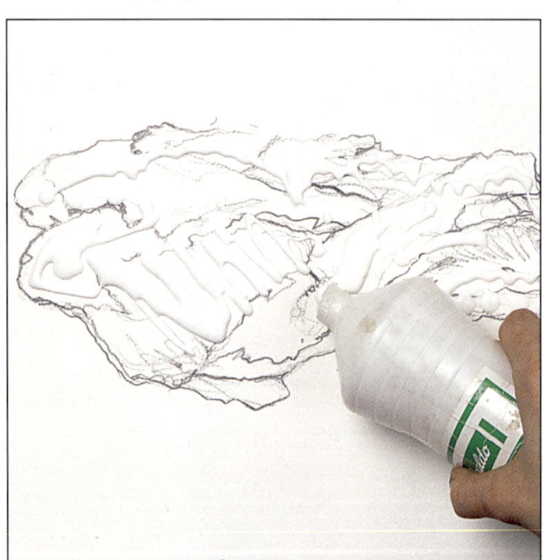

1 ▲ **Draw the bark and apply the glue** Use a 6B pencil to draw the bark, varying the pressure to create light and heavy lines. Observe which areas have the heaviest texture and pour PVA glue over these parts of your drawing, using the bottle as though it were a drawing tool. Let the glue form ridges that stand proud of the surface.

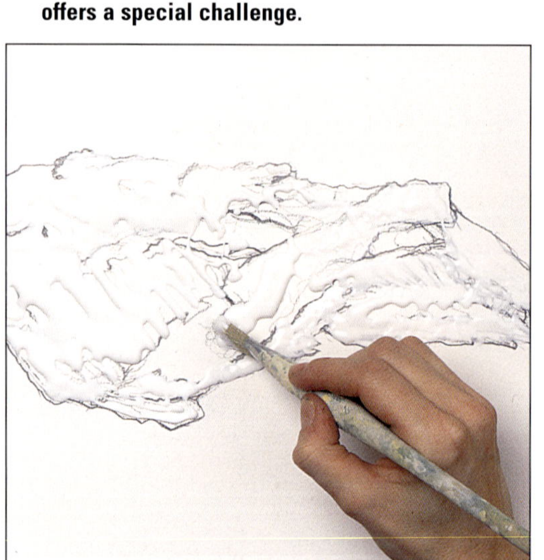

2 ▲ **Create a 3-D surface** Re-create the bark's gnarled texture by using a flat hog's hair brush to move the glue around on the paper. Make stabbing marks in the surface of the glue or dab the brush with a stippling motion, leaving some areas raised. Allow to dry overnight.

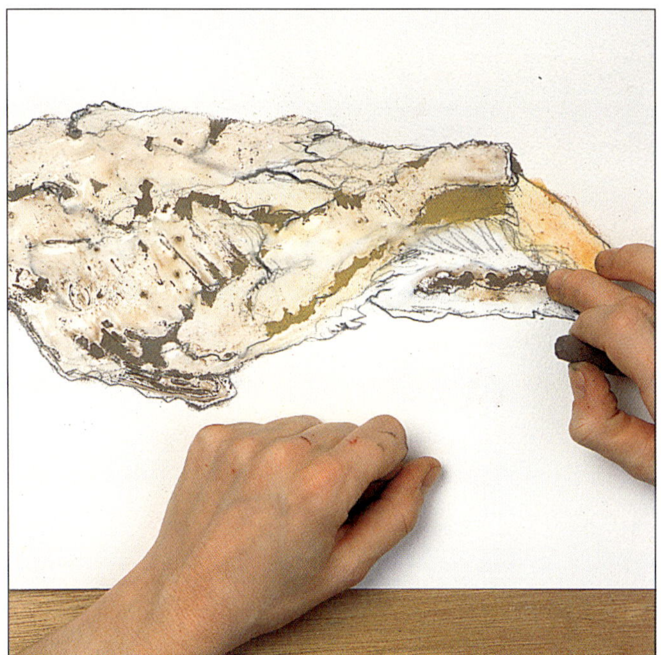

3 ▲ **Apply pastel colours** Check that the glue is completely dry. Using burnt umber for the dark areas and raw umber for the light areas, apply pastel to the patches of bare paper between the glued areas. Then rub with your fingers to spread the colour over the surface of the glue. The pastel blends into the glue to create mottled patterns.

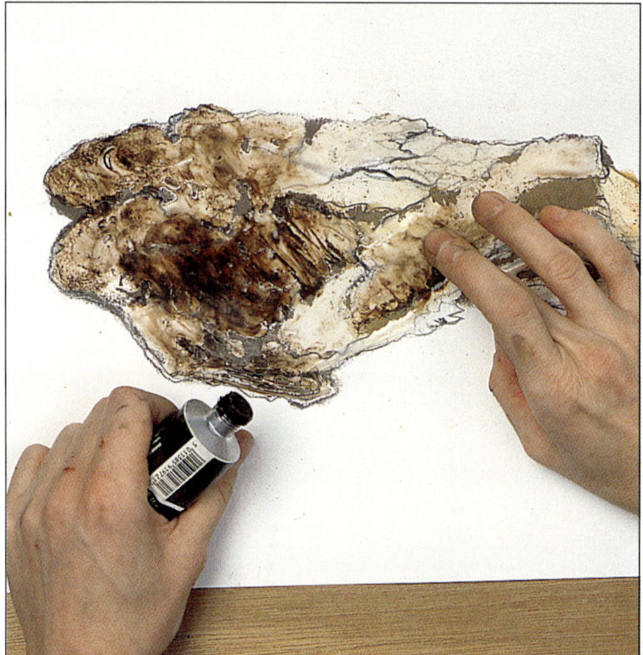

4 ▲ **Add acrylic colour** Squeeze a small amount of burnt umber acrylic paint from the tube, pick it up on the tip of your finger, then rub it gently over the areas where the bark is dark in tone. Apply the paint thickly for the darkest parts and skim lightly over the surface where the colour is lighter. The paint settles into the indentations on the glued surface, once again creating interesting mottled patterns.

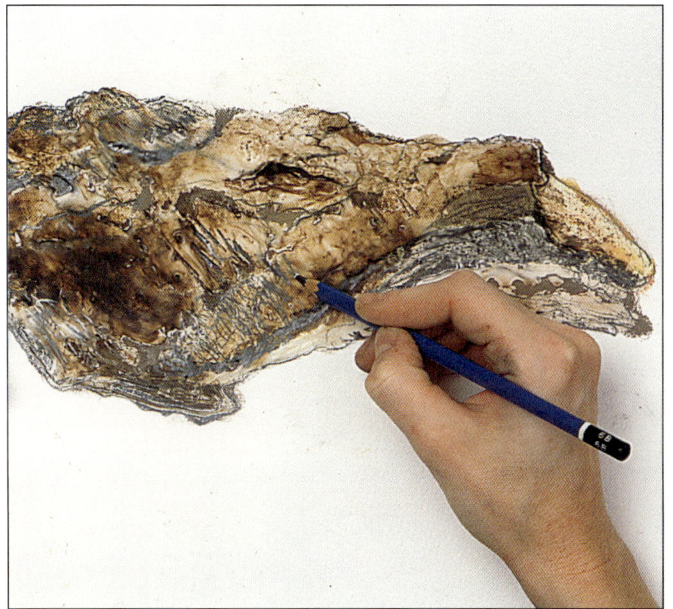

5 ▶ **Add linear details** Finish off by working over the surface with a 6B pencil and a 6B graphite stick, making random lines and hatchings that suggest the cracks and fissures in the bark. Add coloured lines, too, using coloured pencils in Van Dyke brown (dark) and golden brown (light). Apply the dark brown to light areas of the bark and vice versa.

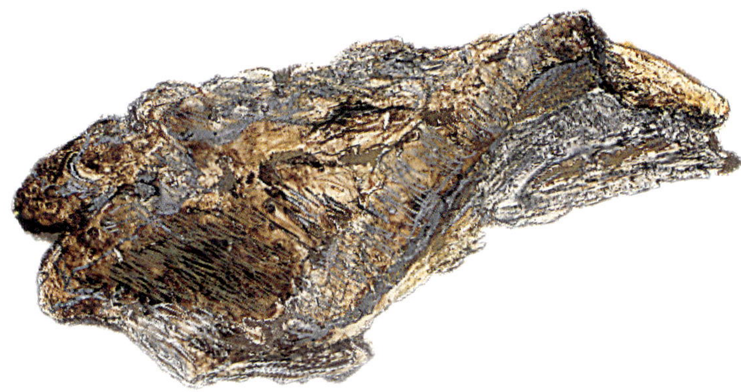

6 ▲ **The finished study** In this interesting three-dimensional study, the richly worked surface not only describes the form of the subject, but also gives it life and character.

Wash-off techniques

Watercolour or ink applied over white paint can be washed off to reveal striking areas of white in the finished picture.

Two wash-off techniques are shown here – the first suitable for misty and textural effects and the second that creates bold, graphic images similar to those produced by woodcuts.

For the seascape, the artist started by applying white gouache all over the support to prevent subsequent colour washes staining it. This allowed the colour to be lifted off with a brush dipped in water, producing soft areas of white suitable for clouds and mist.

In the boats picture shown here, certain areas are painted in white gouache, then the whole image is covered with black waterproof ink. When soaked with water, the gouache dissolves, taking with it the covering layer of ink. This leaves white areas with an attractive texture created by remaining ink marks.

Water-soluble white

Any thick, water-soluble white paint can be used for these wash-off techniques. Our artist chose gouache simply because that was the material closest to hand. Poster colour or Chinese white watercolour work equally well, although the latter may prove expensive for painting large areas. Acrylic white is not suitable for this techynique because the paint dries with an impermeable surface that cannot be washed off.

White paint applied to an off-white support will probably show up sufficiently well for you to see what you are doing. However, when working on a pure white support, it is a good idea to tint the paint with a touch of yellow ochre or another colour with a similarly weak tinting strength. This makes the paint visible, but doesn't stain the support.

▼ You don't need specialist equipment to make wash-off paintings. A watercolour set (A), Chinese white or white gouache paint (B) and waterproof Indian ink (C) are all that is required for the initial painting. Water (D) and a sponge (E) or brush will enable you to wash the paint off. For the support, a piece of mountboard (F) will be strong enough to survive the most vigorous of wash-offs.

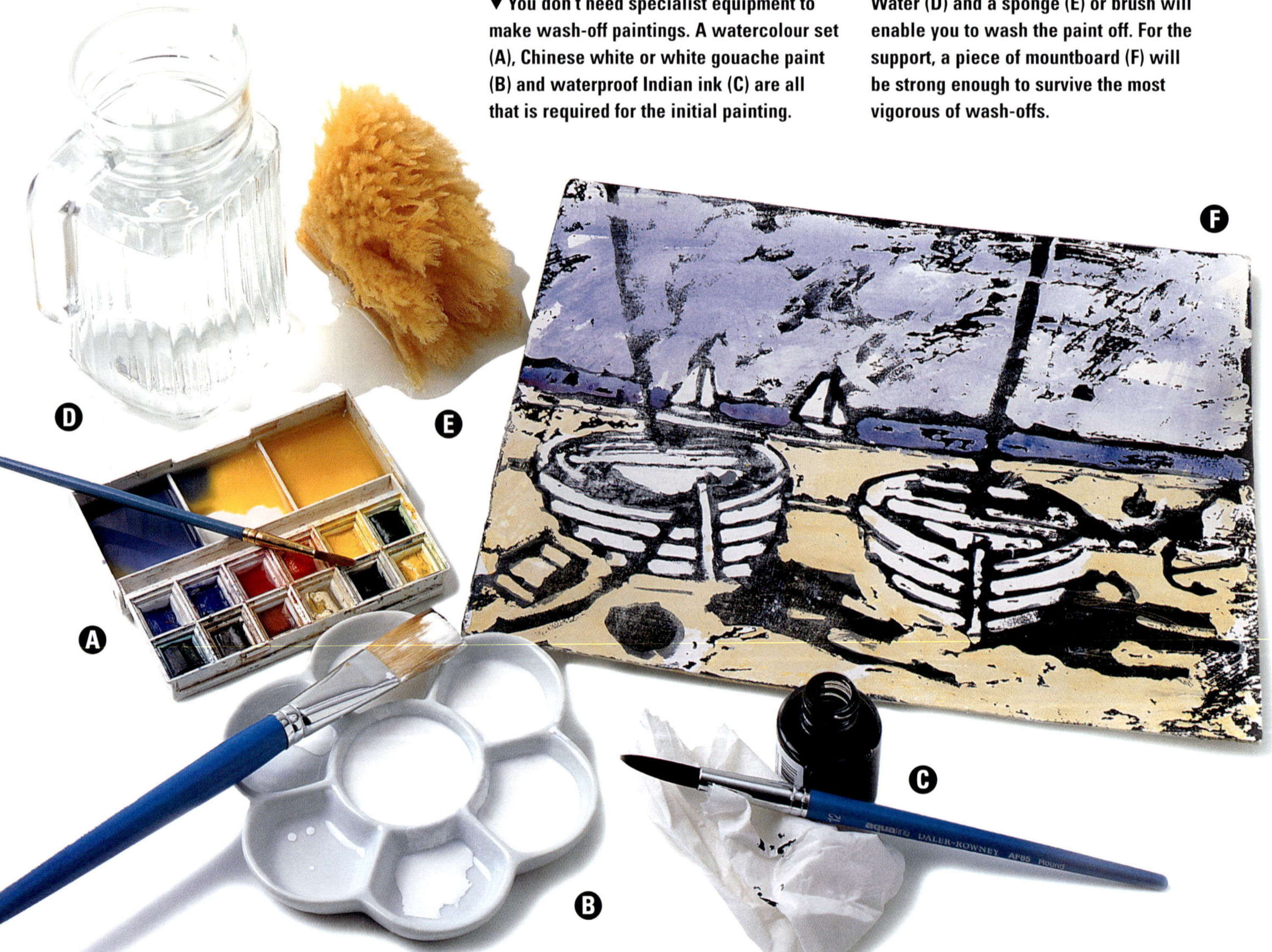

CREATING A WOODCUT EFFECT

For this painting, start with a broad outline drawing in waterproof Indian ink. Then block in cast shadows and other dark areas as solid shapes. When the ink is dry, apply thick white gouache to the exposed areas, deliberately leaving untidy edges along the black lines. These ragged lines help to create the woodcut effect in the finished picture.

Next paint the entire support with waterproof Indian ink. When it is dry, flood the picture with water. This washing off dissolves the white gouache, leaving areas of the support exposed. Elsewhere, the waterproof ink remains intact. Some flecks of black are left behind, even in the gouache areas, giving the image an attractive printed quality. You might feel that the work is complete at this stage. Otherwise, tint the white areas with watercolour as shown here. The result is rather like a stained-glass window.

For this painting, you need a piece of mountboard (or very heavy watercolour paper), two brushes – a No. 4 round and a 25mm (1in) decorator's, black waterproof Indian ink, white gouache, a sponge, and ultramarine and yellow ochre watercolours. Note the washing-off process soaks the paper – if the support is too flimsy, it will simply disintegrate.

1 ▼ **Outline the main features** Start by painting a simple, bold outline of the subject, using black waterproof ink and a No. 4 round brush. Paint in the shadows and buoys in solid black.

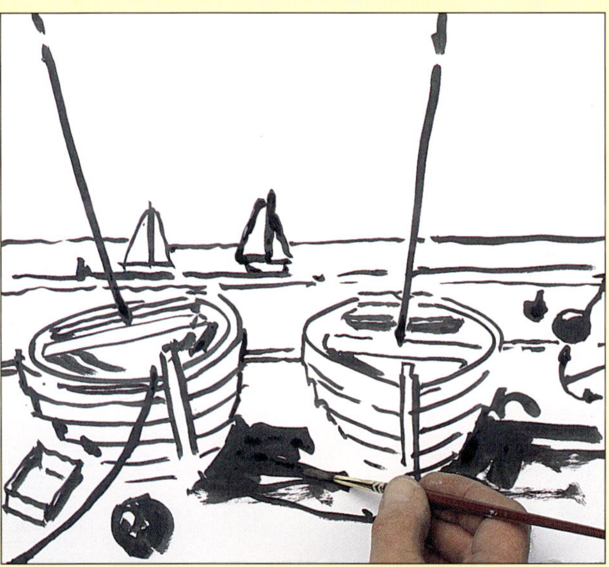

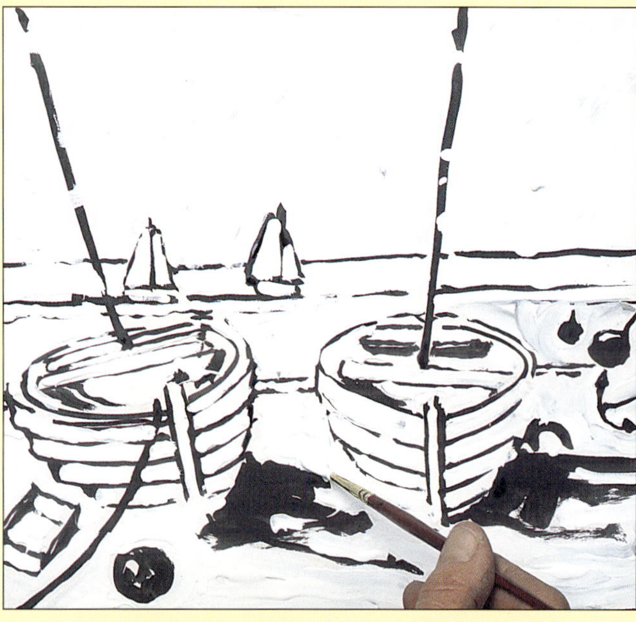

2 ▲ **Fill in with white gouache** Block in the spaces between the outlines with thick white gouache. Work with loose, bold strokes, taking the white sketchily up to the black lines to create untidy edges. Leave streaks of unpainted board (or paper) when blocking in the sky. This deliberate imprecision will produce an attractive textured effect in the finished picture.

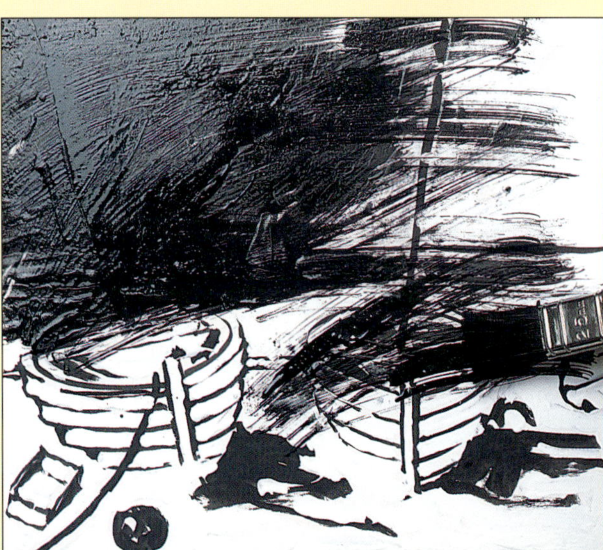

3 ▲ **Paint on black ink** When the work is completely dry, start to paint over the entire picture area in waterproof Indian ink, using a 25mm (1in) decorator's brush.

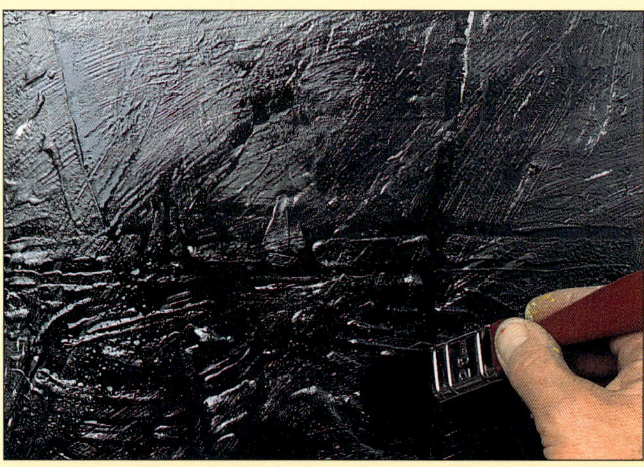

4 ▲ **Cover the paper with the ink** Continue applying the Indian ink until the whole picture is covered in solid black. Allow to dry – this may take a few hours.

5 ▸ **Wet and rub the paper** Flood the whole picture with clean water, while at the same time gently rubbing with a brush or sponge to dissolve and remove the areas of white gouache and the black ink covering them.

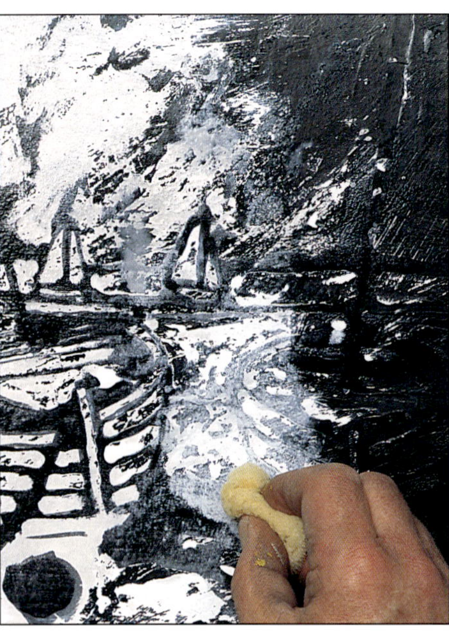

6 ▾ **Complete the rinsing process** Rinse the painting once more to remove excess white gouache and black ink. Allow it to dry.

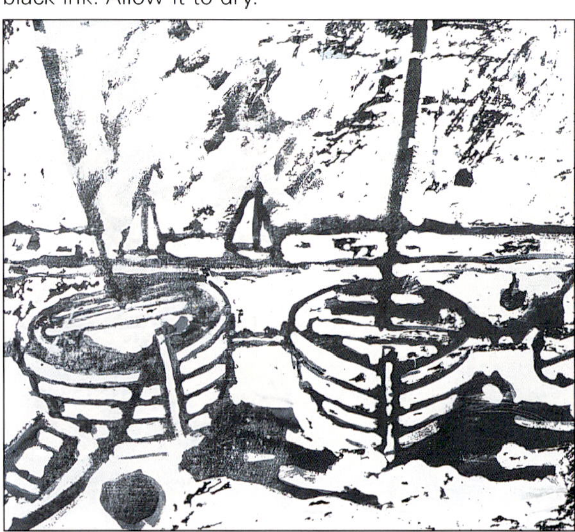

7 ▾ **Colour the sky** Mix a very dilute wash of ultramarine watercolour. Apply this to the sky with the decorator's brush, using broad horizontal strokes.

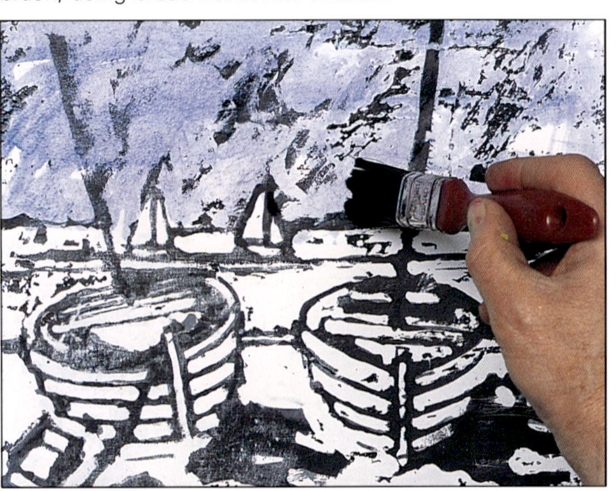

8 ▾ **Fill in the beach** With the same brush, loosely block in the sand with dilute yellow ochre watercolour, taking the colour around the boats.

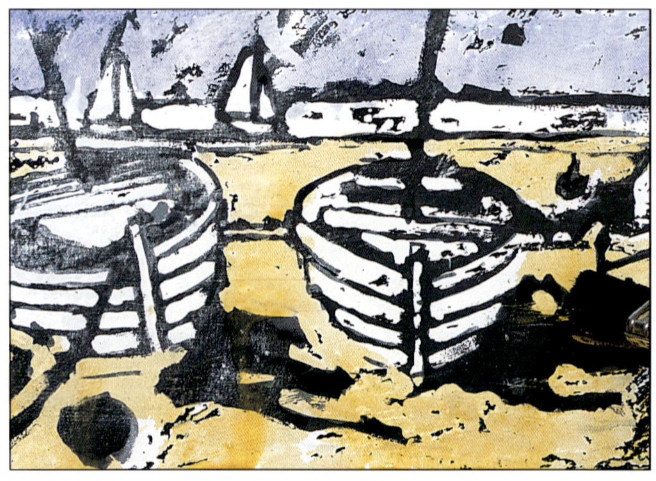

9 ▾ **Paint the sea** Mix a wash of ultramarine darker than the one used for the sky. Brush in the strip of sea.

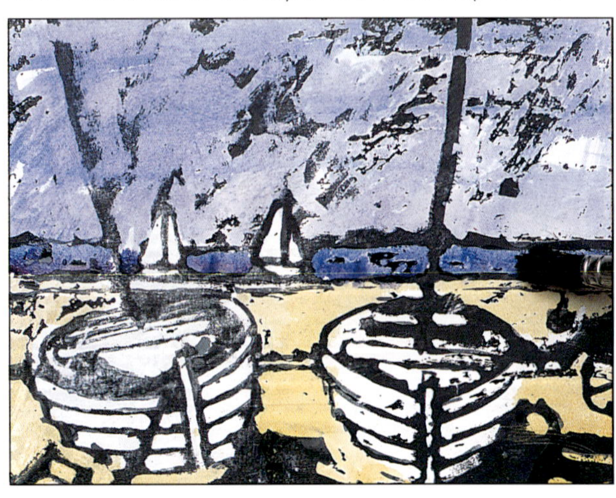

▾ **The finished painting has an attractive grainy appearance where ink marks are left on the sky and beach.**

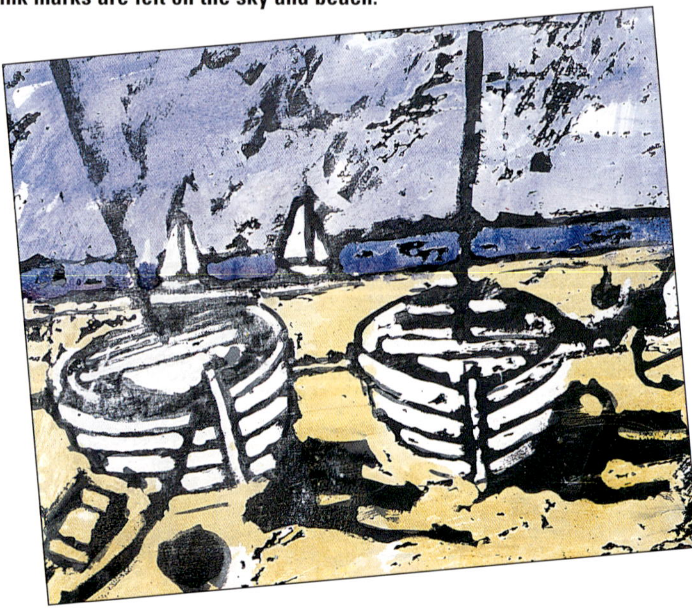

CLOUDS IN THE SKY, TEXTURE ON THE BEACH

Hazy, atmospheric effects can be created by covering the support with white gouache before applying watercolour. The colour can then be dabbed off in the final stages, as it has not had the chance to stain the support. This technique works best with a rapid, loose application of watercolour. On a highly worked painting, the watercolour might disturb the underlying white gouache, causing the colours to go cloudy. For this picture you need: a piece of white mountboard, a 25mm (1in) decorator's brush, a 25mm (1in) soft flat brush, white gouache, paper tissue and four watercolours – Payne's grey, ultramarine, alizarin crimson and yellow ochre.

1 ▸ **Apply white gouache** Dilute white gouache to the consistency of single cream and apply all over the board, using a 25mm (1in) decorator's brush. Work in even, horizontal strokes, keeping the paint as flat as possible – ready for the watercolour to be applied in step 2. Allow to dry.

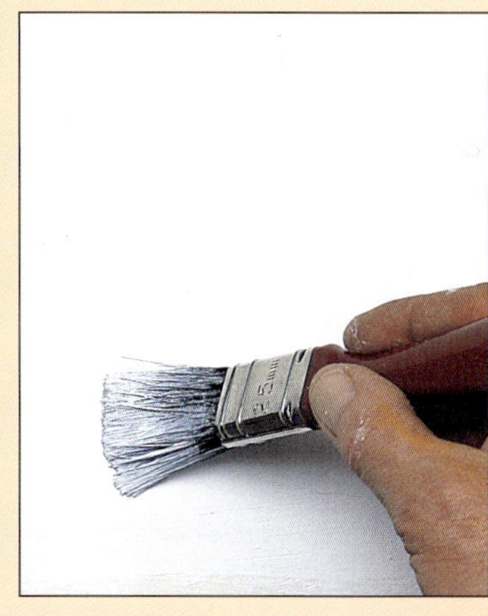

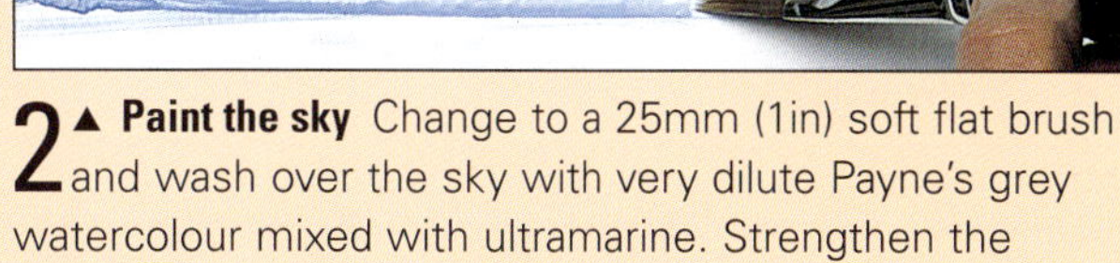

2 ▴ **Paint the sky** Change to a 25mm (1in) soft flat brush and wash over the sky with very dilute Payne's grey watercolour mixed with ultramarine. Strengthen the colour towards the horizon.

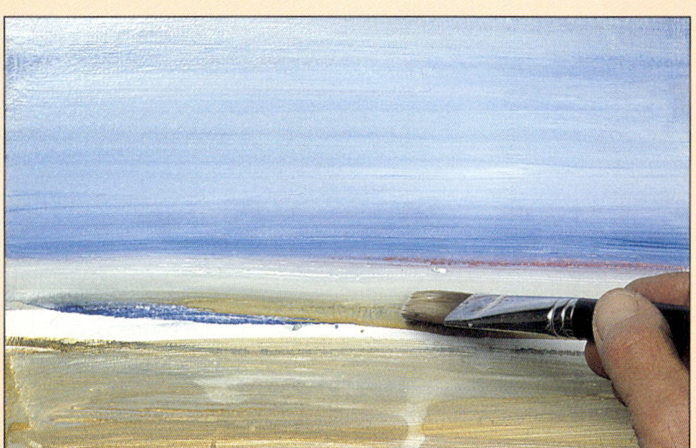

3 ▴ **Brush colour over the beach** Add a streak of dilute alizarin crimson to the horizon. Suggest the beach in dilute yellow ochre mixed with a little of the sky colour.

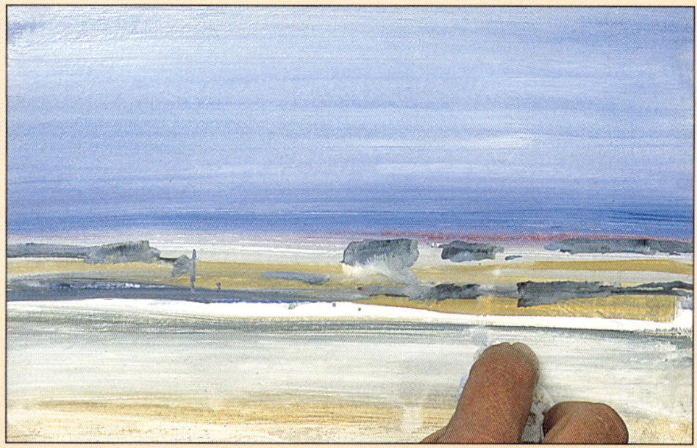

4 ▴ **Wipe off paint** Add the rocks as short strokes of Payne's grey watercolour. Use a paper tissue to wipe off some of the newly painted beach – this lighter tone gives an impression of wet sand.

5 ▾ **Add clean water** Wash the brush and apply dabs of clean water to the beach and sky. This dissolves the colour to create patchy white cloud and a pebbly texture.

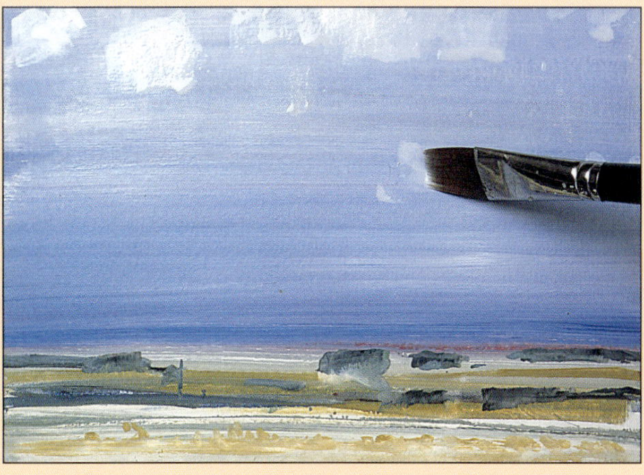

▾ **The wash-off technique used for this seascape has created a delicate effect with plenty of white to lighten the overall tone.**

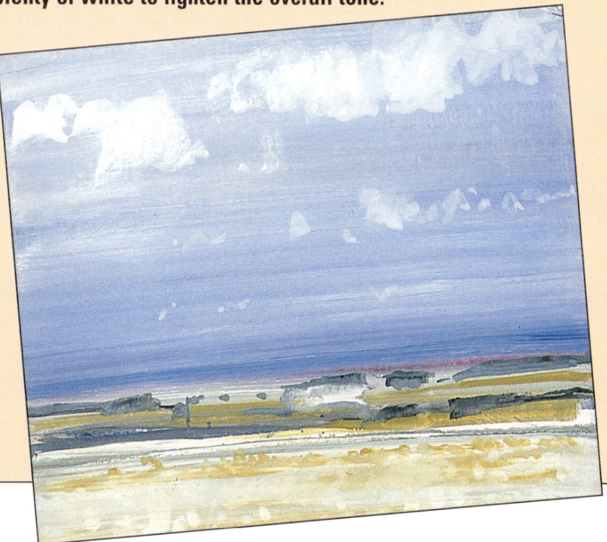

Mixing orange

In the first of three sections covering the secondary colours, we look at the secrets behind rendering a variety of oranges.

The basic rules of colour mixing are usually taught to us in primary school. There, while painstakingly scribbling one coloured pencil over another, we discover that red and yellow make orange. Easy!

As orange is a secondary colour, it can be mixed very simply by combining the two primary colours next to it on the colour wheel – that is, red and yellow. In terms of paint, the equivalents of these primaries are cadmium red and cadmium yellow.

The range of oranges

However, cadmium red and cadmium yellow alone will probably not provide you with all the oranges needed for painting a wide range of subjects. Instead, you should experiment with the many other reds and yellows that are available to the artist.

We tend to associate orange with the bright, acidic colour of the fruit – but think also of the variety of mellow tints in autumn leaves or the earthy colours of sand and brickwork. As this still-life arrangement shows, 'orange' is a very general label used to describe a wide range of colours.

Experimental mixing

Depending on the brand and type of paint, there are up to 20 yellows on a manufacturer's colour chart. Counting the earth colours, the yellows include lemon, cadmium yellow, chrome yellow, aurora, aureolin, Naples yellow and Indian yellow, as well as yellow ochre and raw sienna. The range of reds on offer is equally wide and includes cadmium red, vermilion, scarlet, rose madder, permanent rose, alizarin, Venetian red, Mars red and Indian red.

In theory, by combining every available yellow with every available red, you could have a palette of hundreds

▶ The oranges in this watercolour came from cadmium yellow, yellow ochre, Naples yellow, cadmium red, cadmium scarlet and alizarin crimson, plus two bought colours – chrome orange and cadmium orange. Sepia and burnt sienna helped darken the cast shadows and top.

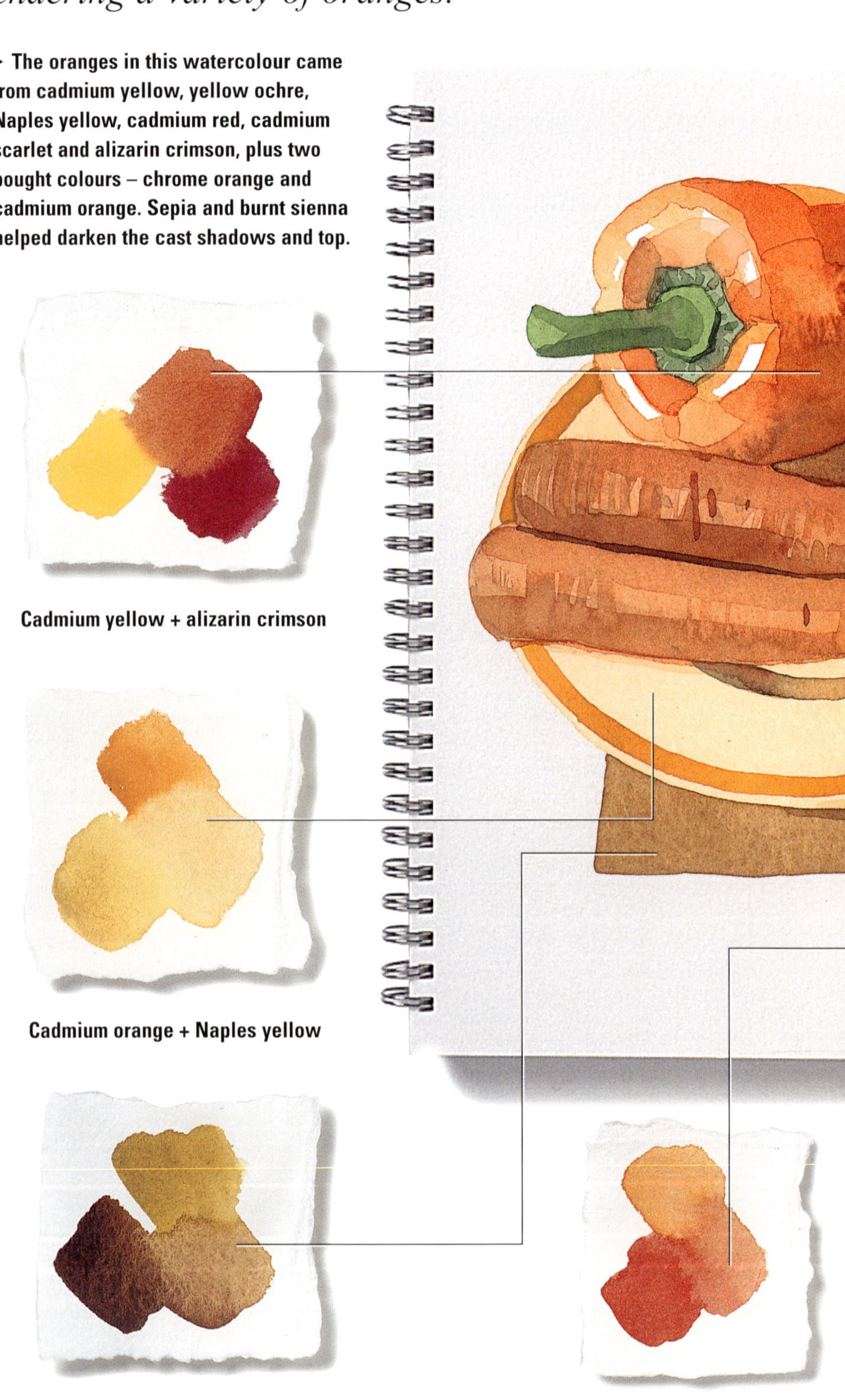

Cadmium yellow + alizarin crimson

Cadmium orange + Naples yellow

Yellow ochre + burnt sienna

Cadmium orange + cadmium red

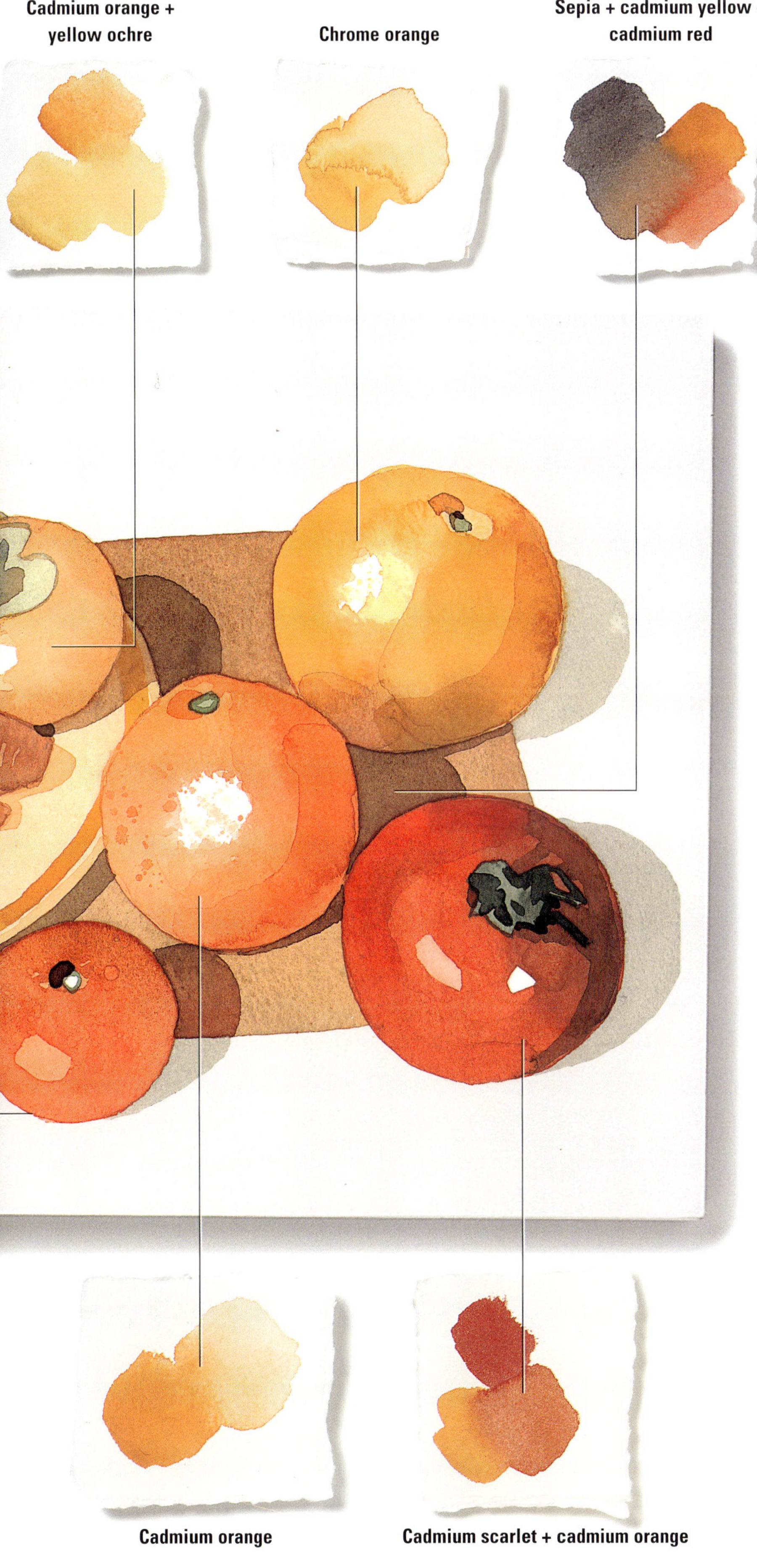

of different oranges at your fingertips. In reality, many of these mixes are so similar that you can't differentiate between them. And as no artist is likely to need such a range of oranges, confine your mixing experiments to the yellows and reds normally on your palette.

Practical mixtures

On the working palette of almost any painter you will find at least two or three reds and two or three yellows. Typically, these will be: a bright yellow, usually cadmium; an earthy yellow such as yellow ochre or raw sienna; and a cooler colour, for instance, lemon. In the painting on the left, the artist chose Naples as the cooler yellow because it is very effective at neutralizing, or 'knocking back', a strong red or orange.

The same palette will probably also contain cadmium red and a cool red such as alizarin crimson. You might also add a third red that falls somewhere between them in colour temperature – for example, cadmium scarlet. A warm earth colour, such as Venetian red, Indian red or burnt sienna, is also useful.

Note that by varying the proportions of any mixture you will get a different result. For example, cadmium red and cadmium yellow will produce a range of results from a yellowish-orange to a deep reddish-orange.

Bought colours

In addition to those colours you can mix yourself, there are also a few manufactured oranges. The most common are cadmium and chrome orange, both of which are strong and bright. The former is slightly lighter, but considered to be more permanent.

A bought orange is by no means essential, but it can provide a consistent starting point for certain standard mixtures. For example, portrait and figure painters commonly use orange mixed with white as a pale flesh tone.

Note that mixing bright yellow with bright red sometimes produces a slightly duller orange than you would expect. To avoid this, try to choose pigments with a degree of natural transparency. For example, yellow mixed with alizarin crimson will give you a brighter orange than when mixed with cadmium red, which is a more opaque pigment.

Mixing green

By mixing and modifying the manufacturers' greens it is possible to expand your palette well beyond the range available otherwise.

For many artists – especially those whoe are interested in the natural world – green is probably the most important colour on the palette. Rural landscapes, flowers and plants, as well as many still-life subjects, call for a variety of greens.

A common misconception

However, the great versatility of the colour green is often underestimated. Beginners sometimes believe that, because green is mixed from blue and yellow, all things green must therefore be painted from equal mixtures of these two colours.

Many first attempts at landscape painting are disappointing for this very reason – simply because the artist has failed to distinguish between the different greens in the subject.

Experiment first

One way to overcome this difficulty is to experiment with green mixtures before starting to paint. Look at the subject and pick out as many different greens as you can. Where there are highlights and shadows on a green area, take note of the light and dark tones these create.

Try your hand at mixing the greens you have detected on a separate sheet of paper. The process will initially be one of trial and error, but you will be surprised at the extraordinary range that can be achieved by mixing and modifying the colours on a very limited palette.

Mixing greens

Start by exploring the possibilities of a pair of colours, and see how many different shades of green you can get. For instance, by varying the proportions of ultramarine and cadmium lemon, you can obtain colours ranging from lime green to deep blue-green. Repeat the experiment, substituting yellow ochre for lemon yellow, and you will create an equally varied range extending from golden green to deep olive.

Modifying a green

Bought greens are also useful – in this fruit-and-vegetable still life, the artist made full use of them. However, they can be very strident – so more often than not you'll need to modify them with other colours. Again, it is useful to experiment and to extend your repertoire before

▶ Although it is possible to obtain greens by mixing blues and yellows, it is often best to use bought greens and, where necessary, modify these with other colours.

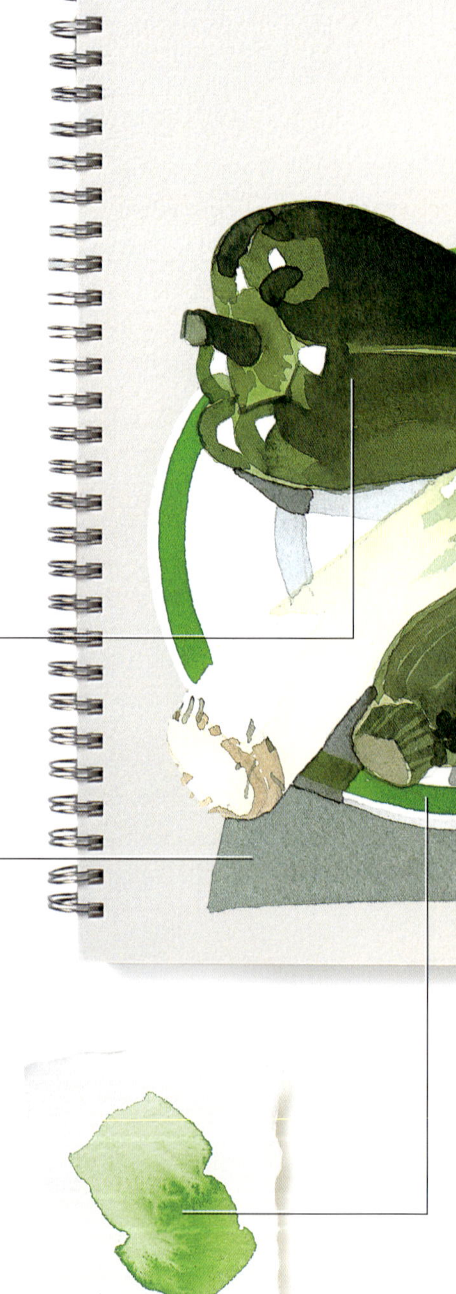

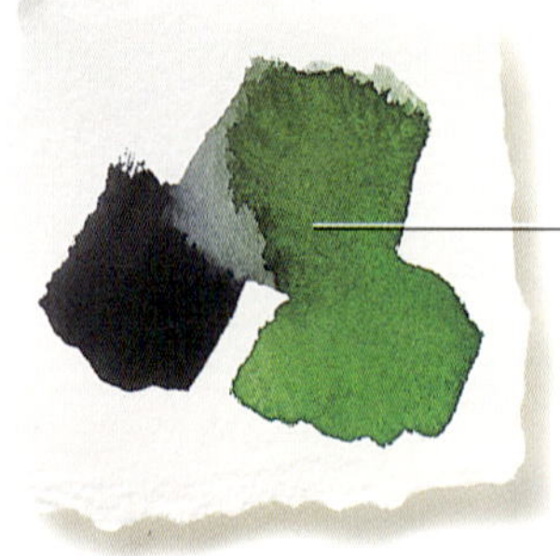

Payne's grey + sap green

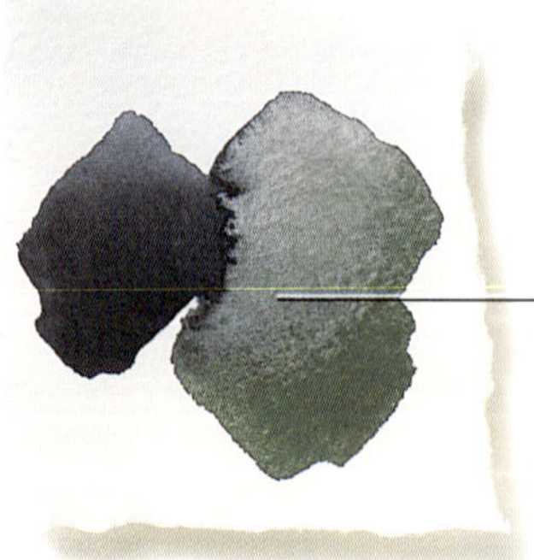

Payne's grey + terre verte

Emerald green

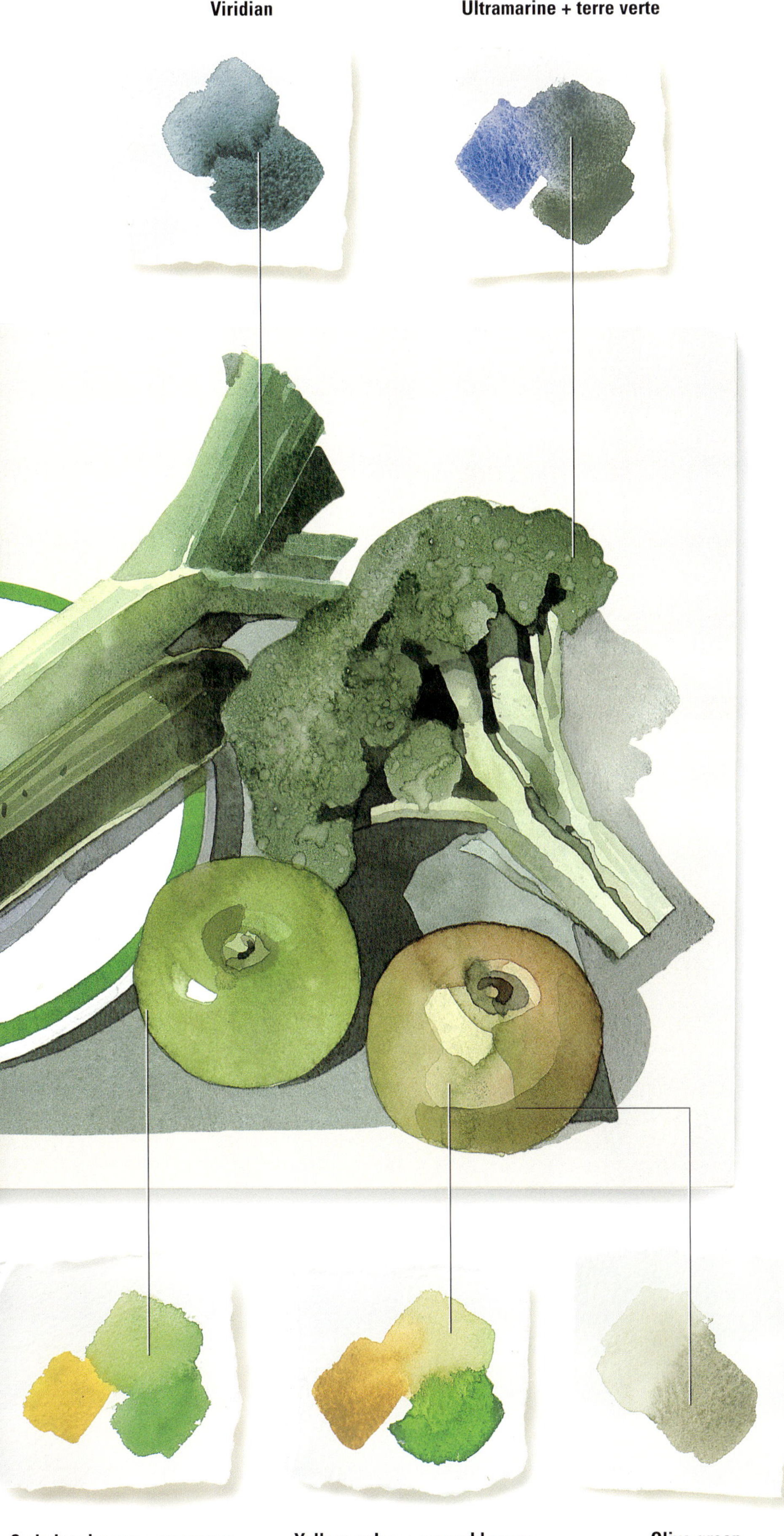

painting. Choose a strong shade, such as emerald, viridian or sap green, and make some test samples. Modify the tone by adding varying amounts of a neutral colour such as raw umber or Payne's grey. This will give you a choice of rich and interesting dark greens. Avoid using black, as this can deaden the colour.

Alternatively, any green can be modified or toned down by adding a little of its complementary colour – red. Try using different reds in varying quantities to produce a range of muted greens and neutrals.

Bought greens

Five manufactured greens were used in this painting. If you have not used these pigments before, now is the opportunity to try out the new colours.

- **Emerald green** is more brilliant than any green you could mix yourself. It is useful for capturing man-made colours, such as the bright green band around the plate here. The clear emerald stands out beautifully from the natural greens of the fruits and vegetables.
- **Terre verte** is the oldest known green. Made from natural earth pigments, it works well when painting vegetation and other organic forms. Here, it is used with a little ultramarine for the blue-green broccoli. The table top and shadows are painted in a mixture of terre verte and Payne's grey to create a cool, neutral and unobtrusive background.
- **Olive green** varies depending on the manufacturer, but it is generally a muted natural green, good for foliage and vegetation. Here, it is used with plenty of water to put a glaze on the shadowed side of the rosy apple.
- **Viridian** is very powerful and needs careful handling. It can easily take over and dominate your picture. Used in small quantities and modified by other colours, it is a useful ingredient in mixtures. Otherwise, viridian is best restricted to specific areas. Here, it is mixed with varying amounts of water for the light, medium and dark tones of green on the leaves of the leek.
- **Sap green** is a warm, leafy green and is often used for painting grass and foliage, especially the picture is set in spring. Here, it is mixed with cadmium lemon for the green apple and with Payne's grey for the dark green pepper.

Mixing purple

Discover how to create rich variations on a theme by mixing bought purples with blues, reds and neutrals.

Purple is rare in nature. The earliest purple pigment came from the shells of the 'purpura', a large whelk found on the shores of the Mediterranean. The Phoenicians are reputed to have ground several million purpura shells to make enough purple to dye their emperor's clothes. The colour they used was known as 'royal purple' and it is still produced today.

Nowadays, purple is a far more accessible colour, but even today real purple pigments are comparatively few in number. The majority of manufactured purples and violets are actually combinations of existing blues and reds.

Purple mixtures

Many artists find it unnecessary to buy ready-mixed purple. Instead, they prefer to make their own by mixing various blues and reds to get the colour they need. Fortunately, it is possible to mix a range of good purples yourself. The brightest of these are achieved by using a cool red, such as alizarin crimson, rose madder or magenta. The addition of white to these mixtures will give various shades of mauve and violet.

If you have ever tried to mix purple using cadmium red, you will know that the result is not a bright colour at all, but a muted brownish-purple. This is because cadmium red contains yellow, which gives the mixture a brown bias.

Mix your own

To discover the potential of the colours on your basic palette, try making some simple two-colour mixtures. Start with alizarin crimson and ultramarine, combining these colours in equal proportions. The result will be a strong, bright purple.

By varying the proportions of the ultramarine and alizarin crimson in the mixture, you can then go on to produce a range of purples with either a red or a blue bias.

Carry out some more tests, this time substituting cerulean blue for ultramarine. As cerulean is a cool, pale blue, the resulting purple will be less bright and slightly more opaque.

It is well worth repeating similar experiments using a number of different blues and reds. The resulting mixtures

▸ The purples in this still life include bought colours used alone and mixed with reds, blues and neutrals (such as Payne's grey or raw umber). Don't forget to try mixing red and blue as well – such as the alizarin crimson and Prussian blue used here.

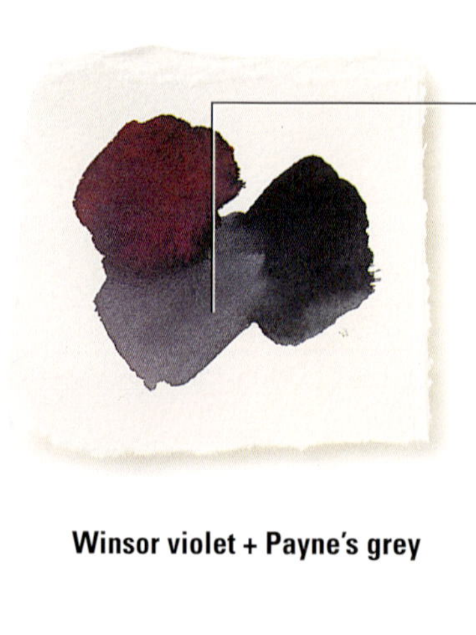

Winsor violet + Payne's grey

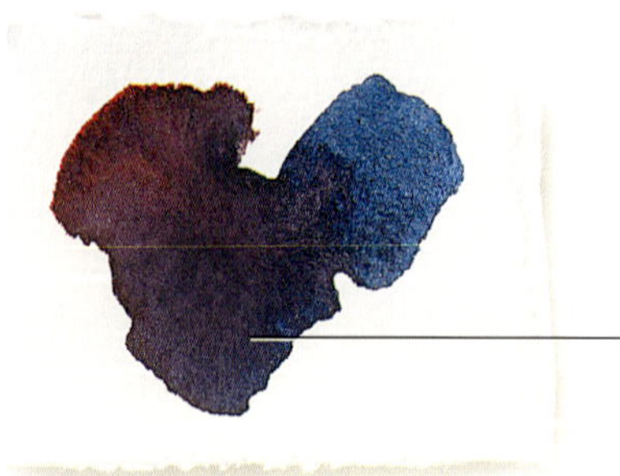

Winsor violet + phthalo blue

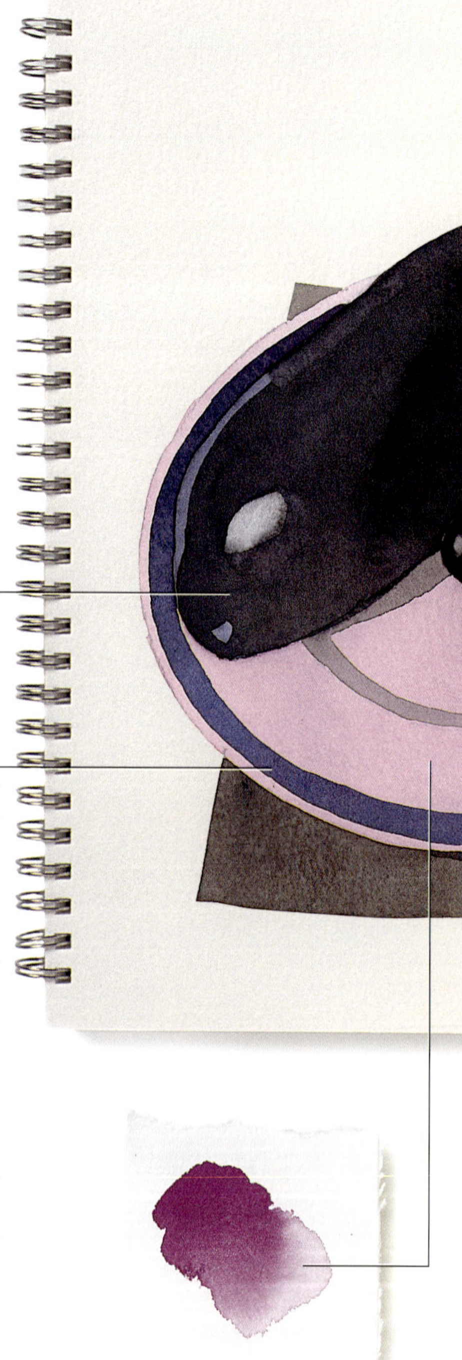

Mauve

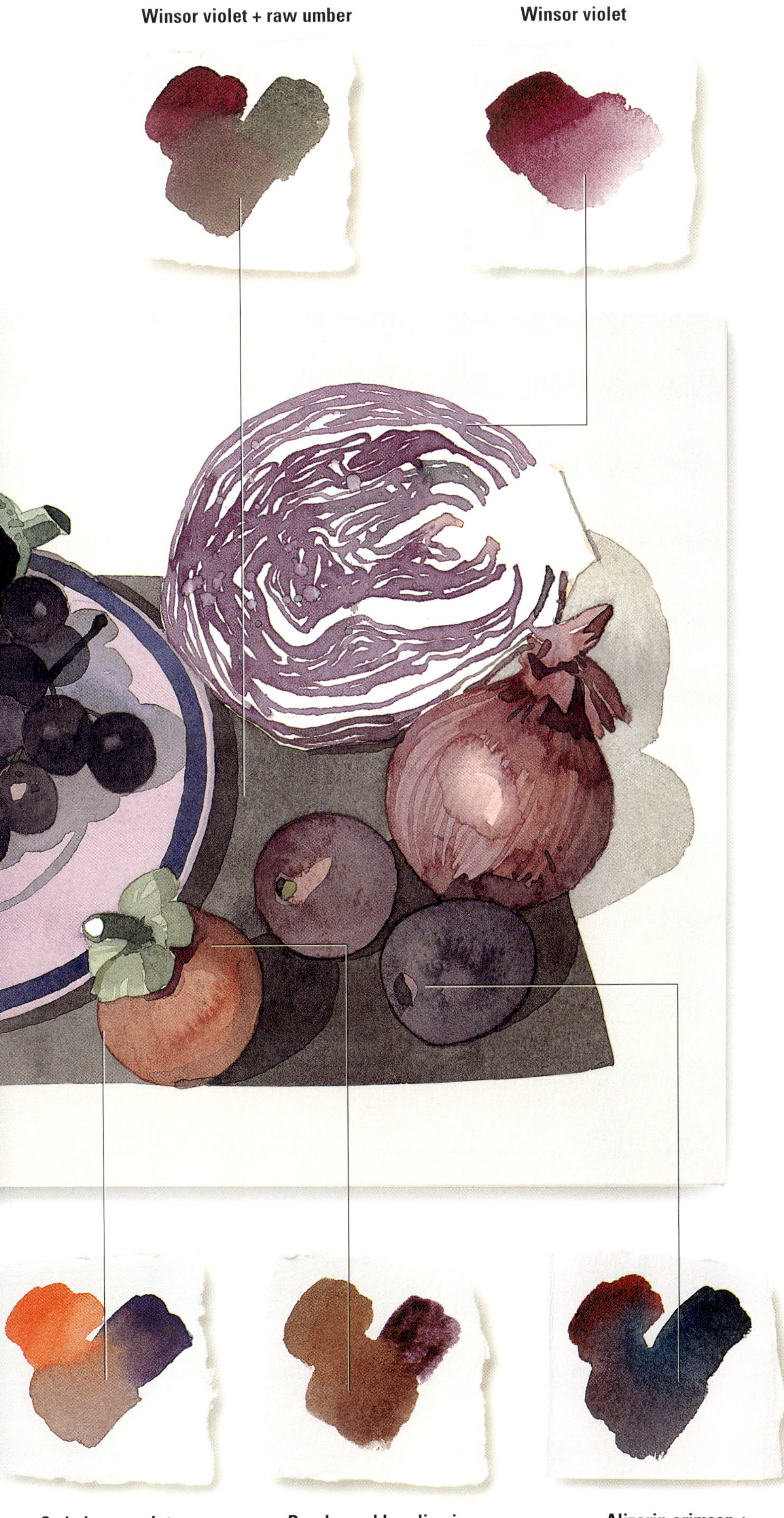

will vary enormously and not all of them will be purple. Some will be brown or muddy grey. Only by trial and error is it possible to have control over your palette and the colours it can produce.

Shadow colours

Purple is frequently used for painting shadows. If you look carefully at those that initially appear to be grey or brown, you will notice that they often contain traces of purple and violet. In this watercolour still life, the thrown shadows are mixed from the purples and violets used on the fruit and vegetables, toned down with neutral colours, such as Payne's grey or raw umber.

You can try mixing your own shadow colours by adding raw umber, Payne's grey or another neutral to any of the purples and violets below. Adding a little of their complementary colour, yellow, can also tone down purple and violet.

Bought purples

Our artist chose four manufactured purples for this still life, modifying these to acquire all the colours needed for painting the fruit and vegetables:

- **Mauve** may have a red or blue bias, depending on the manufacturer. The mauve used for the plate in this painting has a definite red tinge and stands out distinctly from the other colours. It is used here as a dilute wash.
- **Winsor violet** is a transparent colour with a powerful staining capacity. A little goes a long way, so use it sparingly. It is shown here unmixed; modified with Payne's grey and phthalo blue to obtain cool purples; and mixed with raw umber to create the neutral tone of the table top.
- **Purple madder alizarin** is a rich natural colour somewhere between brown and purple. It is popular with landscape artists for painting the warm tones of foliage and trees. Purple madder alizarin is mixed with a little Winsor violet for the dark shadow on the persimmon fruit.
- **Violet carmine** is a clear, transparent purple, used here with cadmium scarlet to depict the cool orange-violet of the persimmon fruit.

Cobalt violet is another bought purple you could try. It is not used here, but it provides an attractive warmish purple that cannot be mixed from other colours.

Details and textures in watercolour

Although watercolours can be used in a free and loose manner, they can also be used to create intricate, highly finished paintings.

The artist for this step-by-step created a sweeping rendition of a Scottish landscape – full of subtle variations of colour and texture – using a simple pocket set of watercolour paints.

In the foreground, features such as the tree branches and intricate shadows are brought into sharp focus using carefully controlled lines made with a fine brush. In contrast to these lines, lively elements have been created by applying the paint in unconventional ways.

Flicking paint

Sprays of seeded grasses, for example, were added in the foreground by gently flicking paint on to the paper. And outstretched, leafy branches have been implied by blowing small pools of wet paint across the paper. These details give the impression of wind blowing across the scene, playing on the grass and foliage as it passes.

In the background, however, little detail has been added. Instead, broad strokes have been used to create the smooth surface of the mountain in a harmonious range of greens, browns and blues. To create these colours, you need constantly to mix small amounts of different colours into your main washes.

It is, therefore, vital to wash your brush often to avoid muddy colours. Dry off the brush on a wad of tissues, or flick the spare water out on to a newspaper positioned on the floor.

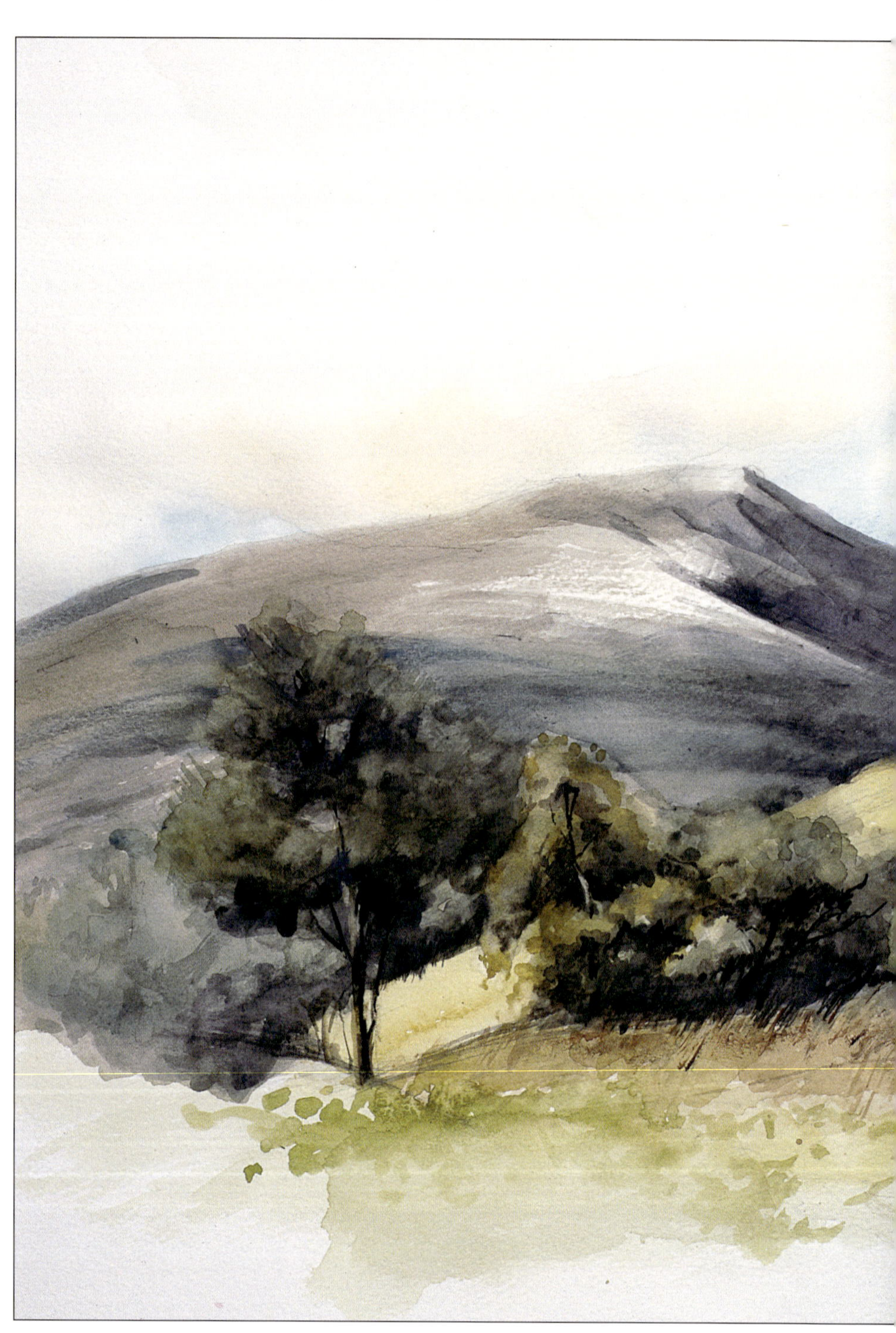

▶ The artist has used aerial perspective to create a sense of depth. The distant mountain is rendered in cool blues and greens, while the grassy areas are painted in warm browns. Note also that the figure in the reference photo (top right) has been omitted to create an unsullied scene.

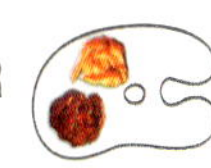

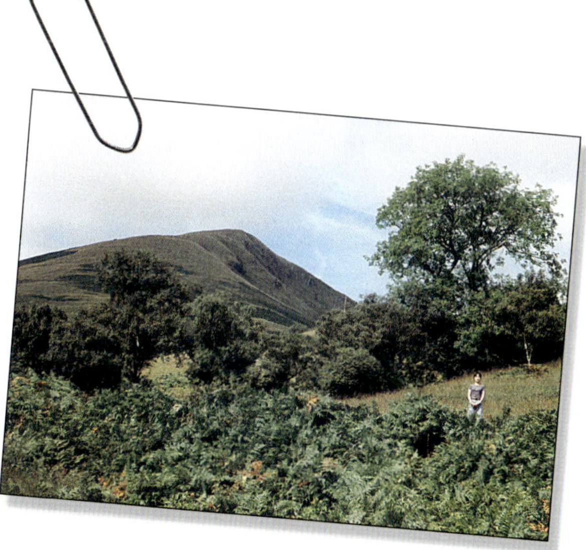

YOU WILL NEED

Piece of 300gsm (140lb) NOT watercolour paper 40 x 60cm (16 x 24 in)

HB pencil

Brushes: Nos. 8, 6 and 2 flats; Nos. 4 and 00 rounds

Large jar of water

10 watercolours: ultramarine; cobalt blue; crimson; burnt umber; emerald green; ochre; orange; forest green; cadmium yellow; black

Large flat mixing dish

Paper tissues

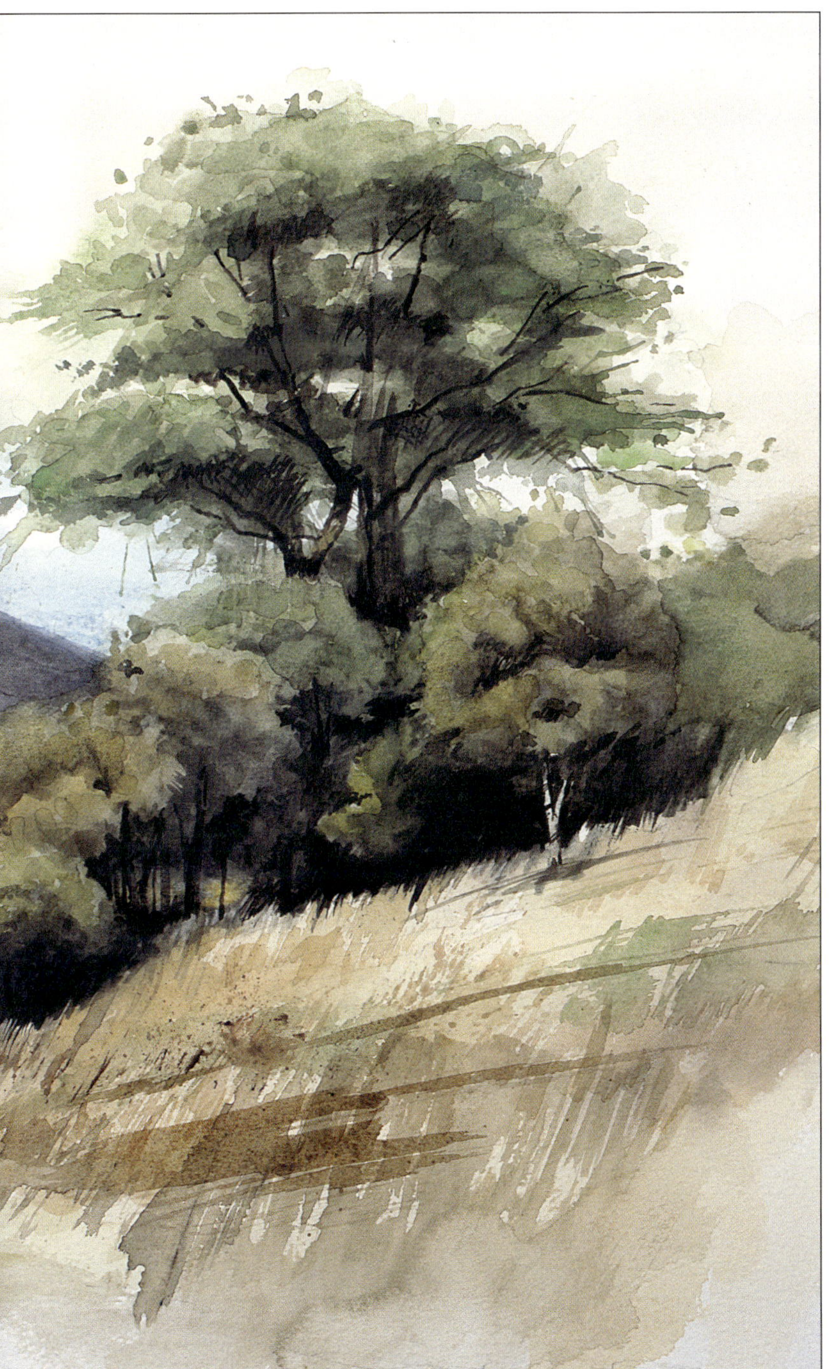

FIRST STROKES

1 ▼ **Sketch out the scene** With an HB pencil, sketch out the main features of your scene. In the palest areas, press only lightly with the pencil, capturing the faintest impression of the ragged outlines of the foliage. In darker areas, you can block in the shadows with a firmer scribbling action. These pencil marks are an important foundation on which to build your detailed composition.

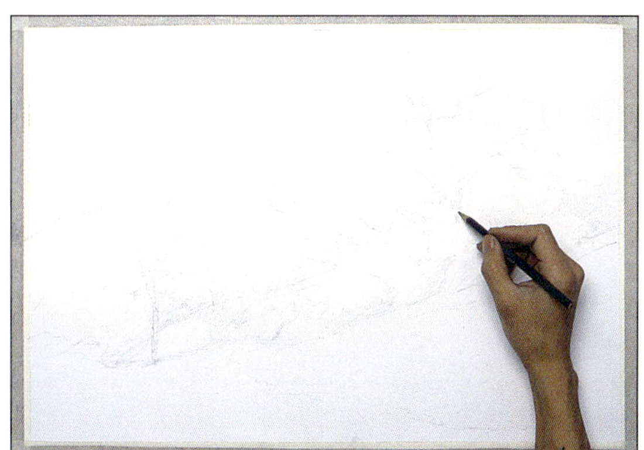

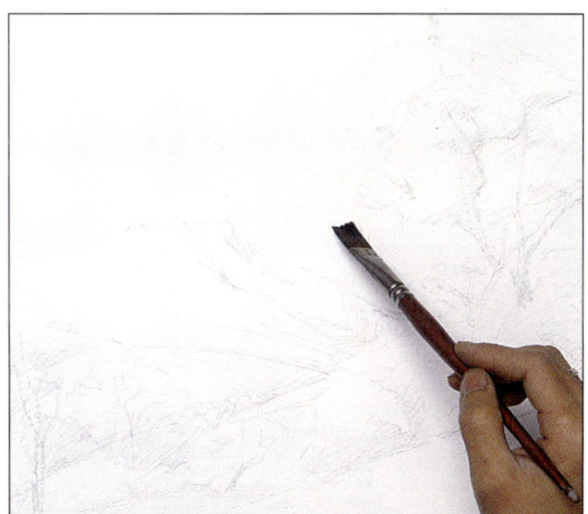

2 ▲ **Prepare the sky** Use a No. 8 flat brush and clean water to wet the sky area, making a neat edge along the line of the mountain. Do not let the area get too wet, or the paper might become wrinkled – but put on enough water to make the paper surface glisten.

3 ▸ Wash in the sky colours Put touches of ultramarine and cobalt blue into a pool of clean water on your mixing dish. Working quickly on the wet paper, boldly mark in the blue sky above the mountain. The water on the paper will make the edges of the colour blend into the white areas. Clean the brush. With tiny spots of crimson and burnt umber, colour a second pool of water and wash in the undersides of the clouds.

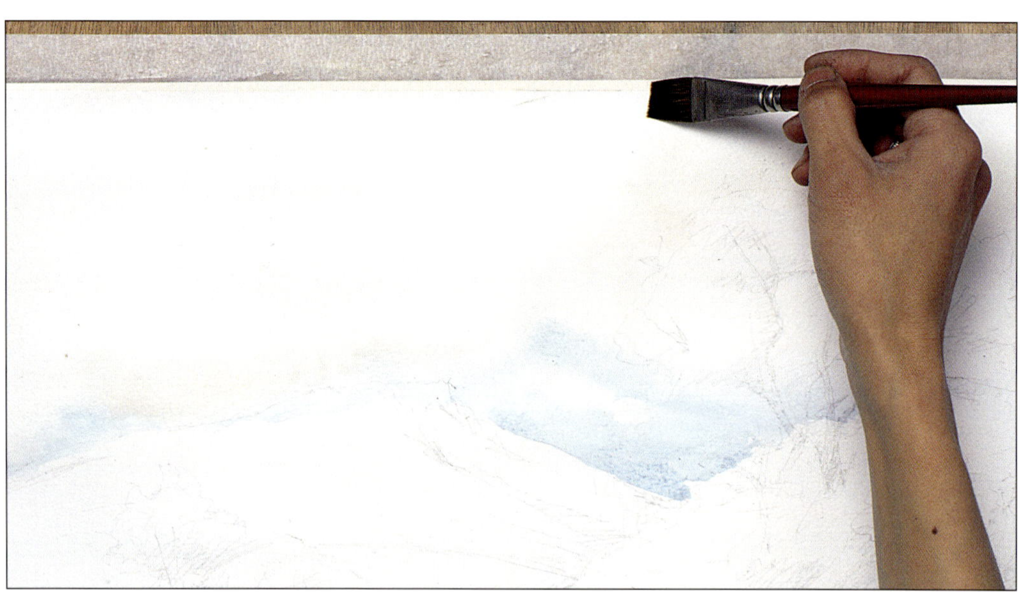

DEVELOPING THE PICTURE

Now that you have established the basic outlines and washed in the sky, you can begin work on the landscape itself. To achieve a range of lively textural effects, use various methods of applying the paint, from dabbing and hatching to spattering.

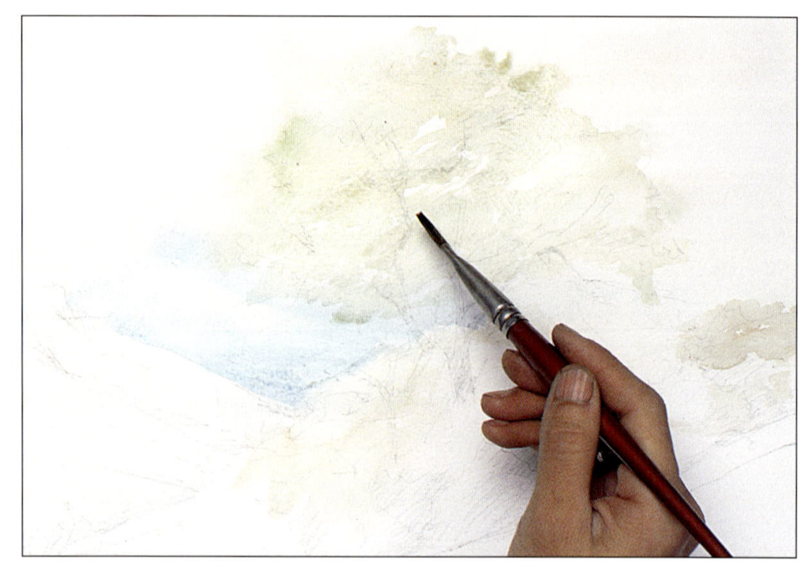

4 ▸ Block in the foliage With clean water, wet the paper in the main areas of foliage. Mix a wash of emerald green with touches of burnt umber and ultramarine. With a No. 4 round brush, block in the foliage, using a dabbing action. Let the patches of colour overlap and run into one another, leaving patches of plain white paper in between.

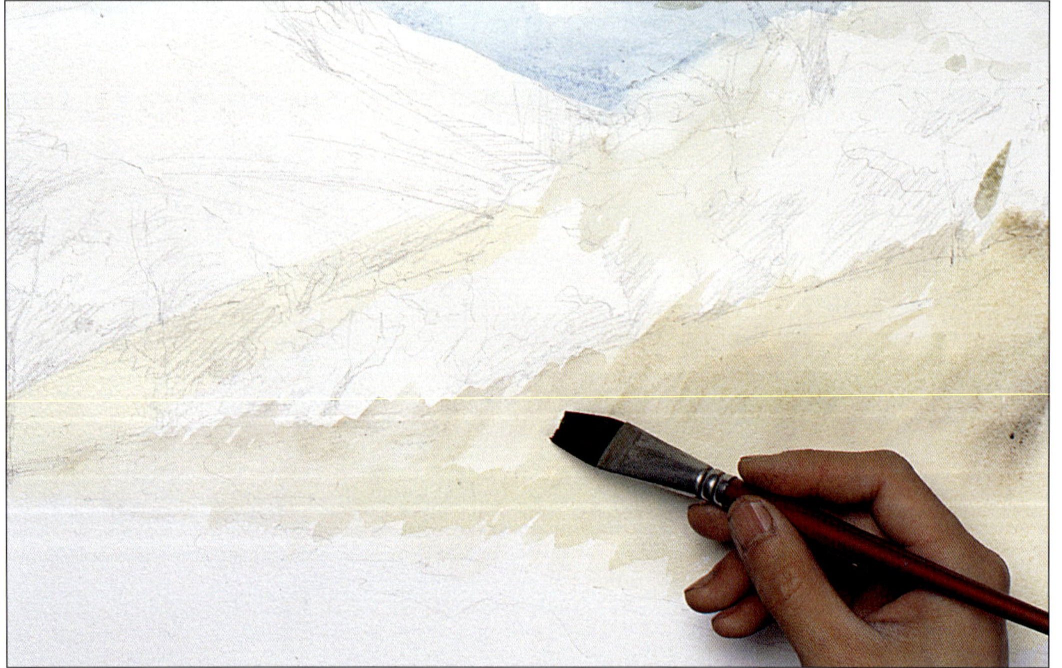

5 ◂ Establish the foreground Wash the paper in the foreground with clean water. Mix a wash of ochre and burnt umber with a touch of orange, then use the flattened tip of the No. 8 flat brush to sketch in the grass. Create strong, textural strokes to make these foreground features stand out. As you work, pull touches of other colours into your wash – emerald green, forest green, burnt umber, ochre and cadmium yellow.

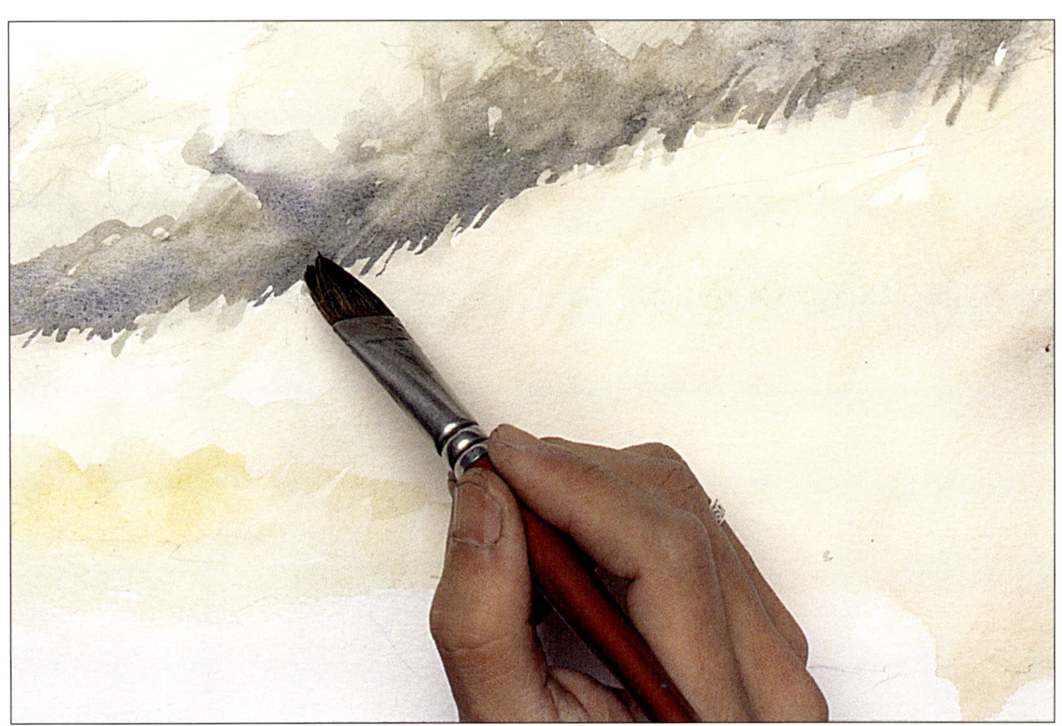

6 ◂ Work into the shadows With a strong wash of ultramarine, forest green and a tiny touch of black, use a No. 8 flat brush to work in the deep shadows under the bushes. Visually, this makes a strong line to draw the eye across the painting. Use tight hatching marks along the edge of the grassy area to give the impression of grasses growing up across the shadows.

7 ▾ Establish the mountain Wait until the sky area is dry so that the edge of the mountain will remain crisp. The mountain is worked on dry paper with a wash of burnt umber, plus touches of cobalt blue and ultramarine to give it a cold, distant appearance. Use long, flat strokes of the No. 8 flat brush following the contours of the mountain. Draw a touch more ultramarine into the mix for the darker (right) side of the mountain.

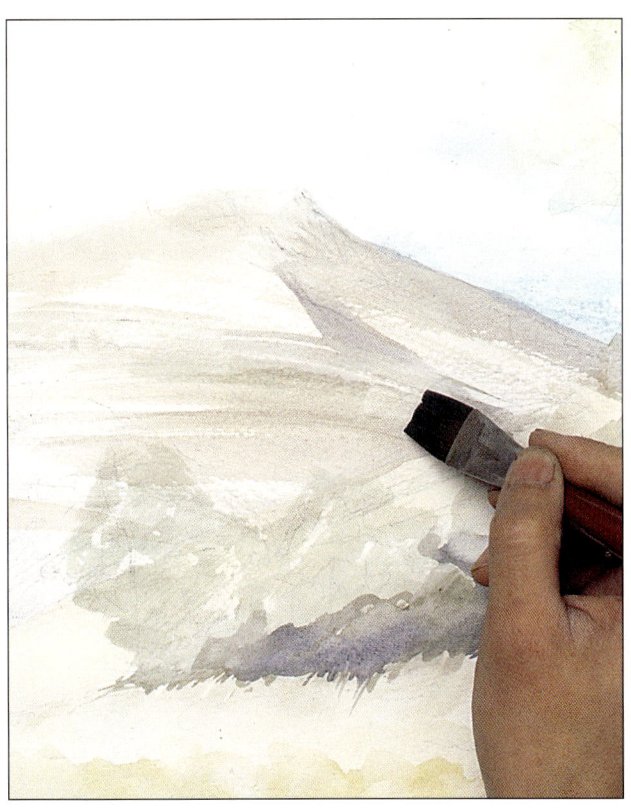

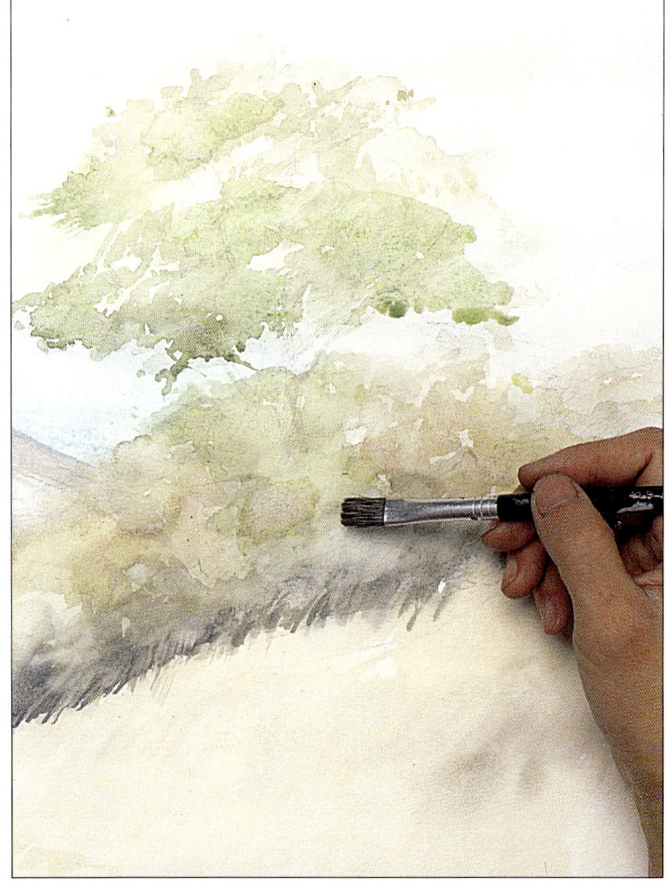

8 ▴ Develop the foliage Using a No. 6 flat brush, dab emerald green with a little ochre and burnt umber on to the leafy areas. For a lively effect, identify pools of green paint around the edge of the tree. With your face close to the paper, blow sharply across the surface to throw spurts of paint outwards from the tree. Remove unwanted spots of paint with a tissue.

9 ▶ Mark in the twigs Use a No. 00 round brush and burnt umber paint to mark in the trunk and main branches of the tree. Some are visible between the green patchy areas. Others stretch out sideways to support external foliage. Refer back to your subject to ensure that your marks remain characteristic of the tree. To mark out the finest twigs, see Expert Advice, opposite.

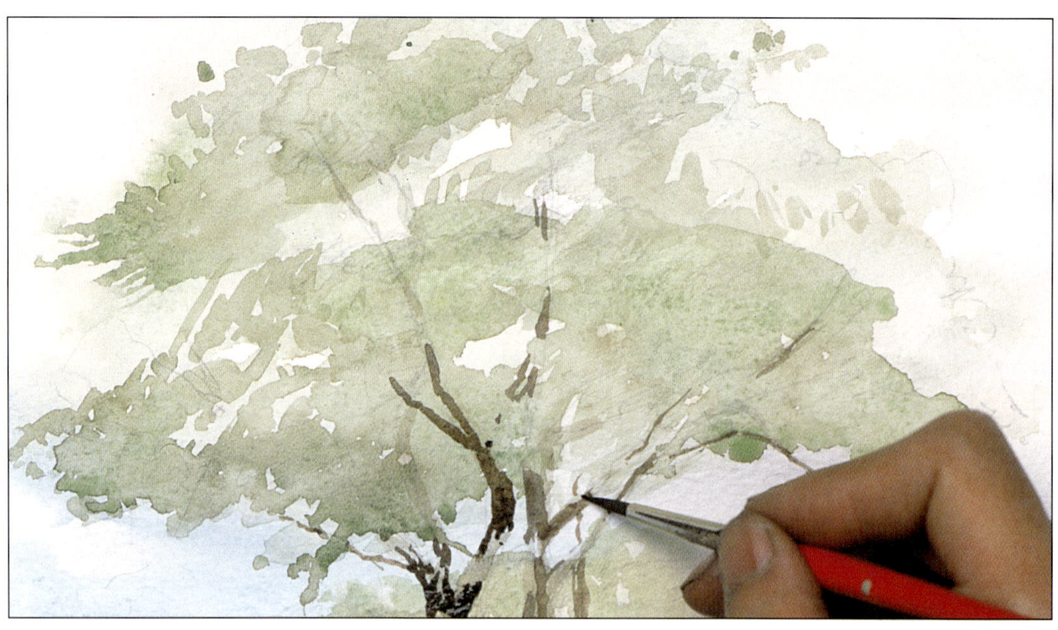

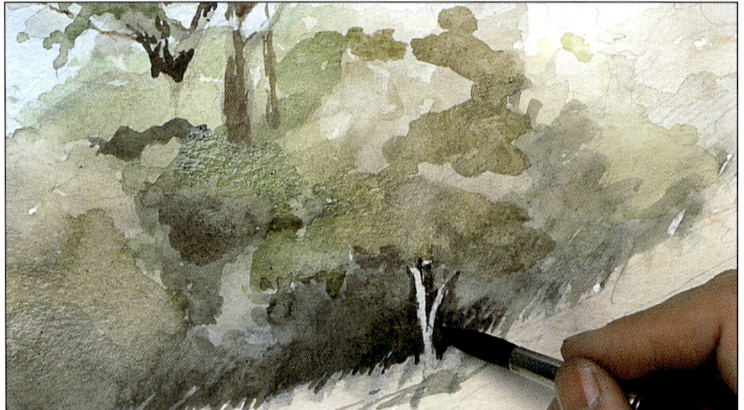

10 ▲ Work a foreground tree To create a light area, draw a wet brush along the line of the trunk. Dry the brush on a tissue, then draw it down the same line to leach out the colour. Use a mix of forest green, ultramarine and a little black for the shadows around the tree. Develop the foliage of the large tree and bushes, using the same colours as in step 8. Add ochre to help the foreground tree stand out.

TROUBLESHOOTER

REMOVING PAINT SPOTS

If paint splashes on to a plain area such as the sky, it can be removed with some quick action. While the paint is still wet, press a clean paper tissue on top of the mark. Add a drop of clean water to the mark, blot with tissue and repeat until the mark disappears.

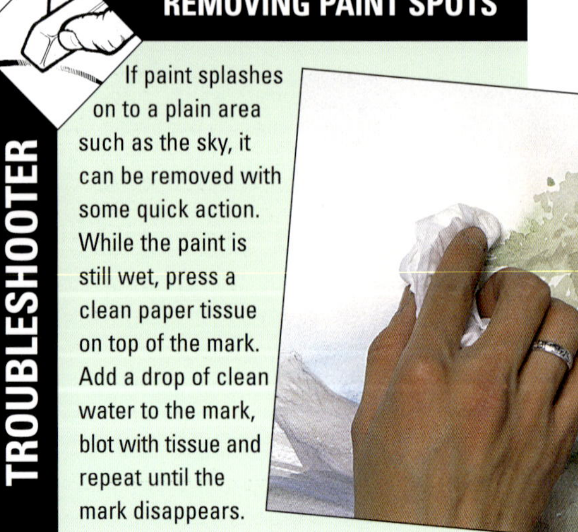

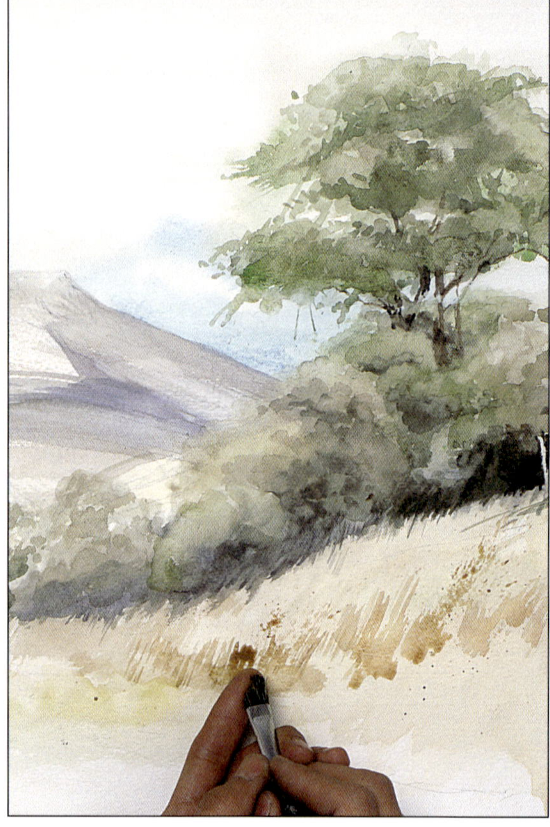

11 ▲ Enliven the foreground grass Add touches of orange and emerald green to ochre and use a No. 6 flat brush to paint in coarse, grassy marks in the foreground of the composition. For a lively texture, make some flicking marks upwards from the base of the grass stems. To do this, load the brush with paint, then hold it in one hand close to the paper and pull the bristles back with the fingers of your other hand. Release with a flick upwards to spatter paint across the picture. Remove unwanted spots of paint quickly with a tissue.

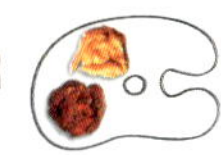

12 ▼ **Develop the middle distance** Using a No. 6 flat brush, mix a wash of cadmium yellow with a tiny touch of burnt umber to block in the field in the middle distance, behind the bushes. Put more burnt umber and a touch of orange into the wash, then use a stiff-bristled toothbrush to scrub the colour across the middle range of the grassy area. Mimic the textural lines of the grasses with your strokes.

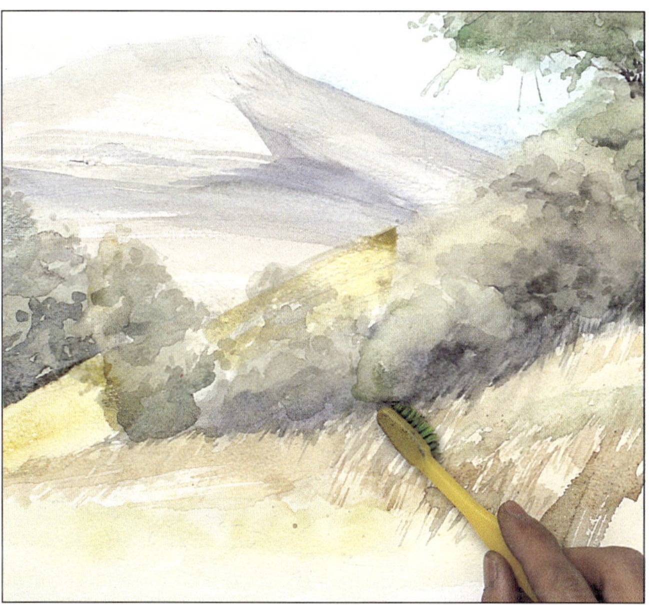

13 ▼ **Deepen the tree shadows** Add a touch of black to burnt umber and, using the tip of a No. 4 round brush, work in the deepest shadows on the trunk and branches of the tree. Use the black paint very sparingly, saving it for really striking details such as these.

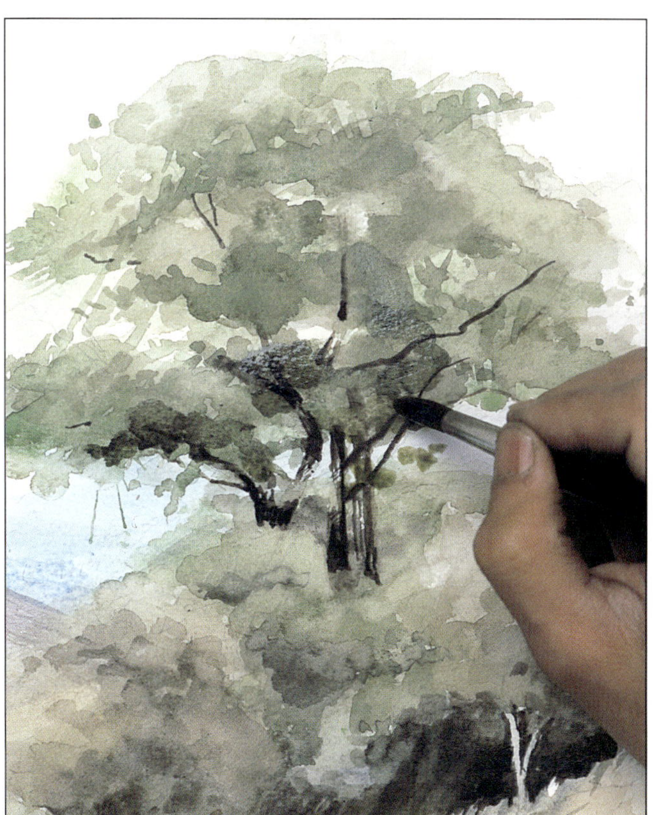

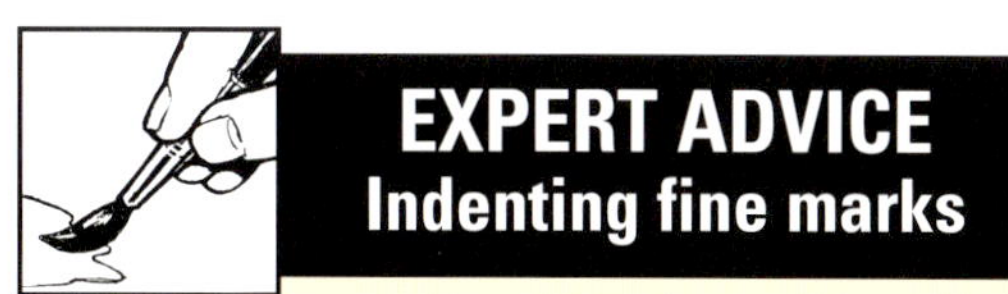

EXPERT ADVICE
Indenting fine marks

Before you paint the finest twig lines in the tree structure, use the pointed wooden end of a paint brush to press indentations into the surface of the watercolour paper. These will make tiny 'rivulets', which will hold the dark paint neatly in delicate twig shapes.

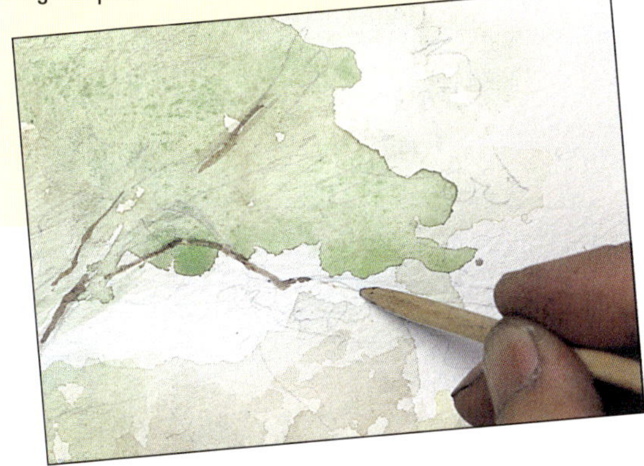

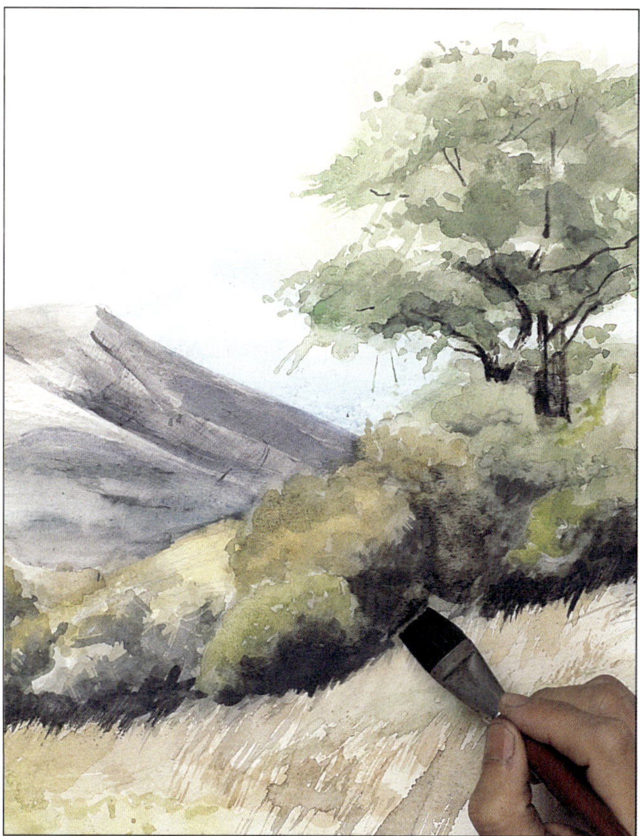

14 ▲ **Strengthen the features** Stand back from the picture and judge the tonal balance between the different areas. Using the No. 8 flat brush, strengthen the main features. Use a wash of ultramarine with touches of black and crimson to deepen the shadow areas on the mountain. Draw more ultramarine into the mix to establish the deepest shadows. Add ochre to emerald green in varying proportions to enliven the upper parts of the bushes.

15 ▼ Add distance detail Use the technique from step 10 to leach out colour from under one of the bushes. With a No. 00 round brush, wash in a mix of cadmium yellow with a touch of burnt umber. Once dry, paint black trunk details.

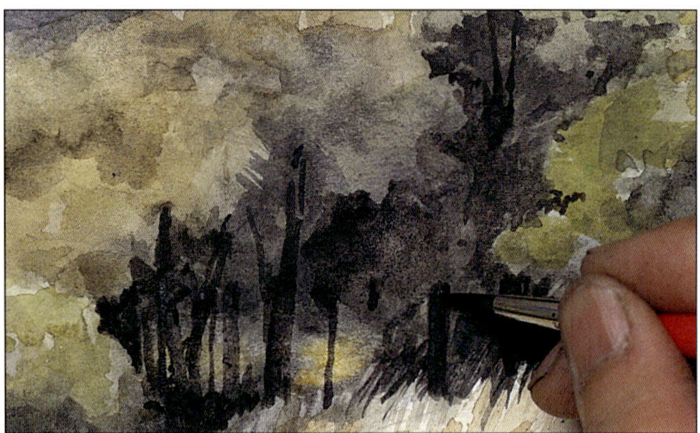

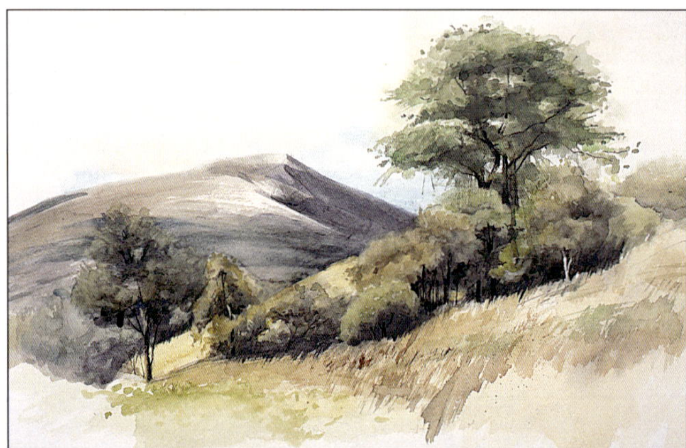

16 ▲ Finalize the balance Using the No. 8 flat brush and a mix of cobalt blue, ultramarine and emerald green, wash in the lower area of the mountain behind the distant trees. Add trunks and branches to the small tree on the left using the techniques from step 13. With the No. 6 flat brush and a mix of forest green and ultramarine, use a dabbing action to develop the leaf detail of both the small and large trees.

A FEW STEPS FURTHER

The composition is now complete, but you might wish to draw out some of the character of the scene with more work on fine detail, such as the grass and branches.

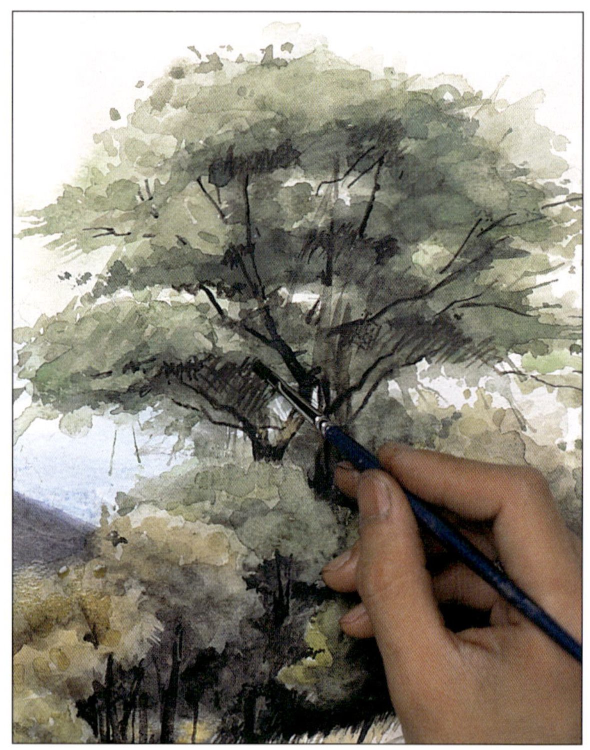

17 ▲ Develop the detail With a strong mix of burnt umber and black, and, using a No. 2 flat brush, paint in more branches and twigs on the largest tree. Strengthen existing branches to the front of the tree, but leave the ones nearer the back more washed out, to give a sense of three dimensions.

Express yourself

Focus on texture

The chosen scene is characterized by contrasting areas of smooth sky, sculpted mountain surface and detailed foliage areas. To focus on these textures rather than the colours, discard your paints and take up a piece of charcoal or, as here, a burnt umber soft pastel. Working with a loose style on NOT watercolour paper, capture the textures with a variety of strokes. Use soft, scribbling motions for the shadows, flowing marks for the contours of the mountain, and a hatching action for the grass. Use the charcoal or pastel on its side to block in larger areas of smooth shadow.

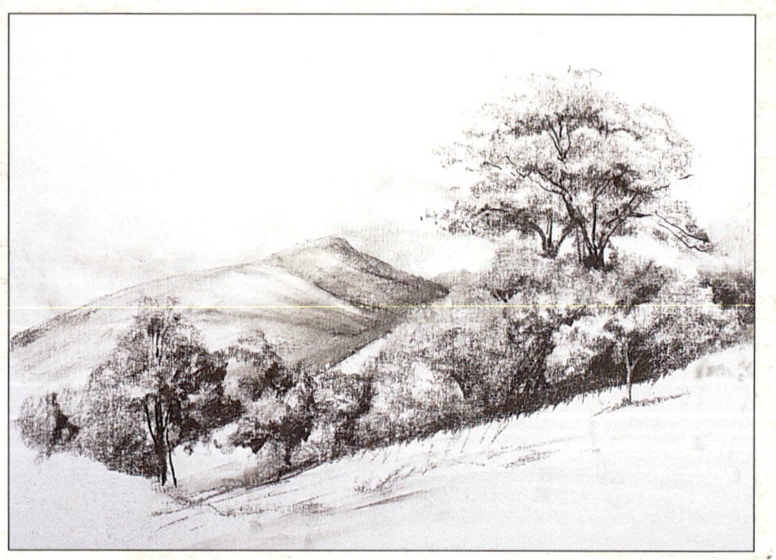

18▸ Add sweeps of colour As a finishing touch, you could convey the impression of the sweeping movements of a strong wind. Make up a strong mix of burnt umber and ochre. With a No. 4 round brush, make bold, slanting marks across the foreground area to suggest the blown and tumbled grasses.

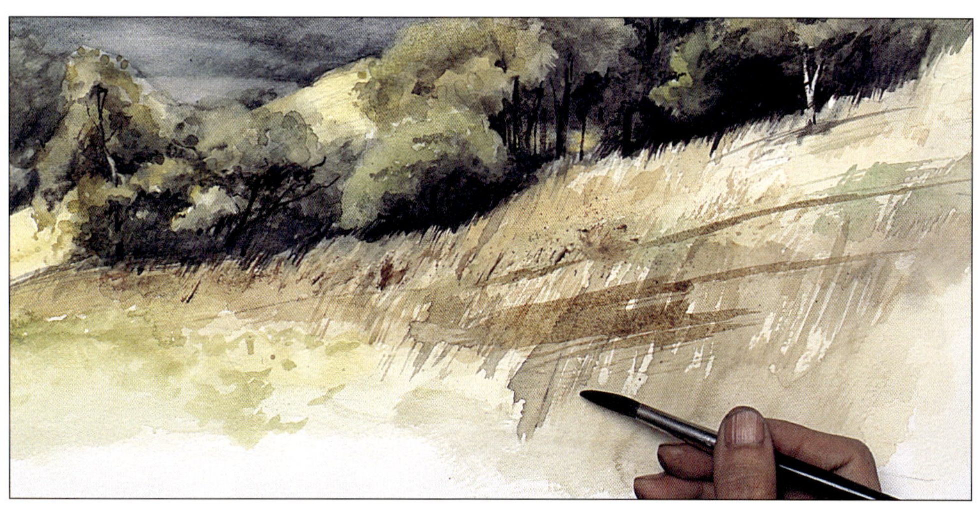

THE FINISHED PICTURE

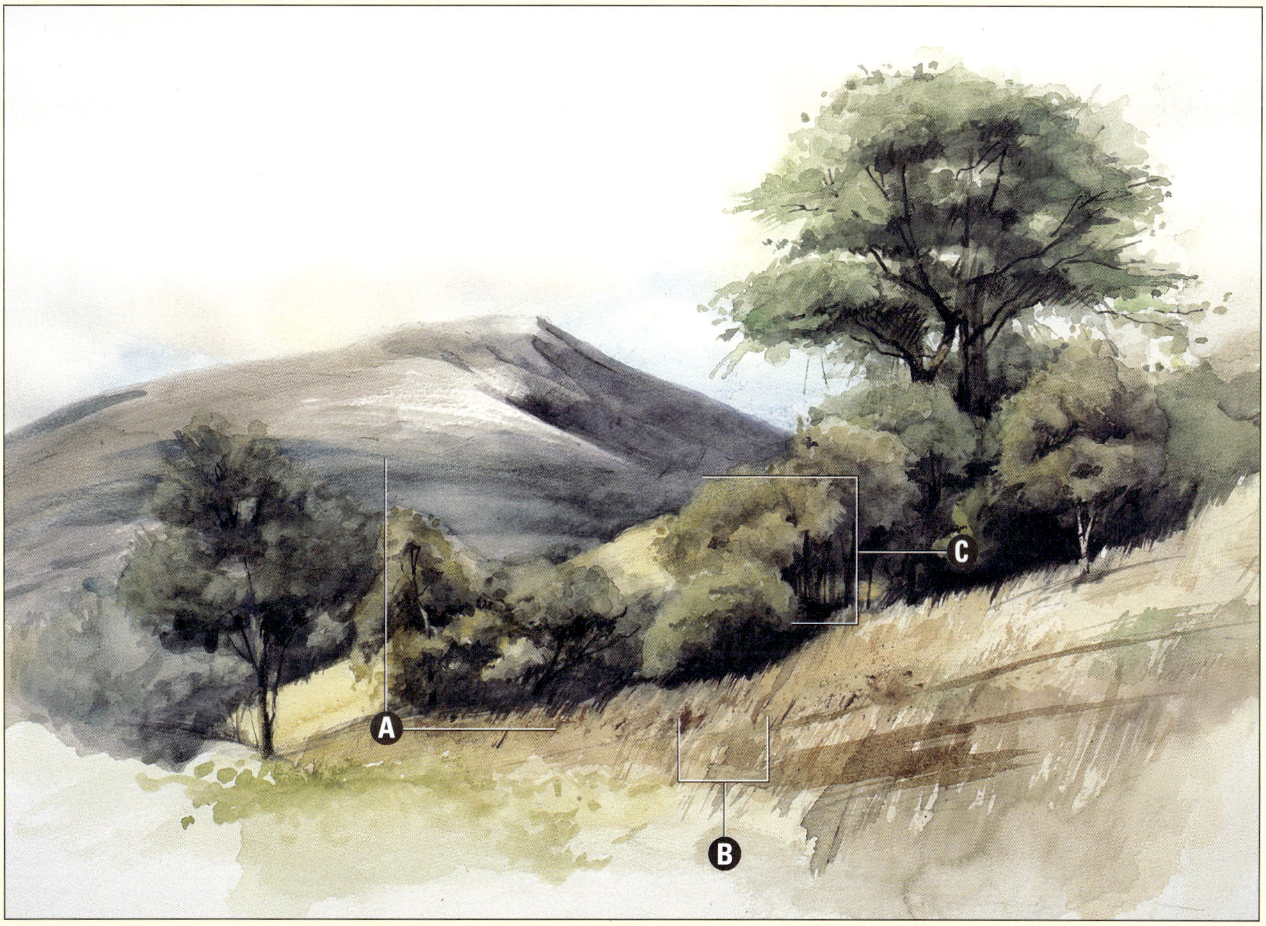

A Sense of distance
The cool blues and greens of the distant mountain recede, helping create a sense of depth. They contrast with the warmer ochres, oranges and browns in the foreground.

B Contrasting textures
Hatched brush strokes and spattered paint created a lively texture for the scrubby grassland. This contrasts with the smooth sky and sculpted surface of the mountain.

C Strong diagonal
The line of trees and the slope in the middle distance help create dynamic diagonals that cut across the picture. They provide a pleasing echo of the sloped profile of the mountain.

Applying paint without a brush

A brush isn't the only way of applying paint. You can use all kinds of other exciting tools and techniques.

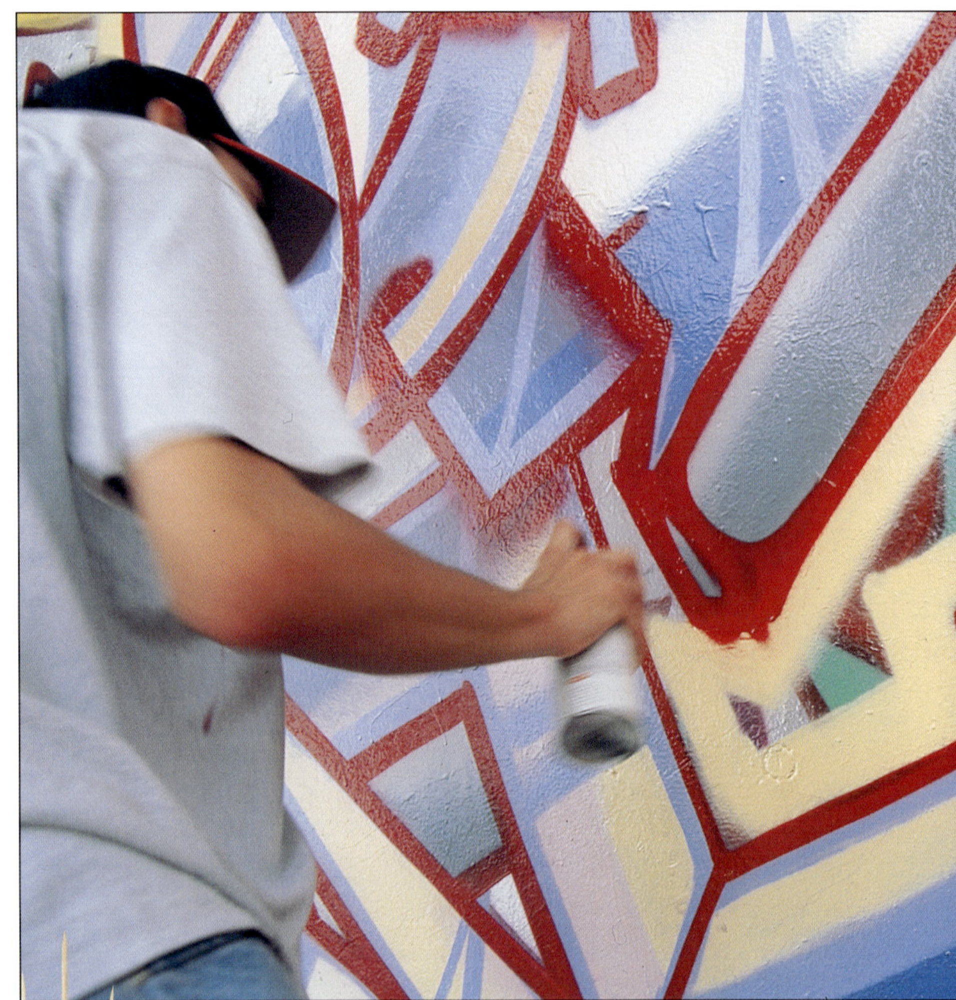

Whereas a regular brush is the most conventional tool for transferring paint onto paper, contemporary artists have developed exciting alternative ways of applying colour. Paint can be sprayed or sponged, dribbled or dabbed. It can be wiped on with a cloth or spread with a knife. In fact, any method of getting colour onto the paper or canvas is valid so long as it produces an effect you like.

Painting with a knife

Specially made painting knives have very pliable blades, which are good for moving paint around on the canvas. But you will need to practise. Initially you may find yourself scraping off the paint as quickly as you are putting it on.

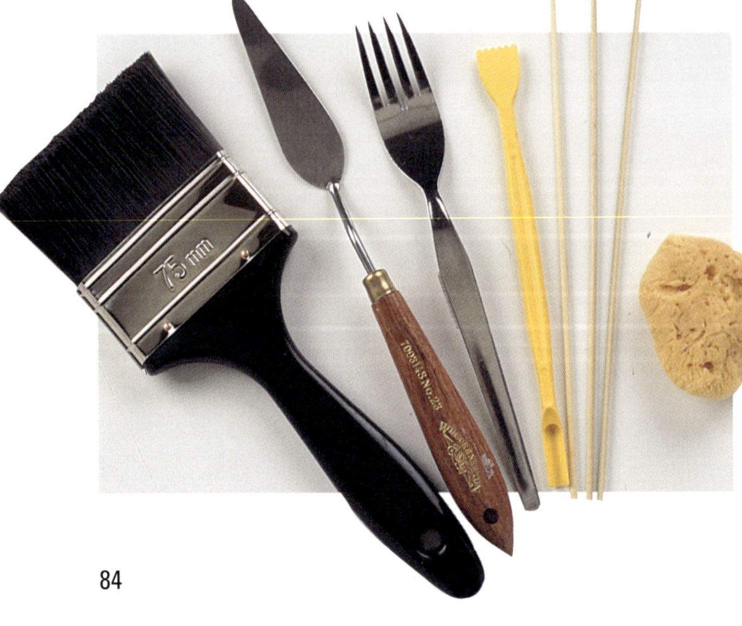

◄ All sorts of things that you wouldn't think of as typical painting tools can be used to apply colour or create texture. Left to right are: a decorator's brush; a painting knife; a fork; a scraper; bamboo skewers; and a natural sponge.

Try painting with different parts of the blade to see what effects you can achieve – use the tip of the knife to dab dots of colour, the edge of the knife to create lines, and so on.

Colour can be laid in thick, flat wedges rather as you would spread butter on a slice of bread. By using the knife in a circular motion you will get swirls and arcs of colour. Pat the paint with the flat side of the blade, and the result will be a stippled effect with the paint standing up in tiny peaks.

Obviously, for knife painting, the paint must be thick enough to hold its

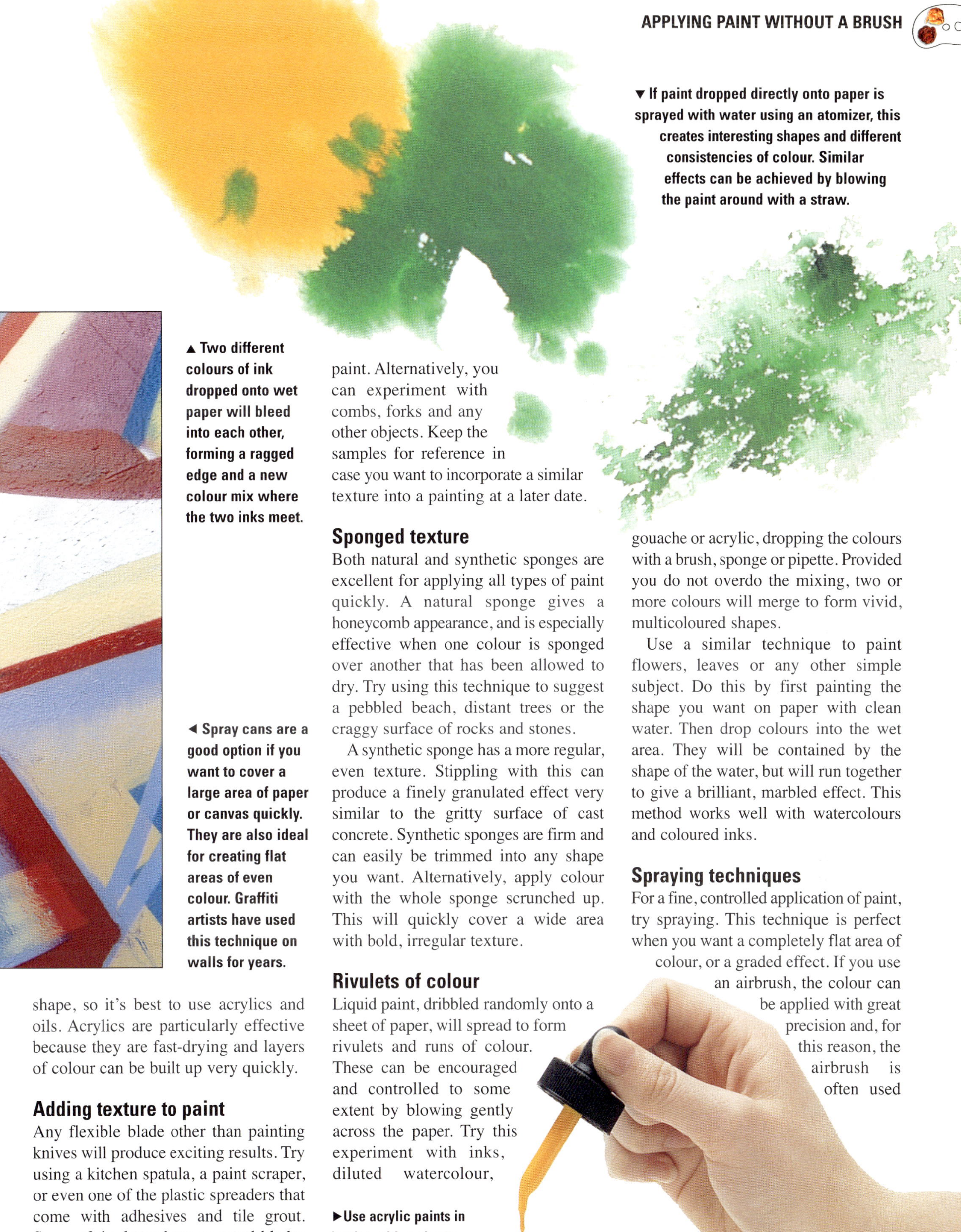

▼ If paint dropped directly onto paper is sprayed with water using an atomizer, this creates interesting shapes and different consistencies of colour. Similar effects can be achieved by blowing the paint around with a straw.

▲ Two different colours of ink dropped onto wet paper will bleed into each other, forming a ragged edge and a new colour mix where the two inks meet.

◀ Spray cans are a good option if you want to cover a large area of paper or canvas quickly. They are also ideal for creating flat areas of even colour. Graffiti artists have used this technique on walls for years.

▶ Use acrylic paints in bottles with a pipette attached to the lid for dropping colour directly onto the surface.

shape, so it's best to use acrylics and oils. Acrylics are particularly effective because they are fast-drying and layers of colour can be built up very quickly.

Adding texture to paint

Any flexible blade other than painting knives will produce exciting results. Try using a kitchen spatula, a paint scraper, or even one of the plastic spreaders that come with adhesives and tile grout. Some of the latter have serrated blades and will give a ridged texture.

The tip of a knife blade can be used to scratch textures and patterns into thick paint. Alternatively, you can experiment with combs, forks and any other objects. Keep the samples for reference in case you want to incorporate a similar texture into a painting at a later date.

Sponged texture

Both natural and synthetic sponges are excellent for applying all types of paint quickly. A natural sponge gives a honeycomb appearance, and is especially effective when one colour is sponged over another that has been allowed to dry. Try using this technique to suggest a pebbled beach, distant trees or the craggy surface of rocks and stones.

A synthetic sponge has a more regular, even texture. Stippling with this can produce a finely granulated effect very similar to the gritty surface of cast concrete. Synthetic sponges are firm and can easily be trimmed into any shape you want. Alternatively, apply colour with the whole sponge scrunched up. This will quickly cover a wide area with bold, irregular texture.

Rivulets of colour

Liquid paint, dribbled randomly onto a sheet of paper, will spread to form rivulets and runs of colour. These can be encouraged and controlled to some extent by blowing gently across the paper. Try this experiment with inks, diluted watercolour, gouache or acrylic, dropping the colours with a brush, sponge or pipette. Provided you do not overdo the mixing, two or more colours will merge to form vivid, multicoloured shapes.

Use a similar technique to paint flowers, leaves or any other simple subject. Do this by first painting the shape you want on paper with clean water. Then drop colours into the wet area. They will be contained by the shape of the water, but will run together to give a brilliant, marbled effect. This method works well with watercolours and coloured inks.

Spraying techniques

For a fine, controlled application of paint, try spraying. This technique is perfect when you want a completely flat area of colour, or a graded effect. If you use an airbrush, the colour can be applied with great precision and, for this reason, the airbrush is often used

PLAYING WITH TEXTURES

Once paint has been applied to a surface, it can be manipulated in any number of ways to create different textures and add interest to a painting. In the examples shown below, a natural sponge, a knife and a fork were used with different hand motions to produce a variety of effects. Experiment yourself using not only the tools mentioned, but also any other potential texture-making implements you may have to hand.

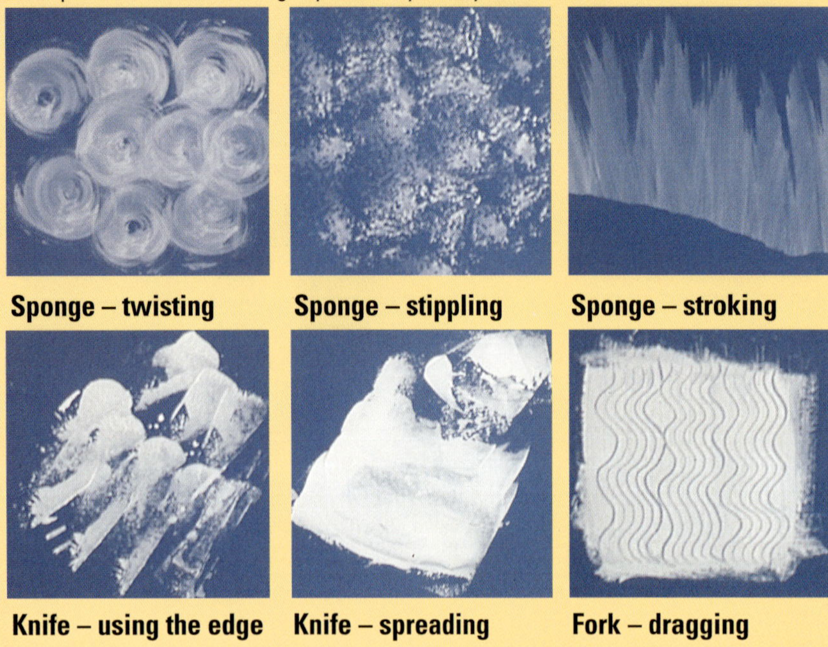

Sponge – twisting | **Sponge – stippling** | **Sponge – stroking**

Knife – using the edge | **Knife – spreading** | **Fork – dragging**

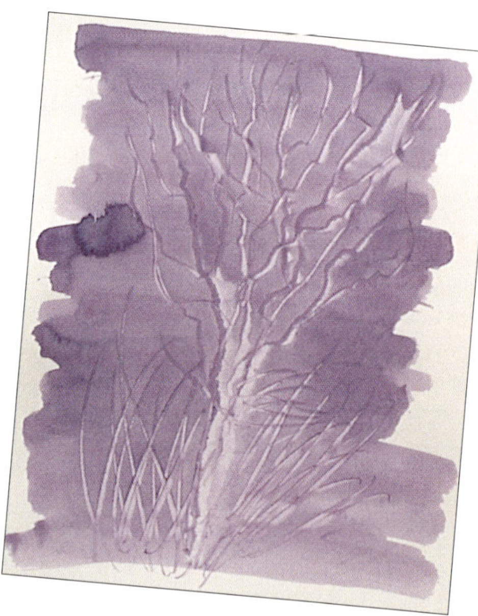

▲ **Create a ghostly tree by washing watercolour onto paper, then scraping out the shapes of the branches using the pointed tip of a painting knife.**

to produce works that are more like prints or photographs than paintings. Because of this, some artists find airbrushed colour very mechanical and prefer the more expressive quality of other textures.

Airbrushing is the most common means of spraying colour, but mouth atomizers can also be used. Colour from a jar or bottle is simply blown through a diffuser, generally giving a more speckled effect than airbrushed colour.

Rapid results

Sprayed colour can provide a useful starting point for a painting, perhaps for filling in a flat background or for painting a large expanse of sky in a landscape. The work can be continued with a brush.

◄ **If paper is first wetted, then paint dropped onto it, the colour will flood into the shape that has been created and be contained by it.**

For an instant result, you can't beat spray paints. Graffiti artists have been using them for years! They come in a wide range of colours including fluorescent and metallic finishes, and are either enamel, cellulose or acrylic based. These paints are perfect for large-scale work, especially for covering large areas quickly. Read the manufacturer's instructions for safety precautions.

Whether you are using an airbrush, atomizer or a spray can, you will need to practise. The trick is to keep the sprayed colour moving slowly and evenly across the surface. Linger too long in one spot and the paint starts to drip and will dry unevenly.

Spattering

To achieve a spattering effect, take a small decorating brush, dip the bristles in paint, then flick the colour briskly on to a sheet of paper. For a finer texture, try the same technique using an old toothbrush. First, dip the tips of the bristles in colour, then drag the bristles back with your finger before letting them go suddenly to flick the colour forward.

Spatter white and red onto a green background, and you have a meadow of poppies and daisies. Also, white paint spattered over blue, green or grey water gives a realistic impression of froth on breaking waves. Spattering can also be used effectively simply to break up an area of flat colour.

A vigorous spatter can cover a wide area, so if you want to aim at a specific spot, use a piece of newspaper to protect the areas you want to remain spatter-free.

Be selective

It is a good idea to experiment and to become familiar with as many approaches as possible before embarking on more ambitious paintings. Have fun and be as innovative and creative as you like at this stage. As a result you will have a mass of skills at your fingertips.

▼ **Spray paints come in a wide variety of colours, including fluorescent and metallic finishes.**

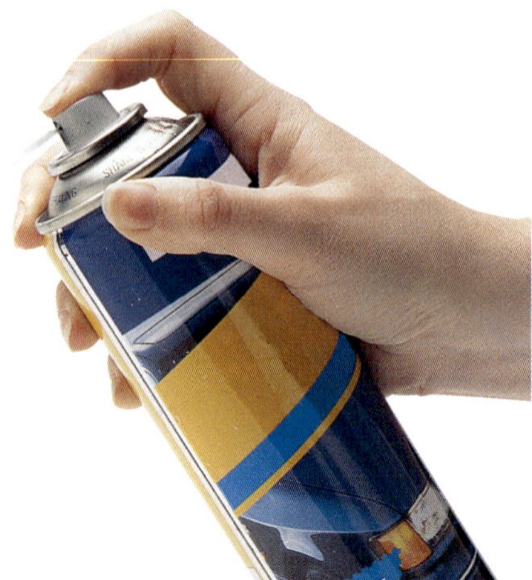

Seasonal palette – spring

A palette for springtime foliage should reflect the beautiful translucent greens of new leaves as well as the sunny yellows of flowering bulbs.

The green shades of spring are exceptionally fresh and vibrant. To capture them accurately in your painting, colour mixing should be kept to a minimum. Remember, the more colours you add to a mixture, the duller and more subdued the result will be. It is a good idea to limit your mixtures to no more than three colours, although, in practice, most spring greens can be mixed from simple two-colour combinations of one blue and one yellow.

Alternatively, why not introduce one of the manufactured greens into your spring landscape? Depending on the subject, there is a good selection of strong, vivid colours to choose from.

Mixing greens

The majority of greens to be found in a spring landscape contain a lot of yellow. Early flowers – including daffodils, forsythia and many crocuses – are also predominantly yellow in colour.

Later in the year, this emphasis changes. Summer flowers bloom in many different colours, and the foliage becomes darker with increased amounts of blue and other shades creeping into the leaf mixtures. For the first fresh leaves of spring, however, yellow is dominant in the garden and countryside, and as such is one of the most significant colours on the landscape artist's palette at this time of the year.

Important yellows

Cool, acid yellows are particularly useful for springtime subjects because, when mixed with blue, they create the sharp greens that are so characteristic of fresh leaves. The coolest yellows on the artist's colour wheel are those with a blue bias. A selection for your palette could include lemon yellow, cadmium yellow pale, Winsor lemon, cadmium lemon and aureolin.

Depending on the blue they are mixed with, these yellows will produce a range of the cool, vivid greens found in a typical spring landscape. The blues used in the watercolour of the verdant garden shown overleaf are ultramarine, cerulean blue and phthalo blue, but it is worth experimenting with other blues to extend your repertoire of greens.

Golden yellows – those with a red bias – produce warm or subtle greens, depending on your choice of blue. Such yellows include cadmium yellow deep, Indian yellow and yellow ochre.

For the garden scene, our artist chose cadmium lemon as a cool yellow, mixing it with one or other of the blues on the palette to make the pale greens in the foreground. For the warmer greens and yellow flowers, yellow ochre was added or used instead of cadmium lemon.

Bought greens

As a general rule, a mixed colour is more easily integrated into a composition than a single colour used directly from the tube. This is particularly so with bought greens, which can be strident and stand out jarringly from the natural colours of a rural landscape.

However, fresh spring foliage is often so bright that it really does show up against the surrounding colours. With such a subject, breaking the rules can pay off and a few splashes of a clear, brilliant green, applied unmixed, will capture this dramatic effect exactly.

Palette for new foliage

This selection of watercolours in greens, yellows and blues provides all the colours you need for the fresh new foliage and flowers in the garden picture (overleaf). The two green colours, sap green and viridian, were used neat in places. However, the main bulk of foliage was created by mixing the two yellows with the three blues to create a range of subtle, harmonious greens.

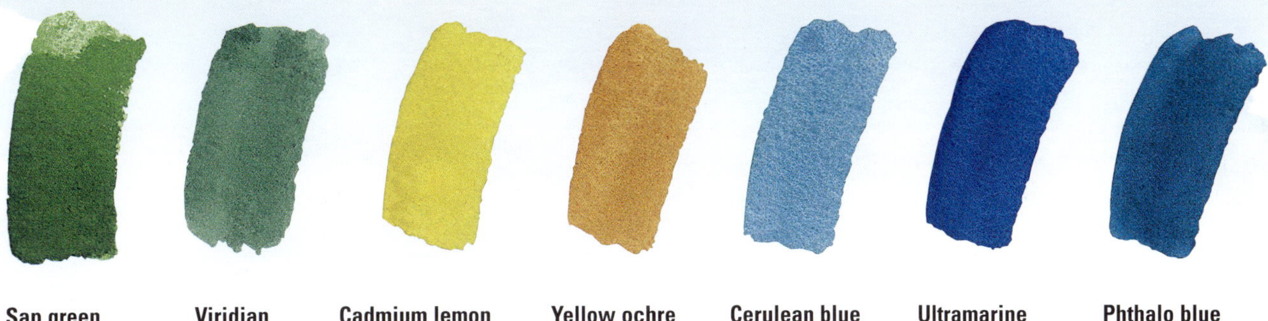

Sap green **Viridian** **Cadmium lemon** **Yellow ochre** **Cerulean blue** **Ultramarine** **Phthalo blue**

GARDEN IN FIRST LEAF

The palette shown on the preceding page was used to achieve the range of greens in this watercolour garden. Pale foliage and flowers in the foreground were painted thinly to allow the white paper to show through. Deeper greens were achieved by using stronger colour mixes with the addition of gum arabic to enhance the paint surface.

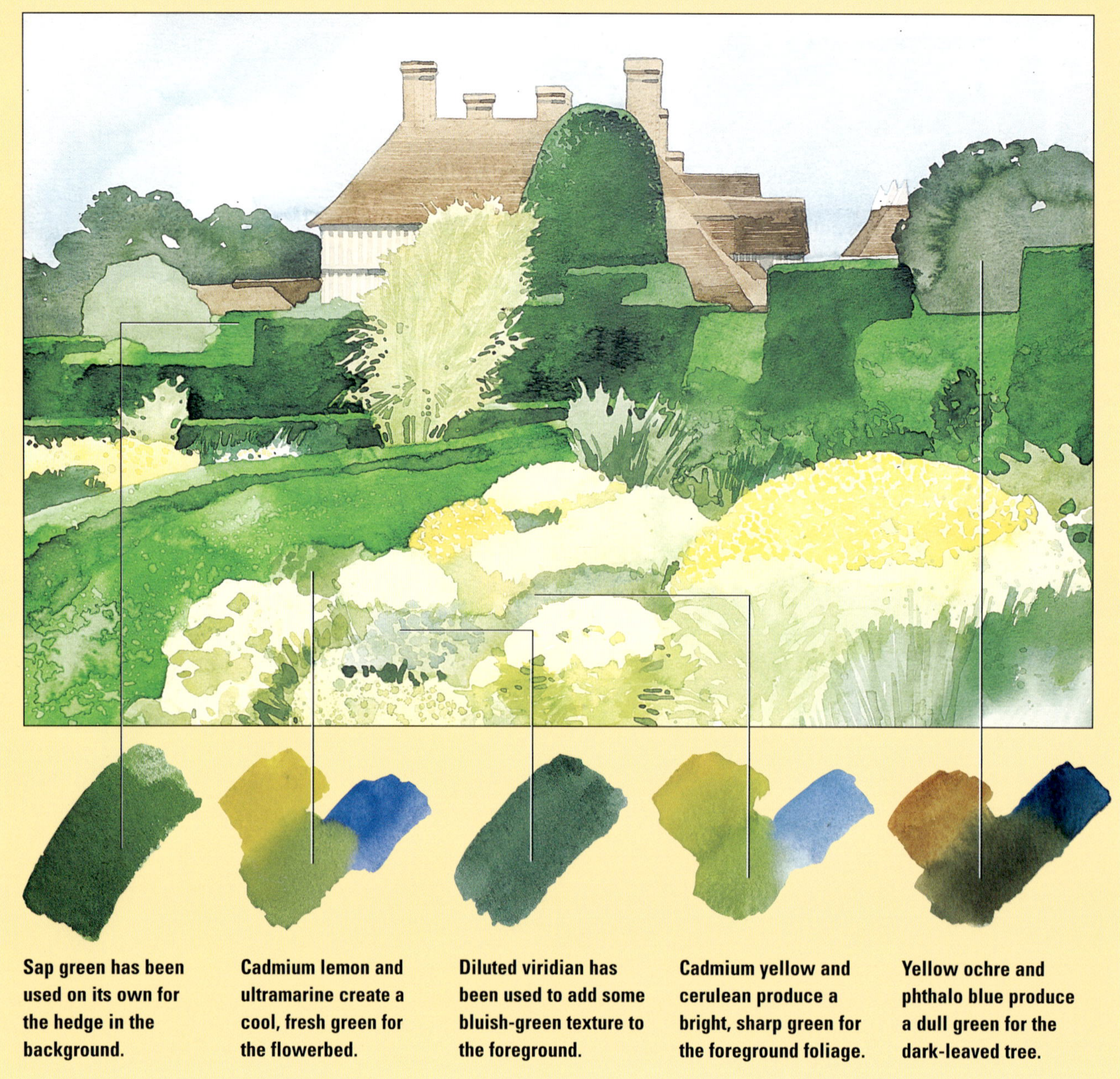

Sap green has been used on its own for the hedge in the background.

Cadmium lemon and ultramarine create a cool, fresh green for the flowerbed.

Diluted viridian has been used to add some bluish-green texture to the foreground.

Cadmium yellow and cerulean produce a bright, sharp green for the foreground foliage.

Yellow ochre and phthalo blue produce a dull green for the dark-leaved tree.

Useful bought greens include emerald, phthalo green, sap green and green-gold. Viridian is also an option, but this must be used in very small quantities only. Applied on its own, viridian can dominate the composition.

In this painting, the hedges and many of the background plants are painted in varying tones of pure sap green. Instead of adding a darker pigment for the shadows, which could dull the colour, gum arabic is mixed with undiluted sap green to create areas of deep green shadow in the hedge.

Transparent colour

Lit by the low sunlight of early spring, colours can appear particularly bright and luminous. With watercolour, you can capture this translucent effect perfectly by applying the paint in a thin layer, so that the white paper shows through the wash of colour. Avoid using white paint in a spring landscape. Adding white to watercolour tends to produce a chalky, opaque effect – particularly unwelcome when you are striving to capture the fresh, sunny colours of spring. To create white flowers and highlights, do as the artist has done in this picture and leave these as patches of unpainted white paper.

Seasonal palette – summer

In summer, the brilliance of the flowers and the diversity of foliage shades offer the artist the perfect opportunity to use a vivid and varied palette.

For the landscape painter, summer is a liberating season. The days are at their longest and, weather permitting, painting on the spot for hours on end can be a real delight. There is time to think about colours, to choose a palette, and to make colour notes and sketches if necessary.

There are no rules or restrictions on summer colours. Unlike spring, with its predominance of cool, yellow-green foliage, or autumn with its mellow earth colours, summer has no particular palette to call its own. The colours can be as bright and varied as the artist chooses or as the subject suggests.

Summer foliage

During the summer months, leaves lose the sharpness of colour that causes many spring trees and plants to look very similar. The greens begin to diversify and each one takes on its own characteristics. Leaves are often tinged with a variety of colours, including silvery grey, blue, mauve and pink. As a result, it becomes easier to spot the different greens both in the garden and in the landscape, and to pick out the local colours of the leaves.

Although greens can be mixed from the yellows and blues on the basic palette, summer is a good opportunity to try out new colours. For foliage, sap green or Hooker's green provides a good starting point. However, if you feel experimental, introduce one or two slightly more offbeat colours, such as cobalt turquoise – a strong blue-green – or green-gold – a glowing, warm shade.

Rendering flowers

For those who love to paint flowers, summer colours are often intensely brilliant and beautiful. Sometimes the colours of nature defy mixing, and only a bought colour from the manufacturer's chart can match the brightness of the subject. This is particularly so when you are painting orange or violet flowers because versions of these mixed from colours on the standard palette are rarely as bright as manufactured equivalents.

Experiment with new colours. Many summer flowers are crimson or deep vivid pinks. Again, these colours cannot be easily mixed, so try a bought version, such as carmine, permanent rose, rose madder or magenta. Not only are these cool reds beautiful in their own right, but they are also excellent in mixtures, especially for capturing the elusive violets and oranges. For example, the orange of the Californian poppies in the picture is a mixture of permanent rose and cadmium lemon.

To capture the effect of light with paint is always a challenge. This is particular the case in summer, when sunlight often plays a dominant role. The transparent quality of watercolour is ideal for painting summer scenes, such as the on the next page, capturing both the brightness and the translucency of the petals. Even though the garden border is dense and colourful, note how the artist has still left quite a lot of white paper showing through to help capture the luminosity of summer light.

Oils and acrylics

There is no reason why a similarly colourful effect cannot be painted using oils and acrylics. The secret to success is to keep colours clean and the mixtures simple. An organized palette will help you to achieve this. Changing your turps or water frequently will also help to ensure that you retain clear, bright colours in your finished work.

Bright, summery colours

There is no single definitive palette for summer scenes – however, make sure you include some bright, hot colours. For the painting on the next page, the artist created the warm flowers from cadmium red, permanent rose and lemon yellow. For the foliage, sap green was the basis of most of the mixes, with the addition of sepia, lemon yellow and phthalo blue.

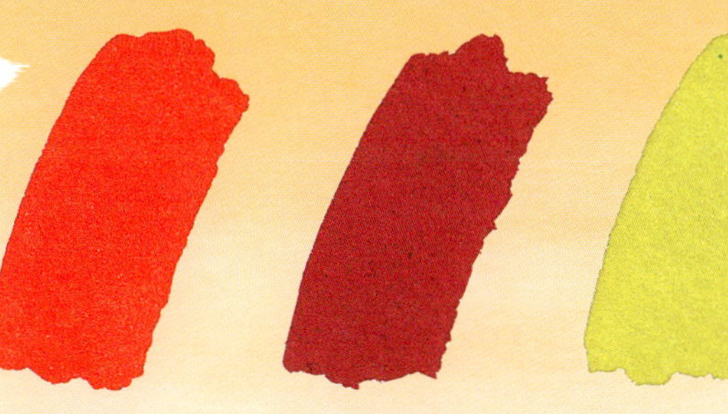
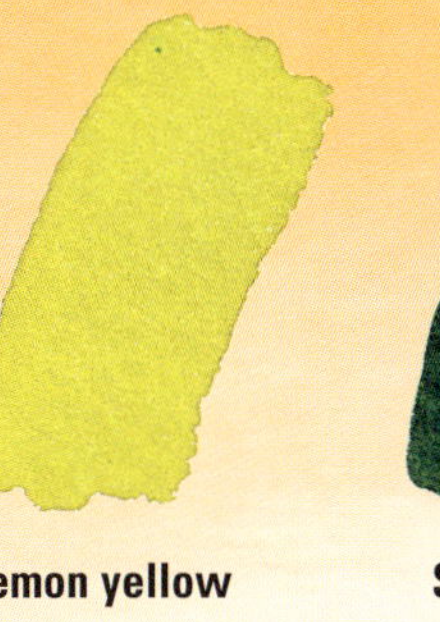
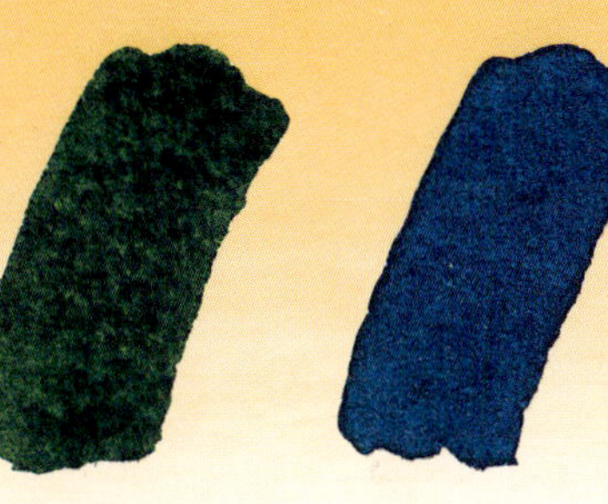
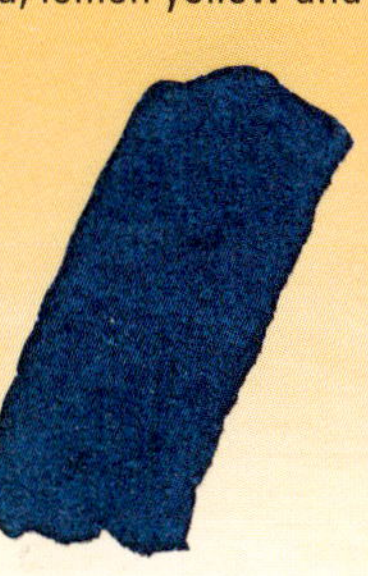

Cadmium red | Permanent rose | Lemon yellow | Sap green | Phthalo blue | Sepia

A GARDEN IN FULL BLOOM

A garden border in summer creates a wonderfully exciting picture – but make sure you don't get too carried away with your bright colours. As always, you should check the colour and tone of each flower carefully. In this picture, for instance, note the delicacy of the pink used for the foxgloves and the subtle changes in the mixes for the poppies in the foreground.

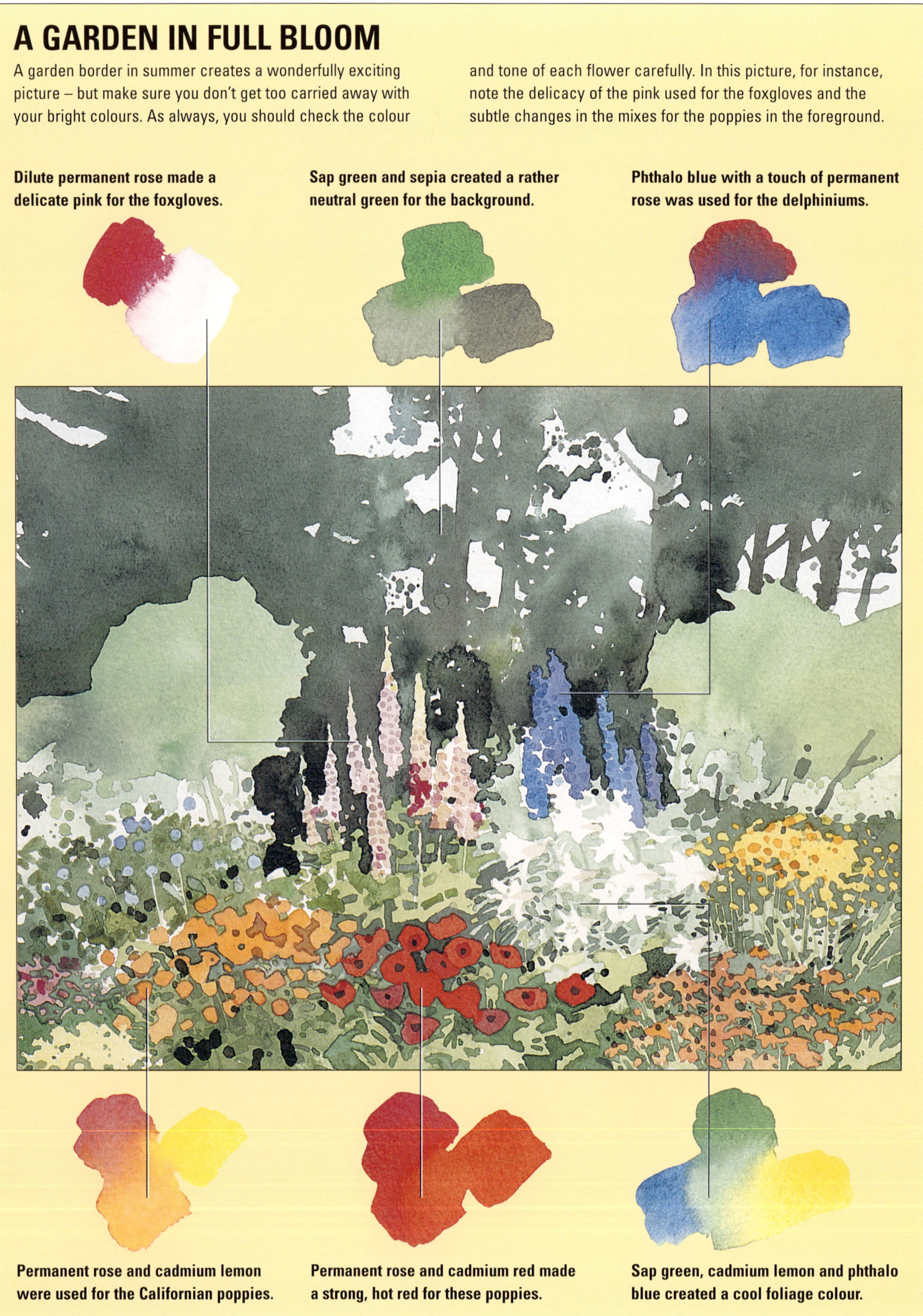

Dilute permanent rose made a delicate pink for the foxgloves.

Sap green and sepia created a rather neutral green for the background.

Phthalo blue with a touch of permanent rose was used for the delphiniums.

Permanent rose and cadmium lemon were used for the Californian poppies.

Permanent rose and cadmium red made a strong, hot red for these poppies.

Sap green, cadmium lemon and phthalo blue created a cool foliage colour.

Seasonal palette – autumn

Whether a riot of copper, crimson and gold, or a restrained display of browns, the colours of autumn leaves define the countryside at this time of year

Depending on the weather and prevailing climate, autumnal trees can be either brilliantly coloured or neutral and understated. New England, in the United States, is famous for its spectacular fall, where the colours of a typical autumn are crimson, orange and gold, often set off by a bright blue sky.

Sometimes, however, autumnal tints are subtler. In a damp climate, the greyness of the weather is often reflected in the colours of the leaves. An overcast day or an autumn mist can make them appear subdued and restrained. Although less dramatic than bold reds and yellows, understated colours can be equally beautiful and will often include mellow earth tones such as umbers and ochres, browns, greys and dark greens.

A quiet scene

For the painting shown on the next page, the artist deliberately chose a rather muted scene. There is no direct sunlight to bring out the colours, so the mixtures are quiet and restrained.

Subtle colours are not necessarily dull colours, however. The bronzes and coppers seen in this painting were mixed from a full palette of pigments, including cadmium red, alizarin crimson and cadmium yellow. The brightness of the palette colours is reflected in the glowing transparency of the mixtures. There are cooler colours, too, particularly in the shadows, sky and green grass.

Be experimental

As the colour swatches on the right demonstrate, autumnal hues can be mixed from the colours you are likely to have on your standard palette. However, if you feel like being adventurous, now is a good time to experiment with more unusual pigments.

For example, brown madder is a rich brownish-purple – an excellent colour for capturing mellow, autumnal tones. Earthy reds – including Venetian red, Indian red and terra rosa – are all warm and natural, ideal for autumn leaves and trees. For shadows, try Mars violet or purple lake. Alternatively, if you have ever wanted an excuse to use the exotic-sounding caput mortuum violet or perylene maroon, these are cool purples that are excellent in autumnal mixtures.

Painting trees

The foliage on any tree is usually multi-coloured, visible as tiny flecks of colour and tone that represent the leaves. The palest flecks are the highlights – reflections caused by the bright light on the leaves; darker flecks are the shadows on the underside of the foliage. A helpful technique for capturing the effect of broken colour in foliage is that which was employed by the Pointillist painters Georges Seurat (1859–91) and Paul Signac (1863–1935).

These artists were referred to as Pointillists because of the manner in which they applied colour. For example, instead of mixing red and yellow to make orange, and thereby losing the intensity of the colours, they would dab separate dots, or points, of red and yellow onto the picture. The two colours merge in the eye of the viewer to create a vibrant orange. A similar approach was used in the autumn landscape here. Loosely dabbing on small patches of colour gives an impression of leaves swaying in the breeze.

Hues for autumn

Although the autumnal landscape shown overleaf is characterized by subtle browns and gentle greens, the artist chose a full palette of warm and cool watercolours to create it (below). You might also try grabbing a handful of the leaves you intend to paint, matching their hues to paint colours, then adding these to your palette.

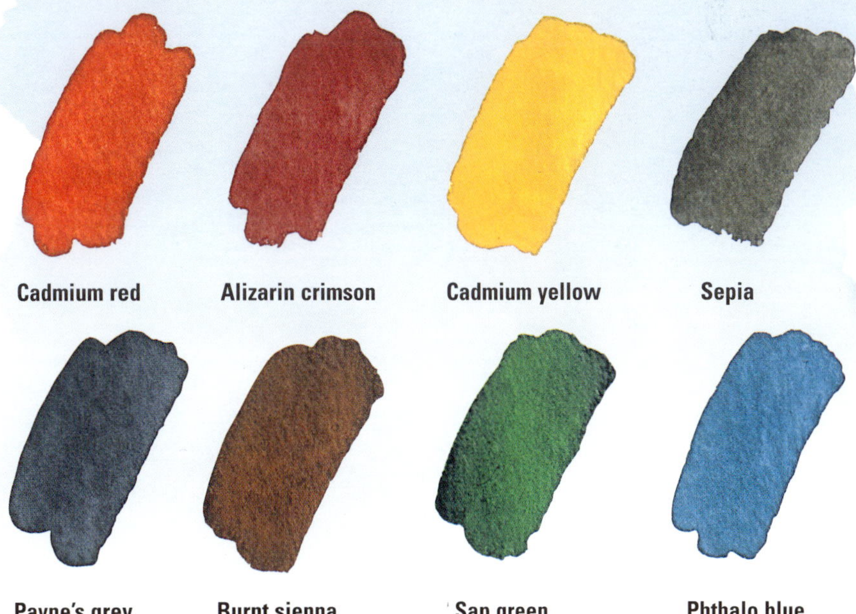

MIXING COLOURS FOR AN AUTUMN SCENE

Not all trees turn brilliant shades of red and gold in the autumn. Here, you can see how the brighter colours in the basic autumn palette on the previous page have been toned down to create the mainly brown shades in this peaceful scene. The brown leaves are set against a pale blue sky mixed from dilute phthalo blue with a little burnt sienna to subdue the colour.

A basic leaf colour is made from cadmium red, cadmium yellow and sepia.

Redder leaves are mixed from cadmium red, burnt sienna and cadmium yellow.

For the distant trees, a mix of burnt sienna and cadmium yellow is used.

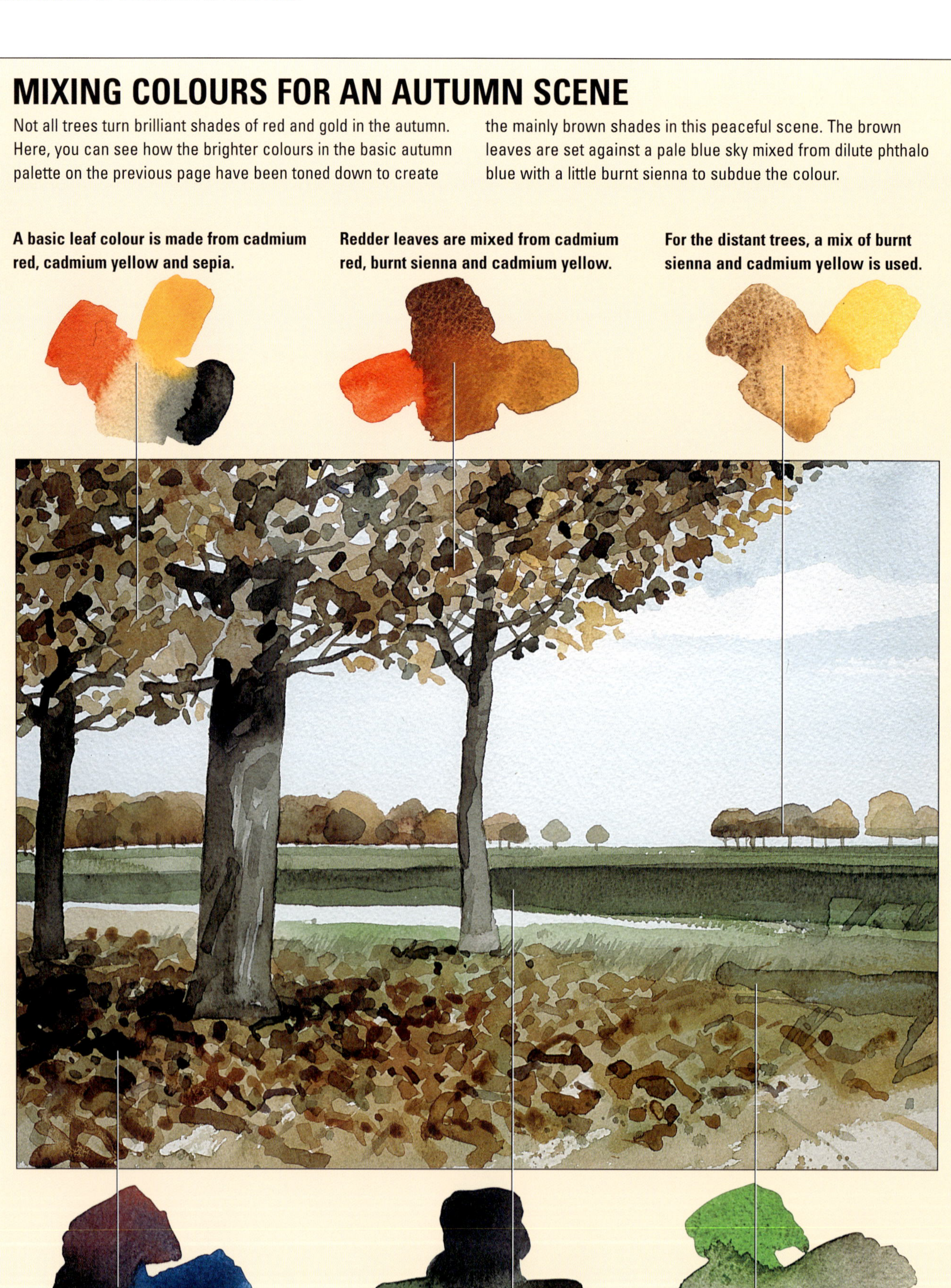

The deep, cool shadows are created with alizarin crimson and phthalo blue.

Dark green tones are made from sap green, Payne's grey and sepia.

A muted green is achieved by neutralizing sap green with sepia.

Seasonal palette – winter

Every season demands a different palette – for a winter landscape, all you need is a small selection of subdued colours.

Even if it isn't covered with snow, the winter landscape rarely contains bright colours. Although bold red and yellow pigments may be invaluable in the other seasons, they are usually unnecessary in winter. Even bright greens may have limited use, as winter foliage tends to be dull and subdued – particularly the dark evergreen of conifers and the faded, grey-green of grass that has lost its summer freshness.

The scene overleaf was painted with a palette of just five muted watercolours (see below), with the addition of a little white gouache in the final stages. The result is a moody, realistic evocation of a rather forbidding winter landscape.

Winter light

With so few local colours present in a typical winter landscape, your choice of colours will be dictated largely by the weather and the light. On a cloudy day, the landscape can almost appear monochromatic – simply a range of blacks, whites and greys with subtle tinges of green, blue and brown. In this case, the emphasis may be on the most neutral colours – Payne's grey and burnt umber.

This was certainly the case for the scene overleaf. The ultramarine used for the sky was toned down with a lot of Payne's grey. And the sap green used for the trees was neutralized by adding both Payne's grey and burnt umber.

Coloured shadows

If you're painting a winter scene in sunshine, however, the brighter colours of the palette come into their own. The sun brings out a spectrum of blues and warm golds that require the addition of ultramarine and burnt sienna. And grass and foliage that are lit by direct sunlight will demand large amounts of sap green in your mixes.

As the sun appears closer to the horizon in winter than it does in summer, it creates characteristic longer shadows. These shadows often contain a lot of colour, particularly blues and greens. Against the bright whiteness of snow, they can appear very attractive – translucent and alive with colour.

Contrasting tones

Snow creates extreme tonal contrasts. The lightest tone is the dazzling whiteness of the snow itself; the darkest tone will be created by the silhouettes of trees and other objects in what is an otherwise white landscape.

Watercolour is the perfect medium for a wintry subject because you can use the unpainted white paper to represent the snow. Inevitably, the bright whiteness of snow makes everything else in the landscape appear dark in comparison. For example, in this painting there is very little detail in the pine trees and fence posts. They are painted as dark silhouettes which stand out as sharp shapes against the white background.

Opaque white

In addition to the five watercolours on the winter palette, our artist introduced a little opaque white in the final stages of the painting. This can be seen in the spattered snowflakes, which lend a decorative and realistic touch to the scene – an effective detail, which you can add to any snowy landscape.

Simply spatter the finished painting lightly with white and grey (made up from a mixture of white and palette mud). The white will show up against the dark

Five-colour palette

A palette of five watercolours was used for the winter landscape on the right. The slightly cool Payne's grey is a good starting point for all your mixes. Use it with ultramarine for the sky and cold shadow colours; with sap green to capture foliage; and with burnt umber and burnt sienna for the warmer tones.

Payne's grey

Ultramarine

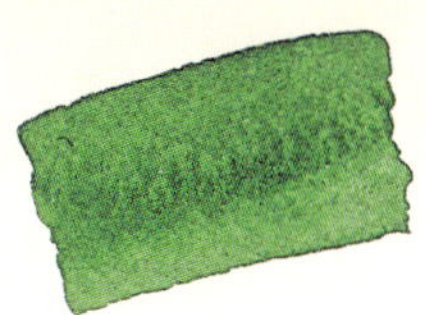

Sap green

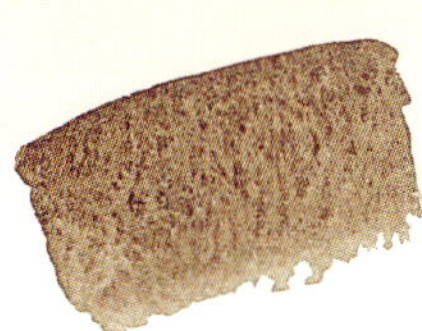

Burnt sienna

Burnt umber

SNOW-COVERED HILLS

Three of the main colour mixes used by the artist for this winter landscape are shown below. Note how the strength of these mixes has been varied in the picture. For instance, the ultramarine and Payne's grey mix is quite dark below the trees, a little lighter in the sky and almost transparent in the bottom left corner. The use of the same mix across the picture helps to give it a visual unity – while varying the dilution prevents it from becoming too repetitive.

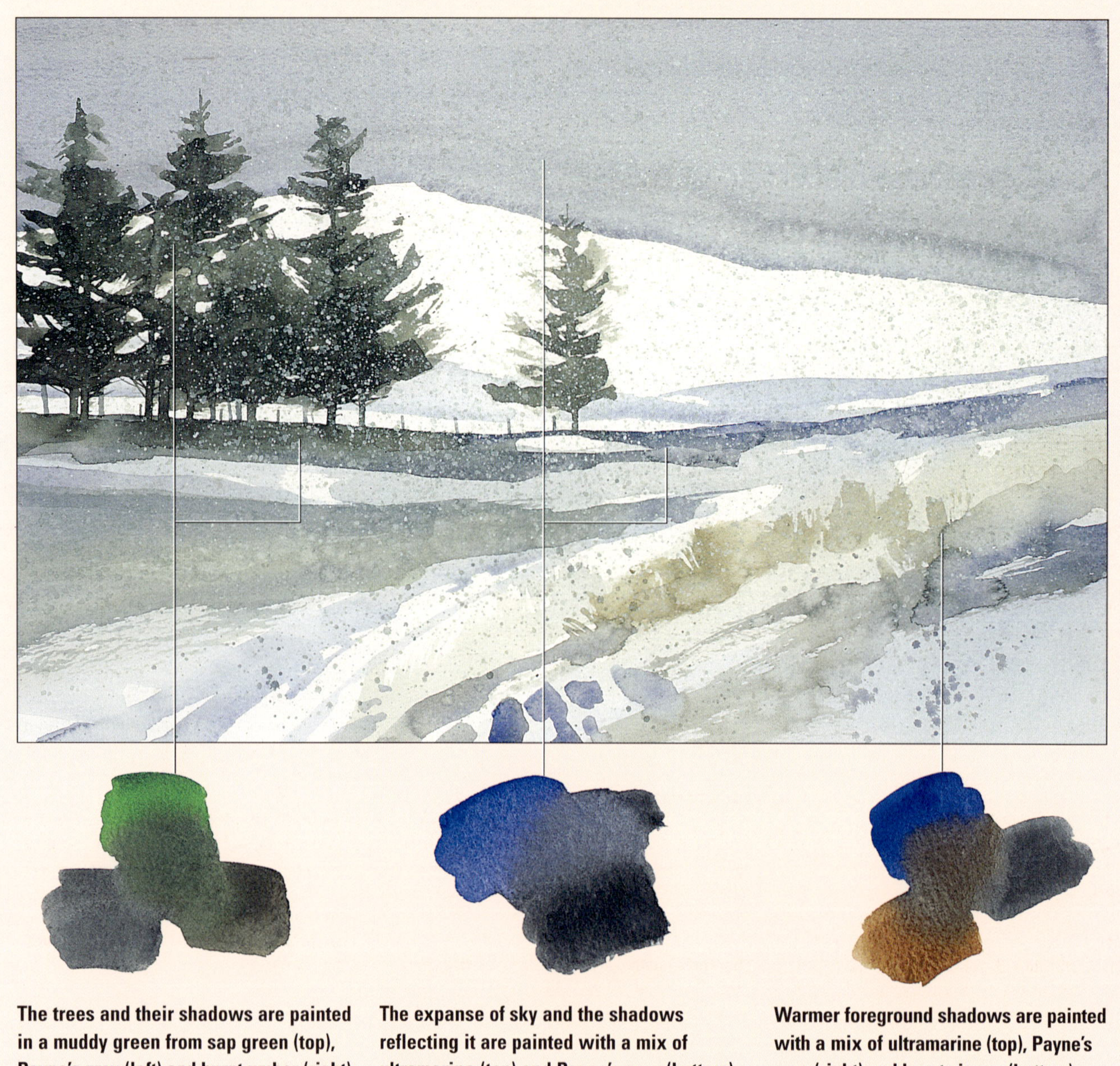

The trees and their shadows are painted in a muddy green from sap green (top), Payne's grey (left) and burnt umber (right).

The expanse of sky and the shadows reflecting it are painted with a mix of ultramarine (top) and Payne's grey (bottom).

Warmer foreground shadows are painted with a mix of ultramarine (top), Payne's grey (right) and burnt sienna (bottom).

tones; the grey stands out from the white snow. You can create a full-scale blizzard by spattering across the entire picture!

Use either white gouache or Chinese white watercolour for this finishing touch. Remember, however, that white paints contain chalk. When white is added to other pigments the resulting colours become pale and chalky, and this can destroy the natural transparency of watercolour paints. Unless you positively want a cloudy, opaque colour, don't mix white with other colours. Reserve it for special effects only.

Cold-weather warning

Painting winter landscapes is exhilarating, but it can also be very cold. You will need to protect yourself against the elements with warm clothing. A padded waistcoat or coat lining keeps your body warm, but leaves your arms free to manoeuvre the paint brush. Fingerless gloves are another good idea, keeping your hands warm, but your fingers free.

Still, the fact remains that painting on-the-spot winter landscapes is a chilly business. A practical, more comfortable alternative to working outdoors is to paint a view from a window. Another option is to make rapid on-the-spot colour sketches and take photos, then do the painting at home.

GLOSSARY

Abstract A style of painting where colour and form (and sometimes the materials and support) make up the subject of the painting rather than it representing objects or people.

Accent A detail, brushstroke, or area of colour placed in a painting for emphasis.

Acrylic paint A type of paint made with synthetic resin as the medium (liquid) to bind the pigment (colour), rather than natural oils such as linseed used in oil paints. It has the advantage of drying faster than oil paint and being water soluble.

Blending Creating a gentle and gradual transition from one colour or tone to another so that no sharp divisions are apparent.

Blotting an absorbent material such as tissues or paper towels, or a squeezed out brush, to pick up and lighten a wet or damp wash.

Binder The substance in a paint which holds together (binds) the pigment and makes the paint stick to whatever it's painted on.

Cool colours Blues, greens, and purples are considered cool colours.

Complementary colours Two colours on opposite sides of the colour wheel. Complementary colours are contrasting and stand out against each other.

Drawing grid A grid of squares made for transferring a sketch proportionately onto a large-scale support.

Dry Brush A painting technique in which, as the name suggests, a little bit of paint is put on a dry brush. When applied, it produces a broken, scratchy effect.

Easel A frame for holding a drawing while the artist works on it. A good sketching easel allows the drawing to be held securely in any position from horizontal to vertical.

Expressionism A movement of the early 20th century that started in Germany in which the artist aims to express their emotions through the use of vivid colours and strong, distorted lines.

Etching An illustration made by drawing through a wax covering on a metal plate, which is then put into acid to eat away (etch) the metal where it has been uncovered. The plate is then inked and printed. Also the process of creating such an illustration.

Eye-level The plane of vision from the viewer to the horizon, i.e. the horizontal line.

Flat colour A section of colour applied in a uniform tone and hue.

Flat wash Any area of a painting where a wash of single colour and value is painted in a series of multiple, overlapping strokes following the flow of the paint. A slightly tilted surface aids the flow of your washes.

Glaze The term used mostly for oils and acrylics for a thin, transparent layer of paint. Glazes are used on top of one another to build up depth and modify colours in a painting.

Gouache Water-soluble paints differing from watercolours in that gouache uses glue to bind the pigments and the lighter tones contain white pigment, which means they're opaque rather than transparent. The white in watercolour comes from the paper.

Graphite stick A thick graphite pencil, used for large-scale work.

Hard edge A hard edge is the term used when the edge of an object is painted in a well defined or definite way. A soft edge is when it is painted so that it disappears or fades into the background.

Half tone Any of the tones in a painting between the darks and the highlights.

Highlight Those parts of a painting that have the lightest tone. In watercolour painting, the white paper is left unpainted to create white highlights.

Horizontal line Where the land (or sea) and sky meet. A term used in perspective.

Hue The actual colour of something, such as red, green, or blue. What we generally, but less technically correct, call colour.

Impressionism A movement that started in France around 1870 which attempted to capture fleeting impressions, particularly the changing light on a surface.

Masking out A technique for leaving areas of paper unpainted when applying washes by first covering them with paper or masking fluid.

Mixed media A painting which combines different painting and drawing materials and methods. Any materials can be used, such as pages from magazines, newspaper, photographs, fabric, soil, or packaging.

Oil Paint A type of paint made with natural oils such as linseed, walnut, or poppy, as the medium to bind the pigment.

Palette The surface on which an artist lays out their colours (paints) as well as the range of colours an artist works with.

Pastel Ground pigment mixed with chalk and gum or oil, then shaped into drawing sticks. Pastels cannot be mixed on a palette like paints, but are mixed on the paper by overlaying or blending.

Primary colours The three colours – red, blue and yellow – that cannot be produced by mixing other colours.

Resist Any material, usually wax or grease crayons, that repel paint or dyes. Lithography is a grease (ink) and water (wet stone or plate) resist printing technique. Batik is a wax resist fabric artform.

Scumbling Dragging a dense or opaque colour across another colour creating a rough texture.

Secondary colours Colours obtained by mixing two primary colours green, violet, and orange.

Sketch A rough or loose visualization of a subject or composition.

Sgraffito A technique in which dried paint or pastel is scratched or scraped off to reveal the colour below. Often used for textural effects.

Stippling A method of painting or drawing that involves the application of tiny spots of colour to create an area of tone by stabbing and dotting with the tip of a brush or pastel, for example.

Texture The actual or virtual representation of different surfaces, paint applied in a manner that breaks up the continuous colour or tone.

Thumbnail Sketch Small tonal and compositional sketches to try out design or subject ideas.

Tone The light and dark values of a colour.

Vanishing point A term used in perspective to describe the point on the horizon where parallel lines appear to meet.

Viewpoint The height from which the artist sees the subject they're painting. It determines where the horizon line is.

Wash A transparent layer of diluted colour that is brushed on.

Wash-off Dislodging an area of water-soluble paint, usually with a bristle brush dipped in water or a damp sponge.

INDEX

acrylic mediums 59, 60
acrylic paints
  applying without a brush 85
  brushes 55 – 6
  liquid acrylics 19
  mixed media 65
  palettes 10, 52, 53
  removing 8, 9, 52, 56
  using 59 – 60, 89

ballpoint pens 19, 22 – 5
Bleedproof Designer's White 29
brush pens 17, 19, 20, 21
brushes
  cleaning 8, 9, 55, 56
  restoring 8, 56
  special 55, 56
  storing 6, 9
  types 54, 55, 56

canvases 8, 60
chalk 42, 61, 94
charcoal 7, 61, 82
  paper 40, 41, 42, 49
  shading 48, 50, 51
cleaning
  brushes 8, 9, 55, 56
  palettes 52, 53
  pastels 10, 39
colour blending and mixing
  acrylic paints 59, 60, 89
  coloured pencils 44, 45, 70
  green 72 – 3, 87 – 8
  oil paints 57, 58, 89
  orange 70 – 1
  palettes 52, 53, 58, 71, 74
  pastels 35 – 6, 37, 38, 61, 65
  purple 74 – 5
  seasonal palettes 87 – 94
coloured pencils 43 – 7, 51, 64, 65, 70
  cross-hatching *see* hatching

dip pens 17 – 18, 26
drawings
  ballpoint pens 22 – 5
  fibre-tipped pens 26 – 9
  graphite sticks 30 – 3, 48, 63
  grids 48 – 51
  marker pens 20 – 1
  oil pastels 34 – 6, 61, 62, 82
  reflections 43 – 7
  storing 7
  see also sketching

easels 8, 11 – 12

fibre-tipped pens 18 – 19, 20, 22, 25
  drawing with 26 – 9
fixatives 7, 39
frottage 63

gouache 23, 24, 36, 52, 94
  wash-off techniques 66, 67, 68, 69
graphite sticks 30 – 3, 48, 63, 65
grids 48 – 51

hard pastels 37, 38, 39
hatching 21, 65
  ballpoint pen 22, 23, 24, 25
  coloured pencils 44, 45, 46
  fibre-tipped pen 26, 28, 29
highlighting 23, 29, 50, 51

impasto effects 60
Indian ink 19, 66, 67, 68
Indian papers 41, 42
inks 19, 21, 66, 67, 68

Japanese papers 41, 42

linseed oil 52, 57

marker pens 17, 18 – 19, 20 – 1
masking fluid 8 – 9, 36
mixed media 61 – 5
modelling paste 60
mountboards 66, 67

oil mediums 57, 58
oil paints
  brushes 55 – 6
  oil pastels and 36
  palettes 52, 53, 57, 58
  using 57 – 8, 89
oil pastels 34 – 6, 61, 62, 82

painting knives 84, 85, 86
paintings
  mixed media 61 – 5
  seasonal palettes 87 – 94
  storing 7
  wash-off techniques 66 – 9
  watercolour details and
textures 76 – 83
paints
  applying without a brush 84 – 6
  removing 8, 9, 52, 56, 80
  storing 9
  see also acrylic paints; oil
paints; watercolours
palettes
  home-made 10, 53
  types 52 – 3
  using 52, 57, 58, 71
paper
  charcoal 40, 41, 42, 49
  marker pens 21
  pastels 38, 40, 41, 42
  sketch books 14
  storing 7
  textured 39, 40 – 2, 49
  'tooth' 39, 40, 42
  watercolours 41, 42
pastels
  cleaning 10, 39
  fixing 7, 39
  hard pastels 37, 38, 39
  mixed media 61, 62, 63, 65
  oil pastels 34 – 6, 61, 62, 82
  organising 10
  soft pastels 34, 37 – 9, 41
  storing 6, 10, 39
  textured paper 39, 40, 41, 42
pencils
  charcoal 42, 48, 50
  coloured 43 – 7, 51, 64, 65, 70
  pastel 37
  push-down 31
  storing 6
pens
  ballpoint pens 19, 22 – 5
  brush pens 17, 19, 20, 21
  dip pens 17 – 18, 26
  fibre-tipped pens 18 – 19, 20, 22, 25, 26 – 9
  marker pens 17, 18 – 19, 20 – 1
  rollerball pens 19, 22, 25
  storing 6, 21
  technical pens 17, 18, 26
putty rubber 33, 63
PVA glue 64, 65

reflections 43 – 7
resist technique 36
rollerball pens 19, 22, 25

seasonal palettes 87 – 94
sgraffito 36
shadows and shading
  ballpoint pens 24
  charcoal pencil 48, 50, 51
  coloured pencils 44, 46, 47, 64, 65
  fibre-tipped pens 26, 27, 28, 29
  graphite sticks 30, 31, 33, 48
sketching
  ballpoint pens 23
  coloured pencils 44
  fibre-tipped pens 27
  graphite sticks 30, 31, 33
  oil pastels 34, 35
  pencils 49, 50, 51, 77
  sketch books 13 – 16
  see also drawings
soft pastels 34, 37 – 9, 41
spattering 86, 93 – 4
spraying techniques 85 – 6
stippling 20, 21, 85
storage
  brushes 6, 9
  paints 9
  paper 7
  pastels 6, 10, 39
  pens 6, 21

technical pens 17, 18, 26
textures
  acrylic paints 60, 85
  brushless techniques 85, 86
  charcoal 82
  mixed media 61, 63, 64
  oil paints 57, 58, 85
  paper 39, 40 – 2, 49
  pastels 82
  watercolours 76, 78, 83, 85, 86
'tooth' of paper 39, 40, 42
torchon 38
turpentine 35, 56, 57, 58

varnishing 59

wash-off techniques 66 – 9
watercolours
  brushes 55, 67
  details and textures 76 – 83
  liquid watercolours 19
  mixed media 36, 61, 62, 63
  palettes 52, 53
  paper 41, 42
  sketch book 15, 16
  textures 76, 78, 83, 85, 86
  wash-off techniques 66 – 9
white spirit 35, 56, 57
woodcuts 66, 67